D0397234

THE
AMERICA'S
CUP

DENNIS CONNER AND
MICHAEL LEVITT

ST. MARTIN'S PRESS NEW YORK

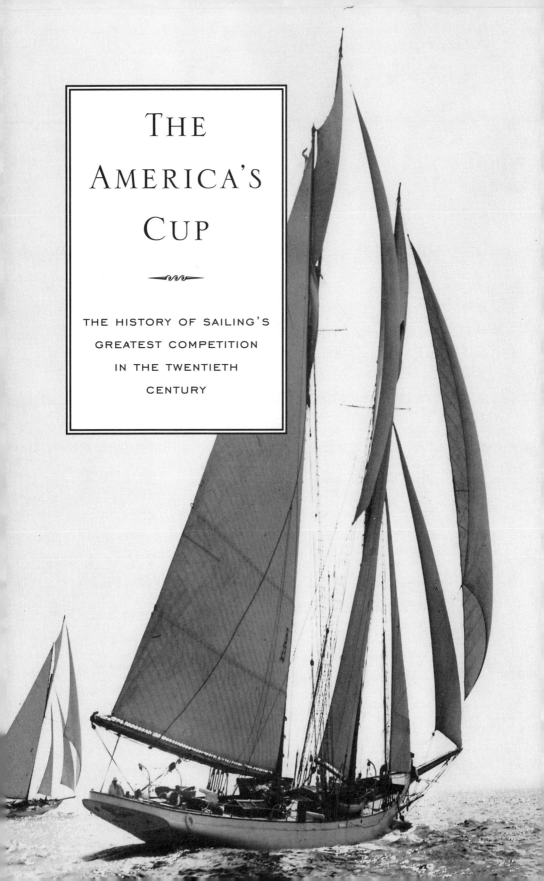

THE AMERICA'S CUP

THE HISTORY OF SAILING'S
GREATEST COMPETITION
IN THE TWENTIETH
CENTURY

Book design by Gretchen Achilles

Library of Congress Cataloging-in-Publication Data

Conner, Dennis.
    The America's Cup : the history of sailing's greatest competition
in the twentieth century / Dennis Conner and Michael Levitt.—1st ed.
        p.   cm.
    Includes bibliographical references (p. 289).
    ISBN 0-312-18567-7
    1. America's Cup races—History.   I. Levitt, Michael.   II. Title.
GV829.C675   1998
797.1'4—dc21   98-12299
                                                                        CIP

FIRST EDITION: JULY 1998

10   9   8   7   6   5   4   3   2   1

I would like to dedicate this book to some of the people who have allowed me to enjoy this great sport: Carl Eichenlaub, Lowell North, and Malin Burnham who gave me a great start; Tom Whidden, Bill Trenkle, and Lynn Soares who continue to make everything possible; Fritz and Lucy Jewett for their friendship and counsel; and my wife, Daintry, for her love and support.

CONTENTS

—◦◦◦—

ACKNOWLEDGMENTS

THE AUTHORS ARE most indebted to Ed du Moulin, who helped edit this manuscript. We wish to thank Jerry La Dow, Dan Nerney, Tom Ehman, and Bill Trenkle for their willingness to read and comment on the manuscript. Journalists and writers who allowed us to use their words include Barbara Lloyd, Roger Vaughan, Jay Broze, John Bertrand, and Bill Center. To them we give our thanks as well as to those who filled in the historical record. The cheerful and competent help of Lynn Soares at Dennis Conner Sports is noted and appreciated. The Herreshoff Marine Museum in Bristol, Rhode Island, allowed us to use its library and photographs. Daniel Forster and Dan Nerney contributed photographs. The authors also wish to thank George Witte, our editor at St. Martin's Press, and Meredith Bernstein, of the Meredith Bernstein Literary Agency.

On a personal note, Michael Levitt, Molly Levitt, and especially Linda Murray Levitt deserve special and heartfelt thanks for bringing this book to fruition. Linda fought the good fight and is terribly missed.

"To sportsmen—manly men, men of gentle mind and simple heart, brave men, fair men; to men who say to the weak, 'May I?'—and to the strong, 'I will!'—to men . . . who look upon the sea, the plain, the forest, the mountains, the rising and the setting sun, and the immutable heavens, with a deep sense of their own littleness in the great scheme of things—I dedicate this book."

—*dedication from* The Lawson History of the America's Cup —A Record of Fifty Years, *published in 1902*

THE
AMERICA'S
CUP

"Like Jupiter Among the Gods, America Is First"

A PECULIAR IF compelling book was published privately in 1902: *The Lawson History of the America's Cup—A Record of Fifty Years.* Three thousand copies were published, and in life's surprising journey, I have come to own two of them. While not a bibliophile or even particularly bookish, I consider them prized possessions.[1] The book has done much to explain my lasting fascination with the America's Cup. It has even helped to explain me to me.

Lawson is unusual because it is two very different books in one: The first is a nearly 300-page history of the first half century, from 1851 to 1901, of the America's Cup. It is most ably and dispassionately written by Winfield M. Thompson, a respected journalist of that time. The second book, although far shorter, is a diatribe from a Mr. Thomas W. Lawson, of Boston, for his exclusion from the America's Cup competition of 1901. A tirade in the America's Cup? It was not the first and certainly not the last.

But before addressing the righteous indignation—the sound and fury—that has been part of so many America's Cups, let's look at the Thompson history. More than any other book before and probably

---

1. The book was republished in 1986 as a limited edition of 1,500 copies by Ashford Press Publishing in England.

since, *The Lawson History of the America's Cup* better explains the complexity, beauty, dazzling technology, and historic and political significance of the America's Cup.

The book begins, naturally enough, at the beginning: in 1851 when *America*, a 95-foot schooner, won a race around the Isle of Wight, in England.[2] This was 75 years after America fought the British to gain its independence, 10 years before this nation's Civil War, and 45 years before the modern Olympics. The America's Cup proved to be a victory of the "New World," America, over the "Old," Britain.

The Lawson History of the America's Cup relates a story that has become famous though it may be apocryphal. Fact or fiction, the story is a paradigm for the event.

Writes Thompson: "As often as the story of the Cup is told, is related the good old tale of the famous dialogue of the queen [Victoria] with her signal-master, who, peering from the deck of the *Victoria and Albert* down the Solent was asked by her Majesty:

" 'Say, signal-master, are the yachts in sight?'

" 'Yes, may it please Your Majesty.'

" 'Which is first?'

" 'The *America*.'

" 'Which is second?'

" 'Ah, Your Majesty, there is no second.' "

On that lazy summer afternoon on August 22, 1851, America—the nation—went from being a second-rate power, at least in the eyes of the British, to a force with which to be reckoned. The newspaper the London *Merchant* wrote pessimistically if prophetically: ". . . The empire of the seas must before long be ceded to America . . . America, as mistress of the ocean, must overstride the civilized world." This is all the more significant coming from "Britannia," which according to legend, verse, and ethos "ruled the waves."

The next day Queen Victoria and Prince Albert visited *America*. When the Queen asked to go below decks to inspect the "ballast,"

---

2. *America*'s dimensions varied considerably depending on the source. The *New York Herald*, in its June 21, 1851, edition, listed her as length on deck: 95'; beam: 23'; draft: 11'; bowsprit length: 32' (17' outboard); and measured displacement: 180 tons.

America, the yacht that started it all in England in 1851. ©MYSTIC SEAPORT MUSEUM, INC., ROSENFELD COLLECTION, MYSTIC, CONNECTICUT. JAMES BURTON PHOTOGRAPHER

Captain Dick Brown, her sailing-master, asked the Prince, who wished to accompany her, to wipe his feet. Responding to the Prince's astonished look, Captain Brown said, "I know who you are, but you'll have to wipe your feet."

Wrote Thompson, the friendly feeling Queen Victoria showed toward Americans in this critical period of this country's development was "of more benefit to this nation than the world knew."

Thompson relates a similar story—this one about Daniel Webster, the nineteenth century's foremost advocate of American nationalism. While addressing a sizable audience at the Statehouse in Boston, Webster, a noted orator, learned of *America*'s triumph in England. He broke off his speech on the opening of railway communication between the United States and the Canadian provinces to proclaim, "Like Jupiter among the gods, America is first, and there is no second."

The America's Cup was a coming-out party for America in 1851, as it was to be for Australia in 1983. In 1983, when *Australia II* ended the 132-year reign of the New York Yacht Club, Bob Hawke, the Australian Prime Minister at the time, declared an "unofficial" national holiday. Any employer who didn't turn his employees loose for the day was a "bum," he opined. When we returned the America's Cup to America in 1987, we were summoned to Washington to meet President Reagan. A picture of that meeting made the cover of *Sports Illustrated* magazine. *Time* magazine's cover showed me. We were treated to a ticker-tape parade hosted by Donald Trump, up an icy Fifth Avenue in Manhattan, and were given a similar parade in San Diego, my home.

When New Zealand won the America's Cup in such all-consuming fashion on Saturday, May 13, 1995, its Governor General, Dame Catherine Tizard, stated it was New Zealand's finest hour since Sir Edmund Hillary became, in 1953, the first person to scale Mount Everest. Jim Bolger, New Zealand's Prime Minister, declared an unofficial holiday for New Zealanders and made the same comparison: "Why not? One of the greatest sporting achievements in New Zealand's history! It's like climbing Mount Everest all over again."

When the crew of *Black Magic* brought the America's Cup home

to Auckland, they were greeted by more than 200,000 wildly cele-
brating people. That's more than half the population of Auckland,
New Zealand's largest city. Peter Blake, the syndicate head, delivered
the Cup to the Royal New Zealand Yacht Squadron (RNZYS) with
the immortal words: "Well, here it is."

The America's Cup has survived—indeed flourished—because it
combines physical skill, courage, technology, execution, heart, intelligence, and team play unlike any other sport. It is wholly modern:
a competition as much for scientists, technicians, meteorologists, strategists, organizers, and those who allocate resources as for athletes. It
is a war game—a space race. The competition is, I believe, as fitting
a measure of a nation's place in the world as any sport is. It was that
way in the beginning, in 1851, and remains so today.

THE AMERICA'S CUP also features controversy. What troubled Mr.
Thomas W. Lawson was an edict of the New York Yacht Club
(NYYC), the trustee of the Cup, that said, in Lawson's words: "No
ship belonging to any American other than a member of a certain
yacht club—their own—would be permitted to defend the nation's
trophy."

To Lawson, a stock market speculator who made his first million
in 1888, when he was 31, it was a matter of sportsmanship—plain
and simple. Indeed, the very first words in his book are: "To sportsmen—manly men, men of gentle mind and simple heart, brave men,
fair men; to men who say to the weak, 'May I?'—and to the strong,
'I will!'—to men . . . who look upon the sea, the plain, the forest, the
mountains, the rising and the setting sun, and the immutable heavens,
with a deep sense of their own littleness in the great scheme of
things—I dedicate this book."

However, the America's Cup has never been "plain and simple."
That's what makes it so grand—so compelling—and that's what
makes it so controversial.

Lawson wished to campaign his aptly named *Independence* in the
America's Cup wars of 1901. The game he wished to play, and the
game I have devoted a considerable period of my life to, is called the
"America's Cup." It might have saved Lawson and any number of

others considerable grief if it had more accurately been called *America*'s Cup. Those italics signal the name of a boat, not a country, and what a difference this typographical convention makes. The competition was called the America's Cup because the boat that won the trophy in 1851—it was then called "The Royal Yacht Squadron £100 Cup" or "Hundred Guinea Cup"—was named *America*.[3] She belonged to a syndicate of NYYC members, including John Cox Stevens, that august club's first commodore.

Their yacht might just as easily have been called *Maria*, and we might be racing for the *Maria*'s Cup. Indeed, another Stevens family yacht, *Maria*, beat *America* handily before the latter yacht ventured across the ocean for England. However, *Maria* seemed too delicate, too high-strung, to make the transatlantic voyage. *America* was, reportedly, the first yacht to cross the Atlantic in either direction.

There was—and is—a Deed of Gift underlying this competition, but like America's Constitution, it has been subject to interpretation. Until most recently that interpretation was done primarily by members of the NYYC—the keeper of the Cup. As one journalist wrote about the 1881 manifestation of that document, "The new Deed is a mixture of bad sportsmanship, bad law, and bad English, made in a hurry by a little clique, and never yet ratified by the NYYC. It is encumbered by meaningless legal verbiage, and its provisions are obscure and contradictory."

That said, when it came to the America's Cup, Lawson exhibited remarkable tunnel vision—as did any number of others before and since. What Lawson failed to see was that the America's Cup *belonged* to the NYYC in the most unambiguous sense of that word. It didn't belong to America; that was merely a sleight of hand.

The NYYC held on to that ornate, even ugly, 27-inch silver trophy for 132 years, as if it was its talisman—its reason for being. And perhaps it was.

Those 132 years, beginning with the first race in 1851 in England and through 24 defenses, represented the longest winning streak in sports, as journalists are wont to say. In 25 total defenses NYYC boats

---

3. The significance of "£100" or "Hundred Guinea Cup" is that's the price the Royal Yacht Squadron paid silversmith R&W Gerard for the trophy in 1851.

won 81 of 93 races. During that era I was involved in two successful defenses of the Cup—with *Courageous* in 1974, where I was starting helmsman and tactician to Ted Hood, and *Freedom* in 1980, where I was skipper. Though I lived in San Diego, and was a lifelong member of the San Diego Yacht Club, I had to sail for the NYYC and be a member of that club. It was their trophy, their competition, and their rules. You may have been an American, but if you weren't invited to their "party," you couldn't attend, Mr. Lawson.

The NYYC had no intention of losing its Cup. Then in September 1983, as skipper of *Liberty*, I lost it to an inspired boat, *Australia II*, and a bare-knuckled group of Australians. To use Lawson's words, the Australians simply said "I will!" and not even the NYYC was "strong" enough to stop them. That despite the fact that the club had, in my estimation, all the ammunition it needed. On the very eve of the contest, *Australia II* syndicate head Alan Bond refused to sign an affidavit, under penalty of perjury, stating that the Australians had complied with all the rules. Nevertheless, the show went on. I couldn't stop them on the water, although I tried my damnedest, losing the Cup 4-3.

It took the loss of the America's Cup for the world—and then America—to rediscover it.

It was different in the previous century. In 1895, some eight years before there was a World Series in baseball, an estimated 65,000 people watched the America's Cup from hired boats off New York City. This was the competition's first venue, which lasted from the first defense in 1870 to the thirteenth defense in 1920. Such popularity, however, wasn't the case when in 1930 the NYYC moved the America's Cup competition to Newport, Rhode Island, and its more rarefied atmosphere. It was out of sight and out of mind—the sporting equivalent of the tree falling in the woods with no one there to see or hear it. Did it even happen? Did it matter?

With the 1983 loss, the trustee of the Cup became the Royal Perth Yacht Club (RPYC). While I was on the outside looking in, my guess is that the RPYC had no intention of losing it either when the America's Cup world reassembled in 1986–87. It was their trophy, their competition, and mostly their rules.

The Australians embraced the America's Cup, as Americans had

The America's Cup was won by America in 1851. It is the oldest active trophy in sports. DANIEL FORSTER

in 1851. They seemed poised to "overstride the civilized world." This was a golden period in Cup history. A renaissance.

It was helped inordinately by a new and exotic and, most important, windy and sunny venue: Fremantle, the port city for Perth, Western Australia. In every way, Fremantle breathed new life into a very old trophy. It was aided, too, by television, including onboard cameras, that made the competition so approachable. Little did anyone realize that the America's Cup, particularly when the racing is close, the wind is ripping, the sun shining, and the plot compelling, is the ultimate television sport.

In 1987 we took a vote on *Stars & Stripes* whether to allow onboard television cameras during the America's Cup. The vote was 10-1 against it. The guys felt it would be an invasion of their privacy. The one vote for it came from me, and that carried the day.

We were fortunate to win it back that year and to present it to the San Diego Yacht Club. The America's Cup was the property of the San Diego Yacht Club and if that club had had a little time to get used to it, perhaps things might have been very different.

In 1987, however, as the America's Cup world well knows, an unexpected and unwanted challenge materialized from New Zealand. The Kiwis, led by Michael Fay, a merchant banker, found a loophole in the rules sufficiently large to drive through a monohull 90 feet on the water and 133 feet overall. Using the terms of Fay's business, it was a "corporate raid" on the America's Cup. We, on the other hand, found a loophole in the rules sufficiently large to drive a 60-foot catamaran through. It was our "poison-pill" defense. After our catamaran beat their monohull, the America's Cup entered the courts where it lived for an unhappy year and a half. For some, that bitter taste still lingers.

At least three salutary things, however, resulted from this unfortunate occurrence. First, a new boat: the International America's Cup Class (IACC) yacht replaced the venerable 12-Meter. The 12-Meter—the boat used in the America's Cup from 1958 to 1987—actually dates back to 1906. Even in 1906, it was not on the cutting edge of racing-yacht design. It was overbuilt, under-rigged, and of shallow draft—no recipe for speed. It was a reaction to extreme boats, like the 144-

foot *Reliance*—the largest boat ever to sail in the America's Cup—that preceded it in 1903. The original 12-Meter was essentially a racer-cruiser, complete with accommodations. Second, a Trustees Committee was formed, consisting of the commodore of each of the clubs that held or had held the trophy—New York, Royal Perth, and San Diego—to keep the America's Cup out of the courts. Third, on-the-water umpiring would keep races from being decided in back rooms—or so the theory goes.

Certainly, as a result of the Trustees Committee, the playing field got leveler, but it still wasn't completely level. If you're the type of person who is bothered by the tilt of the table, you'll never appreciate the America's Cup. For better or for worse, fairness has become a story line—an important theme—of the competition.

The Kiwis didn't think our boat switch from *Stars & Stripes* to *Young America* in 1995, or the three-boat "final" that year, were fair. I didn't feel the fiberglass hull on *Kiwi Magic* was legal in 1986–87 and said so unambiguously; and I didn't feel their backdoor challenge in 1987–88 was legal either, and said so clearly—perhaps too clearly.

I did not think that the wings on the keel of *Australia II* were legal, and I did not believe that Ben Lexcen designed that boat without help from Dutch technicians. Similarly, I didn't feel that the third boat the *oneAustralia* team allegedly built in 1995 was legal either. While the International Jury wasn't troubled by this controversy, perhaps Mother Nature was, because their third boat broke up and sank on Sunday, March 5, 1995—now known as "Black Sunday" to Australia's sailors.

I have been a lightning rod for many conspiracy theories; not all of the attention was deserved. Bill Center wrote in the San Diego *Union*, on May 5, 1995:

"It goes with the territory if you're Dennis Conner.

"At the first hint of controversy in the America's Cup, Conner's name comes up.

"Defense compromise? Conner must be behind it. Boat switch? Conner must have rewritten the rules. When his *Stars & Stripes* almost sank March 26, rumors quickly sprouted that Conner might have pulled the plug.

"And so it goes, all the way down to *Stars & Stripes'* miraculous come-from-behind victory over *Mighty Mary* that sent Conner's team into the America's Cup against Team New Zealand. Conner paid the women off, right? . . .

"Public perception aside, the compromise that kept Conner alive in the defense finals was not his undertaking. And someone else wrote the possibility of a boat switch into the rules.

"Still, Conner is smart. Street-smart at the America's Cup game. If there is an opening in the rules, Conner will seize it . . ."

Fighting or using the rules is a crucial part of the event. Once the Australians recognized that the America's Cup is fought on two fronts, on land as well as sea, they claimed the Cup—the first challenging nation to do so. Using the rules cleverly allowed Paul Cayard, who skippered *Il Moro* for the Italians in 1992, to derail the seemingly invincible New Zealanders, again led by Michael Fay. Steering well clear of such controversy in 1995 allowed the Kiwis to remove the Cup so easily, after its eight-year sojourn in San Diego.

The Royal New Zealand Yacht Squadron (RNZYS), the victor in 1995, promised a new dawn: a "fair" America's Cup. Just before its victory, the syndicate head Peter Blake waxed, "If we are fortunate enough to win this event one way or another we are going to clean it up. We are not going to have rules that are different for one side than the other . . .

"We'll have an event where people will want their sons and daughters to get involved in sailing because they see that at the end of the day they can have a fair sporting chance of getting through and actually winning the America's Cup."

Let me tell you, it's a lot easier to sound lofty when you're faster by a country mile than the rest of the world. That group lost only two races in 1995—one of which was in the protest room.

Indeed, immediately after *Black Magic* won, the RNZYS announced it had accepted what amounts to a "vest-pocket challenge" from the New York Yacht Club, and released a startling 22-page document, the "America's Cup XXX Protocol," outlining the next event, to be held in the year 2000. Vest-pocket challenges are backroom deals pioneered by the NYYC, where the defender accepts the "first" challenge from a group of its liking. This first challenger typically becomes the Challenger of Record, or words to that effect, and is charged with running the challenger-elimination matches at the next event. It is a powerful position. This deal and the discussions with the New York Yacht Club must have been in the works for weeks before *USA 36*, the boat I used, figuratively sank in the Pacific.

Meanwhile, Bill Koch, head of both *America³*, which defended the Cup in 1992, and *Mighty Mary*, "the women," which sailed in 1995, had hoped to be first. As *Black Magic* crossed the finish line after winning the fifth and final race, Koch and Robert Gill, Commodore of the diminutive Wianno Yacht Club on Cape Cod, where Koch has a home, motored up to them. After Koch ceremoniously presented them with several bottles of champagne and his congratulations, Gill challenged the Kiwis, obviously for Koch. However, he had been beaten to the punch by Robert James, then Vice Commodore of the New York Yacht Club, who watched the final race from the yacht belonging to the New Zealand syndicate. Talk about strange shipmates.

The deal between the Royal New Zealand Yacht Squadron and the New York Yacht Club has apparently obviated the Challenger of Record Committee (CORC), which represented the challengers since 1992, and the Trustees Committee, which kept Cup disputes out of the courts.

For example, the New York Yacht Club formed the America's Cup Challenge Association (ACCA) to replace CORC. "The Board of Directors of ACCA will be made up of seven members, four elected by the NYYC and three by all of the other member challenges," reads a NYYC press release, dated February 2, 1996. You don't need to be a mathematician to realize that New York gets what it wants. On the other hand, a democracy is no way to steer several ships—representing diverse nations—through troubled waters. Ask any admiral.

Also, according to the America's Cup XXX Protocol, the Trustees Committee will be replaced by the Arbitration Panel.[4] This will consist of two members from RNZYS and two from NYYC, the likely Challenger of Record. These four members will select a fifth. De-

---

4. The protocol keeps it, however, as an alternate approach if NYYC withdraws as the Challenger of Record.

pending on who that fifth is, this might well remove the San Diego Yacht Club and/or the Royal Perth Yacht Club—both former holders of the Cup—from any input in its administration. It also returns the NYYC to its position of "guardian of the hen house"—at least the one in which the challengers hang out.

If an "ill wind," it may be that nothing unholy will come of this alliance. To be fair, New Zealand could have found a challenger a whole lot weaker than New York.

New Zealand announced that there will be only one defense group, not several as there have been in the past. This policy will help it inordinately in fund-raising, as potential sponsors know they will be backing a boat that will be in the match, where the eyes of the world are upon the boats and, of course, on sponsors' logos. The challengers can provide no such guarantees. Is that fair to the challengers? Is that fair to a host of New Zealand America's Cup skippers, such as Chris Dickson, Rod Davis, John Cutler, and Leslie Egnot, who were associated with other teams in 1995? They may well be left off the New Zealand squad in the year 2000.

Also announced in the first protocol was that the defender would be allowed to campaign four boats, versus two boats for each of the challengers. After a hue and cry this was amended almost a year later in a revised protocol. Now the defender will only be allowed to campaign two boats, like the challengers.

Mind you, I'm not complaining about it. I'm just pointing out inconsistencies between what Peter Blake—now Sir Peter, on the strength of his America's Cup performance—promised a new dawn, a "fair" America's Cup—and what he seems to be delivering.

Addressing the issue of fairness: In a casino the house has the odds in its favor, and if you don't like those odds, you don't play. Would you have any sympathy for a tapped-out gambler whining, "It's not fair!"? In the America's Cup, the defender historically has had the odds in his favor. Thus, how competitors play the roll of the dice or tilt of the table is part of the game. Those who can stand the heat do the best in this game. Contesting the rules isn't always pretty, but this isn't a beauty contest. If you want fair watch Little League.

. . .

THE TITLE OF this book is *The America's Cup—History of Sailing's Greatest Competition in the Twentieth Century*. It begins at the turn of this century—at the point where *Lawson* stops. It ends at the end of the twentieth century when the Kiwi stewardship begins.

I feel somewhat more qualified to write my history than Lawson his. In the 21 years I have devoted to the America's Cup, boats I have skippered have won the trophy three times. This ties the record of Captain Charlie Barr, who skippered three winning America's Cup yachts in 1899, 1901, and 1903, and Harold "Mike" Vanderbilt, who skippered winning boats in 1930, 1934, and 1937. If you count *Courageous*, where I was starting helmsman and tactician, I have been on boats that have won four Cups. In seven competitions, I have been in the America's Cup match, or finals, six times. I have won more than 100 races in America's Cup trials. I am also the first man to lose the Cup (1983), the only man to win it back (1987), and, yes, the only man to lose it a second time (1995).

Beyond winning, I am proud, too, that I have also helped change the America's Cup from a clubby and cliquey sport, of interest to very few people, to a sport where even a poor boy from San Diego—now even a girl—can play.

For 132 years, the America's Cup was a private party for the NYYC—for members only. It was paid for by its membership, which included J. P. Morgan and Cornelius "Commodore" Vanderbilt. When Commodore Vanderbilt's progenitor and namesake, "Commodore" Cornelius Vanderbilt, died in 1877, his fortune was $100 million—more money than was in the U.S. Treasury on the day of his death.

However, for those of less substantial means—I'm the son of a commercial fisherman—or for those of us who depend upon corporate largess, the more who hear and see the tree fall, the merrier. That is one of many reasons for writing this book.

Joining me in this effort is author Michael Levitt, with whom I've already written three books. His *America's Cup 1851–1992: The Official Record* won a Benjamin Franklin Award for the outstanding book on sports in 1992. Also his book *Upset: Australia Wins the America's Cup*, which he co-authored with Barbara Lloyd, was critically acclaimed and a best-seller in the field.

Like Lawson, what Levitt and I have endeavored to do is to describe the complexity, beauty, dazzling technology, controversy, and historic and political significance of the America's Cup. We focus, too, on the personalities: Sir Thomas Lipton, Commodore Harold "Mike" Vanderbilt, Ted Turner, Alan Bond, Ben Lexcen, Michael Fay, Tom Blackaller, and, yes, Dennis Conner, to name a few, because to succeed here you have to be willing and able to wage war.

The America's Cup isn't merely a "Faster, Higher, Stronger" sport, to use the modern Olympic motto, but a sport that involves those qualities, as well as generals, lieutenants, foot soldiers, sailors, scientists, designers, tacticians, meteorologists, strategists, and a host of other technical types reaching for the stars.

CHAPTER 2

THE TURN OF THE CENTURY
A "GILDED AGE"

—◦◦◦—

ON APRIL 12, 1903, in Bristol, Rhode Island, a young girl's voice chimed, "I christen thee—*Reliance!*" With that a very bearded man gave an almost imperceptible nod. This was the boat's designer and builder Nathanael Greene Herreshoff, known as the "Wizard of Bristol." Then the huge gleaming-white hull of *Reliance*—the largest boat ever to sail in the America's Cup—started slowly backwards out of the shed where she was constructed to meet her element and future.

Herreshoff, then age 55, had designed and built *Vigilant*, which had successfully defended the America's Cup in 1893. She was, wrote Winfield M. Thompson in *Lawson*, the "prototype of a vicious kind of yacht, whose existence has been more of a curse than a blessing to the sport of yacht racing."[1] *Vigilant* was nothing compared to what followed from Herreshoff. He subsequently designed and built such America's Cup defenders as *Defender* in 1895, *Columbia* in 1899 and again in 1901. Ahead of him was *Resolute* in 1920. But no sailboat was more awe-inspiring, more audacious, and more American than *Reliance*.

---

1. Bill Koch sounded a similar refrain nearly 100 years later, in 1991, when first sailing an International America's Cup Class (IACC) yacht in blustery conditions. He said, "The guys who designed these boats are idiots."

The abundant Reliance *at her launching was the largest boat to compete for the Cup.* ©MYSTIC SEAPORT MUSEUM, INC., ROSENFELD COLLECTION, MYSTIC, CONNECTICUT. JAMES BURTON PHOTOGRAPHER

From the beginning, America's Cup boats were to be examples of the technical skills of a nation, and *Reliance* was all of that and more. She was 143 feet, 9 inches overall, but 201 feet when measured from the tip of her boom to the end of her bowsprit. *Reliance* was also a sloop—or "great-single sticker"—that flew 16,600 square feet of sail off a mast that finally ended 200 feet above the water. That is sufficient sail area to equip six International America's Cup Class (IACC) yachts today. *Reliance*'s mainsheet measured 1,000 feet. Sixty-six men sailed her!

Reliance was not seen by the press or the public until her launching. Indeed, Captain Nat had little use for the press or even his fellowman. Rather than addressing his employees directly, he would scribble instructions with the stub of a pencil, and woe to him who didn't follow them to the letter.

A New York newspaper reporter once paid a local kid to row

Herreshoff designed and built defenders Defender, Columbia, Vigilant, Reliance, *and* Resolute. COURTESY HERRESHOFF MARINE MUSEUM, BRISTOL, RHODE ISLAND

him around to get a glimpse of *Reliance* being built. They were chased away by Herreshoff employees who threw red-hot rivets at them. As Herreshoff said about the press, "No well-regulated factory of any description should have its doors open to prowlers and loafers, and not even to reporters..."

Even European royalty couldn't escape his scorn. For example,

Reliance *sails upwind off Blithewold in Bristol, RI. The lawn of the estate, now a museum, was used to dry her sails.* COURTESY HERRESHOFF MARINE MUSEUM, BRISTOL, RHODE ISLAND

Herreshoff designed *Ingomar*, a schooner, which was 122 feet overall and 86 feet on the water. Under the command of Captain Charlie Barr, the skipper of *Reliance, Ingomar* raced most successfully in England and Germany in 1904. The German Emperor, Kaiser Wilhelm II, was so impressed by her that he ordered a similar boat from Herreshoff, despite the fact that his own *Meteor III* was only two years old and quite successful. "Captain Nat started to design the new schooner for the Kaiser with much enthusiasm for she was to be a large vessel and the Kaiser had plenty of money in his own right, which was not the case of some other monarchs and princes of the day," wrote L. Francis Herreshoff, Nathanael's son, in his book *The Wizard of Bristol.*

The Kaiser cabled Herreshoff to know the dimensions of his new yacht; upon receiving them, he made some changes, primarily to her draft. The water was too thin around much of Germany for her to float. Herreshoff was outraged. He wrote back, "If you want the yacht as I designed her you can have her, but I will not design a yacht for anyone of dimensions my experience shows are not suitable." The project stopped then and there and never restarted. Herreshoff neglected to inform the Kaiser of this fact. When the Kaiser found out about it, he was apoplectic.

Herreshoff, born in Bristol in 1848, attended Massachusetts Institute of Technology and worked as an engineer in Providence building steam turbines before joining his brother John in the Herreshoff Manufacturing Company. They started building launches and small steamers during the boom years in the North following America's Civil War. The brothers built the U.S. Navy's first torpedo boat and technically advanced light steam power plants.

This period in America became known as the "Gilded Age," a phrase coined by Mark Twain—a period of rapid industrialization, ruthless pursuit of profit, corruption in government, and conspicuous consumption. The Herreshoff brothers started building yachts, the right toy at the right time.

In its heyday the Herreshoff Manufacturing Company employed 300 people. Yet, the only thing that identified the company was a sign on a building that read, "Office."

"Whose office?" was the inevitable question of strangers. Anyone living in Bristol could tell you: " 'J. B.' Herreshoff's—Captain Nat's brother, John."

J. B. Herreshoff was blind; he lost one eye to glaucoma and the other was poked out when he was 14 by his brother Charles. It was J.B. who ran the business. "J.B. was human if [Nathanael] was too busy to be," wrote L. Francis Herreshoff.

With Nathanael Herreshoff, it's difficult to separate the builder from the designer. He not only dreamed these things up, but figured out how to build them. This was no easy task. Exaggerated waterline, through overhangs forward and aft, was pushed to its extreme by Herreshoff with *Reliance*. For example, her measured waterline was 89 feet, 9 inches, but she was 143 feet, 9 inches overall. When the boat heeled, the overhangs, fore and aft, became waterline. This increased sailing length and, thus, speed, when the breeze blew.

When it didn't blow, the boat stood tall, which minimized wetted-surface drag.

Reliance also had nine belowdeck winches—a "first" that is usually attributed to *Intrepid*, a two-time defender of the America's Cup that arrived 64 years later. Belowdeck winches meant their weight as well as that of the crew's was kept low in the boat, increasing stability. *Reliance* was wide on deck, too, to allow the plethora of crew to lie flat on the weather rail, helping to keep the boat more vertical and, thus, more powerful. She had two steering wheels, also a first.

The boat's rudder was plated, of thin bronze sheets over a frame that left it hollow. When weather helm got excessive, as it often did in this huge scow-shaped behemoth, water was allowed into the rudder making it heavier. As the boat heeled, the heavier rudder dropped more quickly to leeward, like power steering, to turn the boat away from the wind.

Consider *Reliance*'s construction. With her exaggerated bow and stern and 100 tons of lead ballast in her keel, this was as difficult a structure to support as a brontosaurus. The method Herreshoff pioneered was called "longitudinal construction," and it was first used on *Constitution* in 1901, another Herreshoff America's Cup contender in that series.

Reliance employed widely spaced steel-web frames running entirely around the hull and across the deck. These thick but lightweight frames resisted athwartships strains far better than numerous shallow frames—the design typical of yachts before *Constitution* and *Reliance*. However, even more radical, supporting the boat fore and aft were longitudinal frames, or stringers, running the entire length of the boat and connecting to the web frames and bronze plating of her hull. This, then, was the "longitudinal construction," and it became the basis of boat as well as airplane construction for the next 50 years.

Nevertheless, *Reliance* was so extreme she could barely tolerate a seaway without denting her prominent bow. Several times during her one summer of useful life she needed a nose job, like a car after a head-on collision. Compare *Reliance* and her cockleshell construction to *Shamrock III*, the challenger from England, which had to make a transatlantic crossing before sailing in the match; this was a requirement of challengers until the 12-Meter era. Wrote *Land and Water*, a British yachting journal, about the unfairness of this clause, indeed the entire America's Cup premise, "To sail a boat that must be seaworthy to cross the Atlantic and compete in the light, fleecy airs off Sandy Hook against a volatile cockleshell kind of racing machine built with all the foreknowledge of a rival's plans and lines of construction must obviously be a stupendous obstacle to a challenger's success."

That wasn't all of it, however. *Shamrock III* had no winches, while those on *Reliance* ran on ball bearings and were practically works of art. They even shifted gears automatically. The English considered winches "unmanly."

This was a chapter in the America's Cup where the boats were the stars. If overshadowed, as any mortal would be, the men associated with the Cups around the turn of the century were giants, too—some of them good, some evil.

In the former camp was Thomas Johnstone Lipton, who challenged and lost five times: 1899, 1901, 1903, 1920, and 1930. In those five challenges, he only won two races, both victories coming in 1920, when the pendulum had swung back to less extreme boats.

His was a friendly, approachable face with a luxuriant mustache that smiles from boxes of Lipton tea to this day. He was a confidant of kings and friend of American presidents. Lipton was a man who won the world by losing. By losing each time he challenged for the America's Cup, he certainly saved the event.

At the risk of overstating it, he even saved relations between England and America. Before Sir Thomas Lipton left to compete in his first America's Cup in 1899, Joseph Chamberlain, the British Colonial Secretary, beseeched him not to strain relations between England and America.

To understand why a British Colonial Secretary inserted himself into the America's Cup, one must turn the pages back to Windham Thomas Wyndham-Quin, the fourth Earl of Dunraven. Lord Dunraven first challenged for the America's Cup in 1889 under the auspices of the Royal Yacht Squadron (RYS), the club that lost the Cup in 1851. The story of Lord Dunraven, a touchstone event in the history of the Cup, also helps to explain why the America's Cup

became sport's most contentious contest. Further, while both represented Great Britain, Lipton and Lord Dunraven were polar oppo-
sites—the yin and yang, the good and bad—of the America's Cup.

Lord Dunraven inherited an Irish title of Celtic origins. His father, a convert to Catholicism, forbade him to see his Protestant
mother, and to keep them apart, the future earl was bundled off to
boarding school in Rome. It was there that he began to display an
"obstinate resistance," as one biographer described it. Those words
absolutely characterize his runs at the America's Cup.

He came to America in 1871, when he was 30, to hunt buffalo
under the tutelage of Buffalo Bill Cody. Lord Dunraven later bought
60,000 acres of land in the Colorado Territory for a game preserve.
He authored books on hunting and theology. He was twice appointed
Under-Secretary for the Colonies, and chaired a panel of the House
of Lords on child labor and workhouses in England. A man difficult
to typecast, he even studied yacht design and raced the one yacht he
designed with considerable success.

Dunraven first challenged in 1889, as described, and provided the
dimensions of his yacht *Valkyrie*. However, when the New York
Yacht Club (NYYC) tried to get the Royal Yacht Squadron, under
whose banner he challenged, to agree to accept the terms of the Deed
of Gift, that club refused. The stewardship of this trophy seemed too
burdensome. The NYYC waved the flag of "mutual consent" as an
olive branch, claiming disagreements could be worked out, but the
RYS was apparently uninterested in such a compromise. Lord Dunraven's first challenge died aborning.

He challenged again in 1892 and again under the auspices of RYS.
The Royal Yacht Squadron, formed in 1815, was the first club in
England to be granted the "Royal" designation. It has been described
as the "most exclusive club in the universe." Dunraven's yacht was
Valkyrie II, and would be 85 feet on the water. The NYYC accepted
this dearth of information. Even the requirement that the RYS agree
to the terms of the Deed of Gift was glossed over. One of the more
interesting points of discussion involving this challenge was that the RYS
professed no interest in being the trustee of the Cup if Lord Dunraven
won it. In effect, the club didn't want its trophy back. The NYYC
was appalled. The Cup had become its talisman—almost its reason

for being. The NYYC said firmly, "It is not agreed that the squadron had the right after having won the Cup to reject custody of it."

The races were finally held in 1893. Dunraven's *Valkyrie II* lost to *Vigilant*, Herreshoff's first America's Cup design, in three straight races. Nevertheless, Lord Dunraven's boat was ahead in one race by more than 26 minutes when the time limit expired. In the final race, *Valkyrie* led before blowing out two spinnakers. She lost the final race by 40 seconds on corrected time.[2] In the context of the times, this was a photo finish.

Dunraven returned in 1895 with *Valkyrie III*. He raced *Defender*, which was the first aluminum yacht and the first American defender lacking a centerboard.[3] When *Defender* was launched in 1895 at Herreshoff's yard, she literally stuck to her ways; the keel wouldn't come loose. She had to be freed by several tugs. The yacht had a good reason for not wanting to touch the water. When the aluminum boat finally floated in saltwater, she started to corrode like a floating battery, which she was. *Defender*'s skipper was Captain Henry "Hank" Haff, who had previously skippered *Volunteer* to victory in the 1887 America's Cup.

Valkyrie lost the first race to *Defender* by more than eight minutes. While Lord Dunraven sailed the race, after it he told the race committee that the American boat added ballast the night before and was now two or three feet longer on the water than when originally measured. This was done, he said, showing his knowledge of yacht design, to increase the waterline length to make the boat faster. Dunraven's evidence was that a drain hole that had been visible before the race was now submerged.

In a word, Dunraven accused the NYYC of *cheating*. He demanded that *Defender* be remeasured, and prior to that a neutral observer be placed aboard to make sure the surreptitiously added ballast wasn't removed. The observer wasn't put aboard, but when the Amer-

---

2. Handicaps were used in the America's Cup until 1930, when J-Class boats were first used. That corresponded to the Cup leaving New York and moving to Newport. Curiously enough, a boat's starting time, on which the handicap was figured, was determined when she crossed the line, not when the starting signal was hoisted, as long as a yacht started within two minutes of the signal.

3. The yacht *America* had a keel, rather than a centerboard, but she wasn't a defender.

ican boat was remeasured the next day, she was found to be one-eighth of an inch longer on the water—an insignificant amount.

Approximately 65,000 people watched the 1895 America's Cup. The course started and finished at the Sandy Hook Lightship out at sea. There was the option of a triangular course or windward-leeward. Both courses were 30 miles long.[4]

Most of the spectators were sportsmen or gamblers, or both, not yachtsmen.[5] They watched the action from sightseeing boats. The captains of such boats were generally cooperative when asked by the NYYC to remain off the course; others, however, would shout, "Who are you to give orders?" It was a valid question. Both competitors sailed with large signs on their transoms saying "Keep Away." This riot of boats particularly troubled Lord Dunraven as in Scotland the summer before, his *Valkyrie II* had been sunk and a sailor was killed while attempting to avoid a spectator craft, the *Satanita*.

In the second race an out-of-control and out-of-position spectator boat, the *City of Yorktown*, forced both *Valkyrie III* and *Defender* apart on the final approach to the starting line. *Defender*, to leeward, passed the spectator boat on the latter's leeward side; *Valkyrie III* passed it on its weather side. Then the two boats converged again. *Defender*, as the leeward boat, had right of way, according to the rules. Eyewitnesses said, and newspaper photographs confirmed, that *Defender* didn't alter course as she made for the line. Meanwhile, *Valkyrie* was apparently early and bore off to avoid crossing the line before the gun. A collision was inevitable. At the last minute, *Valkyrie* luffed. This action caused her main boom to foul *Defender*'s starboard shroud, which sprung from the spreader. Without support, the topmast curved ominously, but didn't break. As *Valkyrie* crossed the line, there were comments such as "shameful!" and "outrageous!" The crew nursed *Defender* around the race course, losing by 47 seconds. However, after the race the NYYC rightfully disqualified *Valkyrie*.

---

4. Until 1887 there was the choice of an inside course that started and finished off Staten Island.

5. The word "sportsmen" was, in those days, a polite term for men who liked to place wagers on sporting events. The early members of the NYYC and the yacht *America*'s owners were "sportsmen." John Cox Stevens, for example, the club's first commodore and *America*'s primary backer, once bet $20,000 on a horse race—a bet he won. He was President of the prominent Jockey Club.

Dunraven argued that rather than his boat falling off to kill time, *Defender* luffed up and caused the collision. He also said the behavior of the spectator boats was impossible and dangerous, and unless the committee could guarantee a "clear course," he would not race. The NYYC said it had no power to keep the course clear. Dunraven, showing his "obstinate resistance," refused an offer by syndicate head C. Oliver Iselin to resail the race, saying that would be an admission of guilt.

For the third race, *Valkyrie* came out under jib and mainsail but without topsails. *Defender* took the start. *Valkyrie* crossed the starting line more than a minute and a half later. As soon as she crossed the line, her tiller was jammed over, and she returned to port.[6]

Dunraven quit, and it was a scandal. Wrote Thompson, ". . . To an American, it is hard to justify what is popularly known as 'quitting.' There is a feeling in this country that a sportsman should 'take his medicine' when once embarked in a sporting venture, come what will. This Lord Dunraven did not do . . ."

Rather than apologizing, Dunraven skulked home to England and then, when safely out of range, published an article in the *London Field*, wherein he accused the NYYC and C. Oliver Iselin of cheating. Coming from that distance it was cowardly.

The NYYC took this slap in the face seriously—likely far more seriously than it deserved. A special panel was convened to review Lord Dunraven's charges. On it were J. Pierpont Morgan, the powerful banker; Edward J. Phelps, former Ambassador to Great Britain; Alfred T. Mahan, the naval strategist, and George L. Rives, a former Assistant Secretary of State. Although all NYYC members, their reputations were above reproach, at home and abroad. The crew of *Defender* testified that the telltale drain hole could be submerged by merely shifting the boom to the port side from the centerline. Also, the nocturnal work that so distressed Lord Dunraven was not to add ballast but to reposition ballast that was aboard when *Defender* was measured. That was perfectly legal. Furthermore, 13 tons of lead would be required to increase *Defender*'s waterline by one foot, tes-

---

6. Haff's victory in 1895 with *Defender* made him the first skipper to defend the America's Cup twice.

tified an engineer. The conclusion was that it would be an impossible task to increase her waterline by two or three feet, as Dunraven alleged, overnight. Similarly, that amount of ballast could not be removed overnight.

When Lord Dunraven arrived in New York to testify at the club, then situated on Madison Avenue, he was granted police protection. He left, however, after one day, before the hearings had concluded, citing the press of business back home.

The NYYC waited for an apology. None came, so on February 27, 1896, the NYYC expelled Dunraven as an honorary member. A newspaper in London wrote, "Lord Dunraven has blundered in taste, and the New York committee have let him down in generous and chivalrous fashion." Nevertheless, what became known as the "Dunraven Affair" nearly killed off the America's Cup. A challenge from England materialized shortly thereafter, but it was withdrawn when the challenger, Charles D. Rose, was accused of "collaborating with the enemy." There was supposedly an attempt by some NYYC members to finance a challenge surreptitiously.

The Cup gathered dust until onto the scene rushed Sir Thomas Lipton, a knight-errant if ever there was one.

Lipton was born in 1850 into humble circumstances in a tenement house on Crown Street, in Glasgow, Scotland. His parents were Protestant farmers, who had fled Ireland with the potato famine. Ultimately, his parents leased a tiny store at 13 Crown Street, where they sold ham, butter, and eggs. Before he was 10 years old, Lipton took an interest in the grocery business and had an aptitude for what today would be termed "marketing." Noticing his father taking a half-dozen eggs in his large hand to present to a customer, the boy said, "Why don't you let Mother serve the eggs, Dad? You see Mother's hands are much smaller than yours, and the eggs would look much bigger . . ."

Lipton quit school when he was 10 to take a job at A & W Kennedy Stationers. From a young age, Lipton knew unambiguously what he wanted, and that was to be rich.

When he was 14, he came to New York with $8 in his pocket. Lipton chopped tobacco in Virginia, worked rice fields in South Carolina, and clerked at a grocery store in New York. He returned to

Scotland in 1869 with a barrel of flour, a rocking chair for his beloved mother, and $500. He worked at the family shop on Crown Street. With his return, business improved. He then suggested to his mother and father that this might be a good time for "extension."

"Who knows," he said, "but there may be a Lipton shop in every city in Scotland." Ultimately, there were 500 Lipton shops in Scotland, Ireland, and England. Lipton did it through savvy marketing, prodigious work, competitive pricing, and ubiquitous and clever advertising.

In 1897 Lipton's became a public company. In addition to the grocery stores, there were packing houses in America and tea plantations in Ceylon. There were riots to buy the stock. That year, Queen Victoria knighted Lipton at her Osborne House on the Isle of Wight. He was so honored for the money he contributed to Princess Alexandra's Royal Dinner for the poorest people in England.

As described in *Lawson*, "Lipton was unique in England, though his type was not uncommon in America. He was a rolling stone, farm-hand, longshoreman, laborer . . . Behold him then in 1897, England's foremost tradesman-prince—not the old-fashioned, staid, proverbial English tradesman, but a tradesman of the hustling strenuous Yankee brand. His grocery and provision shops were on every corner and his income from them was so great that he was enabled to donate a princely sum to the Queen's charities. [Lipton] was at heart, a real Yankee."

In 1898 Lipton purchased *Erin*, a steam yacht. On *Erin* and her successor, he would entertain kings, princes, presidents, and a grandfather and mother of a president-to-be. The Prince of Wales, who would ascend to the throne in 1901 as King Edward VII, was a frequent visitor aboard *Erin*, enjoying Lipton's company. This caused the King's nephew, the aforementioned Kaiser Wilhelm II, of Germany, to inquire why the King of England went yachting with his grocer.

Once, during Cowes Week, a regatta still held on the Isle of Wight, the Royal Yacht signaled *Erin* with the message, "No Kings today," meaning King Edward VII wouldn't be visiting his friend. Asked what to answer, Lipton said, "No only aces!"

In his autobiography, Lipton tells the story of how during Cowes

Week he was entertaining several American friends on *Erin*. Lipton noticed the royal launch heading for his yacht. There was, he said, great excitement on the part of the American ladies aboard. They began practicing their curtsies in anticipation of a royal visit. Lipton ordered his crew to stand by. He wrote, "Who do you suppose jumped out of it? My old friend, 'Honey Fitz,' otherwise Mr. John F. Fitzgerald, the Mayor of Boston, and his two young daughters. 'My word, Fitz,' I exclaimed, 'But you have arrived in great style.' 'What do you mean?' he asked blankly, 'I took the best boat I could see available to bring me over to you.'" Apparently, the King's boatman had never entertained such a request before and assumed this direct American had permission from the King to borrow his boat.

Lipton was a lifelong bachelor, and the Mayor was apparently promoting a marriage between his daughter Rose and Lipton. Ultimately, Rose Fitzgerald married a Harvard graduate, Joseph P. Kennedy. One of their nine children was John Fitzgerald Kennedy, the thirty-fifth president of the United States.

Many believe Lipton's first challenge was encouraged by his friend the Prince of Wales, who wanted, it is believed, someone to erase the memory of Lord Dunraven. Edward VII was an enthusiastic racing sailor, and his *Britannia* would become famous. As a 10-year-old in 1851, he had watched alongside his mother, Queen Victoria, as *America* finished first in that famous race around the Isle of Wight. The King was a sportsman and *bon vivant*; he was the complete opposite of his mother and father, Prince Albert, who defined the straitlaced style of the Victorian age. Rudyard Kipling once described Edward VII as a "corpulent voluptuary"; nevertheless, he was very popular.

As L. Francis Herreshoff wrote, "... As both prince and king, Edward was the most fond of yachting of any English monarch since Charles II, but while Queen Victoria was alive, he had little money of his own. However, several times after an unusually satisfying sail or race on his yacht *Britannia*, he would telegraph Watson, her designer ... (to) order a much larger and better yacht than *Britannia*. Watson, of course, had to say 'Yes, your Highness,' but after he got back to Glasgow, he never did anything about it for he knew the prince could not pay for the yacht ...

Guests surround Lipton on his motoryacht, Erin. *Rose Fitzgerald (Kennedy) is second from right.* ©MYSTIC SEAPORT MUSEUM, INC., ROSENFELD COLLECTION, MYSTIC, CONNECTICUT

"Nevertheless, Prince Edward was the principal figure that brought yachting in the eighteen-nineties to a greater popularity than it ever had before or since, for many wealthy English and Scots took up yachting on a grand scale during his life, and even some of them like Sir Thomas Lipton, who had no particular love for it."

Sir Thomas challenged in the name of the Royal Ulster Yacht Club in Ireland. Lipton had been proposed for membership in the Royal Yacht Squadron by the King, who was later Commodore and then Admiral of that club, but his application was denied. Commoners such as Lipton—even "England's foremost tradesman-prince"—were unacceptable to the membership.

In 1899 Lipton's *Shamrock,* designed by William Fife Jr., met *Columbia,* another Herreshoff design, considered one of the most beautiful boats ever built. Wrote W. E. Robinson in *The Rudder* magazine, "Nothing so handsome in naval architecture was ever seen . . .

The fair Columbia, *a Herreshoff design, was the gem of the ocean in 1899 and 1901. She was the first two-time winner.* COURTESY HERRESHOFF MARINE MUSEUM, BRISTOL, RHODE ISLAND

To all came the impression that here was the acme of American genius and skill in building for the defense of the America's Cup . . ."

Following the Dunraven affair, the course was patrolled by six torpedo boats and six revenue cutters. The U.S. government helping to patrol the racecourse was a first in the history of the America's Cup, and required a special act of the United States Congress.

Another first was the introduction of the Marconi wireless for the transmission of news from the racecourse. Crowed the *New York Herald* on October 1, 1899, "The value of the Marconi system of wireless telegraphy will be furnished to the western world for the first time during the yacht races by Signor Marconi and his corps of assistants who will report every moment of the contending yachts to the *Herald* . . . This will be an unparalleled feat in the history of journalism."

Lipton lost three races by decisive margins to *Columbia*, which was skippered by Charlie Barr, making his America's Cup debut as a defending skipper. After the loss, Lipton announced, "I will try again."

Lipton's second challenge was for 1901. His *Shamrock II*, designed by George L. Watson, was the first America's Cup yacht to be tank-tested. But before leaving for America, *Shamrock II* was dismasted, with King Edward VII aboard. The King, who was seated in the companionway and smoking a cigar, was not hurt, however. After ascertaining that none of the crew was hurt, he lit another cigar.

Thomas W. Lawson, of Boston, tried to muscle his way into this America's Cup. The NYYC tried to persuade Lawson that all he needed to do was to charter his *Independence*, designed by Bowdoin B. Crowninshield, to a club member, and thus sail under the NYYC's flag. This charterer would be in nominal charge, but Lawson and his crew could continue to sail her. The NYYC hammered away at this theme in endless correspondence, but showing "obstinate resistance" to rival Lord Dunraven's Lawson refused to listen. Instead, he began his book.

Herreshoff designed and built a new boat for 1901, *Constitution*, to be skippered by Uriah Rhodes. The fair *Columbia* was back with Charlie Barr, a Scotsman and recently naturalized American, as her skipper. She was manned by a crew of Swedes and Norwegians, most of whom had been aboard her in 1899, as had Captain Barr. She belonged to J. P. Morgan and his cousin Edwin D. Morgan.

J. Pierpont Morgan, who formed J. P. Morgan & Company, con-trolled railroads, created U.S. Steel, and financed a considerable part of the Franco-Prussian War of 1870, and the Boer War of 1899–1902. He staved off several financial panics in America and was described by a biographer as a "one-man Federal Deposit Insurance Corpora-tion." Wall Street speculators like Lawson, who made and lost for-tunes overnight, were anathema to him.

Morgan became Commodore of the NYYC in 1897. The club moved to its present site on Manhattan's West 44th Street in 1901; the land was donated by J. Pierpont Morgan. Once asked by a mil-lionaire what it costs to own a yacht, Morgan said, "You have no right to own a yacht if you have to ask that question." It became a cliché. Morgan watched the 1901 America's Cup from the deck of his 304-foot *Corsair*. During the summer, he used *Corsair* to commute to Manhattan from a home upstate on the Hudson.

Herreshoff obviously wanted his new yacht, *Constitution*, to win. So when the Herreshoff sail loft said it would only make sails for *Constitution*, not *Columbia*, J. P. Morgan grew so incensed that he brought the English sailmaker Ratsey and Lapthorn to City Island, New York, to make sails. As a result, Morgan and Herreshoff didn't speak again until the former was on his deathbed. Not selling sails to the competition would have a strange resonance in 1977, when Lowell North, a sailmaker and skipper of *Enterprise*, refused to sell Ted Turner, skipper of *Courageous*, North sails (see chapter 6).

Barr so aggressively hounded Rhodes during starts in 1901 that sometimes the bowsprit of the 131-foot *Columbia* was over *Constitution*'s afterdeck. The feisty Thomas Fleming Day, editor of *The Rudder* magazine, characterized Rhodes's handling of *Constitution* as "boat murder." The writer continued, "Barr simply made a monkey of the other man. He forced him to do whatever he wished, and shoved and jostled the *Constitution*, the latter's skipper giving way in the most complaisant manner. The *Constitution* crowd seemed to be deathly afraid of Barr, and whenever it came to a close question their only anxiety seemed to be to get out of his way . . . Their excuse for this cringing was that they did not want to have the boat injured; a most childish excuse, and one that no experienced man would make . . ."

It got so ugly out there that Barr was disqualified from a race on the very day he was named the defender. So *Columbia* ruled the waves, becoming the first defender to make an encore appearance. Two other defenders would match her in later years: *Intrepid* in 1967 and 70 and *Courageous* in 1974 and 77.

I sailed aboard *Courageous* in 1974, as her tactician and starting helmsman. My model for that appearance—indeed in sailing—was "the redoubtable Charlie Barr," as he came to be called.

While Lawson's *Independence* wasn't a recognized defender, she sailed eight races that summer—six against *Columbia* and *Constitution* and two matches against *Columbia*. Under the command of Captain Hank Haff, a two-time winner of the America's Cup, she lost all of them. She had her moments, however, particularly on a reach. One observer described *Independence* as "going at steamship speed and giving an exhibition of heeling such as we have never before witnessed." L. Francis Herreshoff wrote the obituary of the "Boston boat," as *Independence* was called: "The *Independence* came in last every time because she was slow in light weather and broke down in a breeze..." She was broken up less than three months after she was launched. *Independence* cost Lawson exactly $205,034.08. He died practically penniless in 1925.

The America's Cup match of 1901 was slow to commence, first because of *Shamrock II*'s dismasting, and then because American President William McKinley was shot in Buffalo. He died of his wounds on September 14. Following the assassination, Vice President Theodore Roosevelt became the twenty-sixth president. Lipton proposed the races be delayed, to which the NYYC agreed to a five-day postponement. Lipton's *Shamrock II* lost three races to Barr and *Columbia*, but in 90 miles of racing, she lost by only 5 minutes and 36 seconds on corrected time. *Shamrock*, in fact, was ahead until the final miles of each race. Lipton announced that he would return.

Lipton's next challenge for what he called the "auld mug" was in 1903 with *Shamrock III*, another Fife design. Herreshoff drew *Reliance*, which was skippered by Barr. The scowlike form of the boat, interestingly enough, was influenced more than a little by Lawson's *Independence*. *Shamrock III*, which was 134 feet overall and 90 feet on the water, lost two races and then went astray in the fog in the third.

Who was Charlie Barr, the first skipper to win three America's Cups? Barr was born in Scotland in 1861. His older half brother was Captain John Barr, the best professional yacht captain in Scotland. Indeed, John Barr skippered *Thistle*, the America's Cup challenger from the Royal Clyde Yacht Club in 1887. Charlie Barr was the mate on *Thistle* in that Cup. When *Thistle* was sold in 1892 to Kaiser Wilhelm II, Charlie Barr came to America, where he worked as a professional captain. He skippered *Vigilant*, a defense candidate, in 1895. His competition was the famous Captain Henry Haff, who had already skippered *Volunteer* to victory in the 1887 Cup. Captain Haff, sailing *Defender*, embarrassed Charlie Barr and *Vigilant*—particularly at the start. Said Barr then, "I have been made a fool of . . ." It would not happen often again.

Barr was a small, wiry, and heavily mustached man. Despite his diminutive stature, he was able to command the tough Scandinavian, British, and Maine seamen who sailed the extreme yachts of the day. L. Francis Herreshoff nicely described the division of labor on an America's Cup yacht then, "There was one head or brain (the captain), several mouthpieces (the mates), and twenty or thirty bunches of sinew, muscle, and leather, which acted instantly at each order." No one led the sinew, muscle, and leather better than Barr. He was a professional sailor who might be paid $3,500 for an America's Cup summer.

In 1904, Barr was Captain of the Herreshoff-designed *Ingomar*, which so impressed Kaiser Wilhelm. The next year Barr skippered the famous three-masted 185-foot schooner *Atlantic* in the Transatlantic Race. She set the transatlantic record, from Sandy Hook, New Jersey, to the Lizard, in England, in 12 days, 4 hours. Commodore Wilson Marshall, the owner, and six of his friends were along for the ride. This record lasted for nearly 90 years.[7] Barr died in 1911.

Lipton challenged for 1907 but on the condition smaller boats be used. He proposed that the Cup be sailed in yachts of about 110 feet overall and 75 feet on the water, boats similar in size to the King's *Britannia*. This was called the "Big Class" in England. The yacht club rejected this idea, as these boats were of "insignificant power and size." In the letter of explanation to Lipton, the yacht club wrote that the trustee [NYYC] could not accept any challenge that purported to add any design limitations beyond those expressly stated in the Deed. In fact, the New York membership unanimously adopted a resolution, which, in part, states, "That no agreement should be made with any challenger which imposes any other limitations or restrictions upon the designer than such as is necessarily implied in the limits of

---

7. In 1993 *Winston*, my Whitbread 60, beat this record in a race. Our time was 11 days, 8 hours. Two other sailboats, *Procea*, a 244-foot monohull, and *Jet Services V*, a 75-foot catamaran, have sailed the course faster. Neither boat was involved in a race, however, as were *Atlantic* and *Winston*, and, thus, could start when conditions were judged most propitious.

water-line length expressed in the Deed." Those very words would reverberate through a New York courtroom some 80 years later.

In 1913 Lipton challenged for 1914. Again he asked that the competition be held in smaller boats. The club said, in essence, challengers don't write rules, the defender does. Finally, Lipton backed down and challenged without conditions. In an astounding move, the yacht club accepted his original terms—the match would be sailed in 75-footers. This challenge never took place because World War I broke out that year. Nevertheless, Lipton's *Shamrock IV*, designed by Charles Nicholson, remained in New York, and waited for a match that finally took place in 1920. The NYYC wanted the races to be held in Newport, where conditions were better, but Lipton demurred. There was far more media attention to be had in New York than in Newport, he concluded.

This was the first America's Cup where amateurs—rather than professional sailors—skippered the defender and challenger. The defender, *Resolute*, was commanded by Charles Francis Adams, of Boston, who later became the U.S. Secretary of the Navy. The challenger was skippered by William P. Burton, considered the best amateur sailboat racer in England. *Shamrock* won the first race when the American defender, *Resolute*, suffered a breakdown and did not finish. This had never happened before, nor has it since.

The initial race in 1920 filled half the front page of *The New York Times*. Lipton was enormously popular in America—an image he worked hard to cultivate. He did it because he gained from it— it was good public relations—and because he loved it. Lipton was one of those public figures who absolutely did not want to be left alone. He opened his *Shamrock IV* to visitors, and 35,000 New Yorkers showed up to take a tour of her. They had to be controlled by the New York police.

Then Lipton's *Shamrock* won the second race by more than two minutes. He was within one win of wresting that "auld mug," from the NYYC. *Shamrock* and *Resolute* crossed the finish line of the third race at the same time, but Lipton's boat, which rated much higher, lost by seven minutes when the handicap was figured in. Lipton was unbowed. He told reporters, "We are going to have the Cup measured up right away so that I can get a box built just the right size to take it home."

Sadly for Lipton, his *Shamrock IV* lost the next two races and the America's Cup. The Americans seemed as disheartened by this as the British, Lipton's countrymen.

Coming so close but failing was a bitter pill. Lipton told the boatyard "to break that boat up; I never want to see her again."

Shamrock IV was cut into fireplace logs; she heated Lipton's house for years.

CHAPTER 3

1930—37

THE J-CLASS ERA

—⁓—

COWES WEEK, WHERE the yacht *America* triumphed in 1851, has long been the annual regatta of the Royal Yacht Squadron (RYS).[1] When Cowes Week began is difficult to say; there is, for example, a painting titled "Cowes Regatta, 1776," hanging in the castle of the RYS. This predates the founding of this most famous British club by 39 years, and coincides with America's Declaration of Independence from Great Britain.

Whatever its beginnings, Cowes Week has long been an important fixture in Britain's social "Summer Season," which begins with the Derby in early June, then Royal Ascot, Wimbledon, Henley Royal Regatta, racing at Goodwood, Cowes Royal Regatta, as it is officially called, and finally, in mid-August, the beginnings of grouse shooting—which is never described as *hunting*—in Scotland.

In his book *Sacred Cowes*, Anthony Heckstall-Smith, the British journalist, related a conversation between an owner who was a member of the RYS and his skipper that took place at Cowes Week sometime in the 1920s.

"The owner (pointing to a cutter with a green hull): 'Brown, that's the *Shamrock* over there isn't it?'

---

1. Cowes Week continues to this day, although its organization is shared by several clubs.

"Brown: 'Yes, that 'er, Sir Walter.'

"The owner (a smile of triumph spreading across his face as he takes courage from success): 'And wouldn't that be the *White Heather* just astern of her, Brown?'

"Brown: 'Yes, Sir Walter.'

"The owner (now completely carried away by success and becoming jocular): 'But damned if I can recognize the white cutter, which is she, Brown?'

"Brown, who appears stricken by deafness, remains silent.

"The owner: 'Brown, I asked you a question. I asked you the name of the third cutter.'

"Brown's face twitches with anguish and he sucks his teeth.

"The owner (heartily to me): 'The old boy's getting deaf.' (Raising his voice) 'Brown, who owns the other white cutter?'

"Brown (as if in pain): 'You do, Sir Walter.' "

This story is told for several reasons. First, owners of large yachts, particularly in England in those days, often owned boats that they never steered—indeed, never set foot aboard. In some cases, they did not even recognize their boats. Sir Thomas Lipton, for example, never steered any of his America's Cup yachts. Professionals did the sweaty work of sailing and steering big racing boats in England.

Was ownership of a big yacht pride of possession? Or was it, as Heckstall-Smith postulates, "But a stepping stone to social success, membership of the Royal Yacht Squadron and a seat in the House of Lords?"

To understand the America's Cup, one has to understand the Royal Yacht Squadron, the epitome of England's gentlemen's clubs. The New York Yacht Club (NYYC) was, in some ways, patterned after the RYS. Their burgees, or club flags, are practically identical; the Royal Yacht Squadron's is a white flag with a red cross and crown; the New York Yacht Club's is a blue flag, with a red cross and a star.

Nothing pleased the NYYC more than a challenge from England, but especially one from the Royal Yacht Squadron.[2] This is one reason

---

2. Between 1870, the first defense, and 1958, the seventeenth, all but four challengers represented yacht clubs in England. The only exceptions to this were Alexander Cuthbert's two undistinguished

why the NYYC was so horrified when in 1892 the RYS, for whom Lord Dunraven would sail, professed no interest in being trustee of the Cup, should its champion win it. It is also why the club assembled such a blue-ribbon panel to mediate Lord Dunraven's dubious charge of cheating in 1895.

The Yacht Club, as the RYS was called when it began in 1815, has had a long list of royal patrons since the Prince Regent became a member in 1817. When he became King George IV, he gave the club the "Royal" designation. It became the Royal Yacht Club and later the Royal Yacht Squadron. King Edward VII, son of Queen Victoria and Prince Albert, was Commodore and later Admiral. This position was also held by his son, King George V, a most enthusiastic yachtsman, like his father.

Since 1857 the RYS has been housed in Cowes Castle, on the Medina River. The castle, on the Isle of Wight in the Solent, was the former home of the Marquis of Anglesey. More properly known as Lord Uxbridge, he was a member of the RYS and Governor of the Isle of Wight.

When the schooner *America* arrived in Cowes in 1851, she was visited by the Marquis, then age 83. Pilot boats like *America* were fine forward and showed their greatest beam amidships, which was then carried well aft. This, of course, is the normal knifelike shape of boats today. Most English yachts were, oddly enough, wide forward and narrow aft—a shape that used to be described as "apple-bowed." The Marquis said then of *America*, "If she is right, we are all wrong." After *America* trounced the British, he said, "I've learned one thing. I've been sailing my yacht stern foremost for the last 20 years."

Wrote Heckstall-Smith, "The castle [of the RYS] was destined to become the most impregnable fortress ever held by the aristocracy of England against the storms and sieges of the combined forces of the new rich and the low bred."

Sir Thomas Lipton, who would challenge one more time in

---

challenges from Canada, in 1876 and 1881 (see chapter 10), James Bell's *Thistle* from Scotland, and Lipton's *Shamrock*'s, from Ireland. The Australians challenged in 1962 and again in 1967, but the English returned in 1964. From 1970 on, there were multiple challengers.

1930—his fifth—was the perfect example of the "new rich and the low bred." Even his great friend, King Edward VII, could not make him a member of the RYS, although he tried.

Lipton took this defeat, as he took them all, with good grace. Another rejected suitor, nicknamed "The Pirate," did not take it quite so well. He decided that a Sir Percy Shelley was responsible for the blackball that kept him on the outside looking in. He sailed his 150-ton schooner, which carried eight perfectly polished cannons, to Cowes and dropped anchor off the Squadron's castle.

"The Pirate" dispatched a launch with a note, demanding that Sir Percy, who was dining with friends, apologize, or else he would begin firing his cannons at the castle within 30 minutes. Sir Percy refused, saying he had nothing to do with the blackball. It was pointed out to him by an Allen Young, who knew "The Pirate," that he was perfectly capable of doing what he threatened. "Even if he is hanged for doing it that would be but small retribution for the damage such a bombardment might do," implored Young. Sir Percy reluctantly apologized. Then "The Pirate" politely dipped his ensign and off he sailed.

Finally, in his eightieth year, Sir Thomas Lipton became a member. Wrote William Blackwood, who collaborated with Lipton on his autobiography, "I think that at heart he was exceedingly pleased at his election to membership of the famous Royal Yacht Squadron— the most exclusive club in the universe, as it has been described . . . Last summer he was racing with the *Shamrock* in the Solent during Cowes Week, but not once did he set foot in the Royal Clubhouse. And many of his friends secretly rejoiced thereat!"

IT WAS THE Seawanhaka Rule, popular on Long Island Sound, that produced *Independence*, designed by B. B. Crowninshield for Thomas W. Lawson, for the 1901 Cup, and *Reliance*, designed by Nathanael Herreshoff for a syndicate headed by C. Oliver Iselin, for the 1903 Cup. Such boats Lipton began to campaign against—albeit in his diplomatic fashion. He thought of them as too big, too expensive, and ill-suited for anything else but *one* America's Cup appearance. *Reli-*

ance, for example, cost $175,000 to build—a fortune in 1903. She was decommissioned 126 days after her launching and finally broken up in 1913.

Even the NYYC—as responsible for the creation of *Reliance* as her designer, Herreshoff—was discomfited by these boats. Thus, on February 13, 1902, a committee was formed to develop a rule to produce more "wholesome boats." Designers, while not on the committee, were asked to submit ideas. Letters came in droves.

The committee settled on a rule submitted by none other than Nathanael Greene Herreshoff—the devil, himself. Length would be calculated in a much more rigorous fashion, so the rule would not be fooled by a yacht's long overhangs. There were penalties for a relative lack of displacement and excessive sail area.

By 1903 the Herreshoff Rule was in use by the NYYC, although it did not affect the America's Cup that year. By 1904 it was adopted by most yacht clubs on the East Coast and the Great Lakes. With the promise of it becoming universal, or at least as "universal" as most Americans cared about, it was called the "Universal Rule." The Universal Rule produced a rating in linear feet, and class boats were designated by a letter, I through S. "I" ended up being the biggest of the bunch; "I" boats were never built. That left the J's to rule the world.

A similar discussion about racing rules was held in England in 1906. Attending were 16 European nations, and the result was the "International Rule," where classes would be designated in meters, such as 12, 10, 8, and 6.

The fundamental differences between the two rules were ably pointed out by Junius Morgan, a member of the NYYC, who would later head the defense syndicate that built *Weetamoe*, a J-Class yacht for the 1930 Cup. He said, "We look toward progress in design. The Europeans seem to wish to crystallize design with a view to retaining the racing life of a boat for the longest period of time."

An unnamed English yachting writer took the opposite view: "I am convinced the Americans are wrong. My reasons go deep, and are fundamental to all things as well as ships. No man, American or any other, can feel full love for anything until time has had her chance to wrap it round his heart. I think it must be agreed that perfection without full love of the thing itself is unattainable."

In 1924, a rules conference was held in London for Americans and Europeans to air their differences. It took five years, or until 1929, for the principals to agree to adopt the Universal Rule for boats that rated higher than 46 feet. This pleased the Americans. However, to appease the English and Europeans, who apparently needed time to savor such things, these boats would be subject to Lloyd's A1 scantling rules, as well as show minimum accommodations and minimum freeboard limits.

The result was the J-Class era in the America's Cup, designed to the Universal Rule. The boats, which all rated 76 feet, ranged in size from 119 feet overall and 81 feet on the water, to 136 feet overall and 87 feet on the water. Since the boats all rated the same, there would be no handicaps. (Handicaps were a pet peeve of Lipton's; indeed, they likely cost him the 1920 match.) Sail area was about 7,540 square feet.

Other changes: the 1930 America's Cup would be moved to Newport, Rhode Island, where better sailing conditions existed. The racing would now be the best of seven, rather than the best of five. "Marconi rigs"—where a single tall triangular mainsail replaced a gaff mainsail and topsail—would be used for the first time.[3] This helped upwind efficiency immensely. Finally, since all boats were built to Lloyd's A1 standards, the defender, which did not have to cross an ocean, had no construction advantage over the challenger, which did.

Sir Thomas Lipton announced another challenge in May of 1929. His timing could not have been worse. In October 1929, Wall Street crashed; this was a symptom but not the cause of the Great Depression. Before it was over, stocks lost 80 percent of their value; 11,000 banks in the U.S. failed; one in four Americans was out of work; and in Europe unemployment ranged from 15 to 25 percent.

The start of the Great Depression did not affect the 1930 America's Cup, however. In America, four new J-Class yachts would be built for the 1930 defense, to meet Lipton's *Shamrock V*. Those five were half of the 10 ever built.

Besides being few in number, as a class their competitive life was brief: just eight years, from 1930, the fourteenth defense, to 1937, the

---

3. They were called this because the stays needed to hold such masts aloft looked like Marconi radio antennas. Another term for such rigs was "Bermudan."

sixteenth defense. Nevertheless, their flowering caught the attention of a deeply troubled world. Gushed a British magazine, "They fill the more popular headlines; their photographs adorn almost every back page; the most domestic doings of their owners are news; we are made aware of their size compared to Trafalgar Square and St. Pancras Station."

The four boats built for the 1930 defense were *Enterprise, Whirlwind, Yankee,* and *Weetamoe.* While none were shaped by Nathanael Herreshoff, who though alive was in failing health, *Whirlwind* was designed by his son, L. Francis. *Enterprise,* the eventual defender, was designed by Starling Burgess, a second-generation America's Cup designer, too. His father, Edward, designed *Puritan, Mayflower,* and *Volunteer*—defenders in 1885, '86, and '87, respectively.

Starling was a poet at heart, who enjoyed reciting Swinburne—while standing on his head. He felt that the blood rushing to his brain improved his powers of concentration and appreciation. He did not even need his hands to stay balanced. It was said he could do calculus in his head. Burgess left Harvard to fight in the Spanish-American War, serving as a gunner's mate. Then he invented and patented a new machine gun, before returning to college.

In 1905 he opened a shipyard in Marblehead, Massachusetts, before turning to aviation—initially as a barnstorming pilot. He designed the first seaplane, and later built airplanes for England during World War I. After the war, he went into a partnership with Frank Paine, the yacht designer. Burgess was married four times. A draftsman who worked for him said, "Starling always loved women and always had a lot of them . . . I think he had three at the time. Anyway, he had hanky-panky with the girls in the office, and he used to chase them around and around the drafting tables, probably to teach them to do naval architecture."

Enterprise was skippered and managed by Harold S. "Mike" Vanderbilt. Vanderbilt was four generations removed from one of America's most significant fortunes. When Cornelius "Commodore" Vanderbilt died in 1877, his net worth was $100 million. David Rockefeller was once asked why there were no yachts in his prominent family. "Who do you think we are? Vanderbilts?" he responded.

Mike Vanderbilt seemed the apotheosis of good breeding. He was

Enterprise, *a J-Class yacht, was the defender in 1930. She was the first of three defenders skippered by Vanderbilt.* ©MYSTIC SEAPORT MUSEUM, INC.
ROSENFELD COLLECTION, MYSTIC, CONNECTICUT

tall, handsome, a born leader, and eminently accomplished. He won the first Bermuda Race in which he sailed in 1910, when he was 26. Vanderbilt had a fertile mind; he was a champion bridge player, and invented the game of contract bridge. He also codified the International Yacht Racing Rules (IYRR) in 1934—after an America's Cup event that sorely tested the racing rules. It is these rules under which we race today. His timed "Vanderbilt start" remains a standard.

Vanderbilt, who graduated from Harvard in three years, before taking a law degree, was the ultimate organizational man. He was Director of the New York Central Railroad—succeeding the late J. Pierpont Morgan. While sailing was the sport—the hobby—of this New Yorker, he ran *Enterprise* strictly by the numbers. For 1930 Vanderbilt insisted his crew wear numbered jerseys. Maneuvers, such as sail changes or jibes, were charted, as football plays are today.

Enterprise's mast, designed by Burgess's brother, Charles, was made of duralumin. It was 12-sided and it took 80,000 rivets to hold it together. It weighed a third less than the competition's masts. *Enterprise* also featured a huge "Park Avenue" boom, so-called because two men could walk abreast on it. It had tracks running all over it, to allow precise shaping of the mainsail.

There were but three races in the Defender Trials of 1930, and they were drifting matches at that. When the NYYC so abruptly chose Vanderbilt's *Enterprise* over *Yankee*, a Boston boat, eyebrows were raised. The committee's motive was, said an anonymous letter in the *Rudder*, "Anything to make a Boston entry appear at great disadvantage when it comes to the America's Cup." It might have been Lawson, who died in 1925, speaking from the grave.

Shamrock V, designed by Charles Nicholson, of Camper & Nicholson, was primitive when compared to the defender. "*Enterprise* had been accused of being a mechanical ship," wrote C. Sherman Hoyt, a yacht designer who was the light-air helmsman on the boat. "As for winches, after looking over our '57 and one varieties,' (actually I think we had 23) and comparing his [Nicholson's] meager few, we both agreed that if we had too many, he had far too few."

In 1930 there were untold numbers in this country who thought Lipton should be allowed to win. Vanderbilt said, "I'll be damned if I'll be the first skipper to lose the America's Cup." Whether intended or not, this was an echo of the infamous words of his great-grandfather Cornelius "Commodore" Vanderbilt, who once told a reporter, "The public be damned."

Lipton was wholly unsuccessful in 1930. He lost four straight races by an average margin of 6:03. A broken main halyard prevented his *Shamrock V* from finishing the third race. In the twilight of his life, he said with consummate sadness, "I canna win; I canna win." Such despondency was shared by many Americans as well. On the night following the day Lipton lost, there was "not a dry eye in an American speakeasy," wrote Ring Lardner, the famous American journalist. After his defeat, the American public donated money to buy Lipton a golden loving cup; on it was inscribed the "World's Best Loser."

The British were quick to blame their failures on the wealth of such NYYC members as Vanderbilt and J. P. Morgan. One English journalist saw it differently, however. "Our failures in the America's Cup cannot be attributed to the 'Almighty Dollar,' for . . . we were towing a host of foolish conventions, traditions, and personal differences far heavier than any bucket ever made. Anyone who has given a thought to the American sportsman's viewpoint must know perfectly well that your American never does anything halfheartedly . . . Mr. Bobby Jones takes his golf very seriously . . . and Mr. Harold Vanderbilt does not exactly go boat-sailing because summer is the closed season for fox-hunting."

The writer continued that it was time for talented amateurs in his country to be given a chance to steer America's Cup yachts. "Mr. Andreae and Sir Philip Hunloke are the only two men in the whole country to whom we can turn for examples of the amateur's skill in first-class racing . . . Is it reasonable to believe that [they] are unique? I think not. The other amateurs should be given an opportunity— they should have been given that opportunity long ago. In America they would have had their chance but in this country we cannot depart from the old regime which is painfully senile . . . Again in this country we've always heaved and hauled on our sheets ten men at a time. Winches, we say, are unseamanlike. 'New fangled gadgets,' we bluster. 'Dammit, sir, they destroy the old traditions of the sea. Man power is the right power.' Blowing out our chests we bawl, 'one, two, three—pull!' and haul our sheets in far too flat, while the Americans, Norwegians and Swedes trim their sheets on nice little winches and sail away . . ."

THE J-CLASS *ENDEAVOUR*, a challenger from England in 1934, came as close to winning the America's Cup as any challenger until 1983. She was owned and skippered by T. O. M. (Thomas Octave Murdock) Sopwith—called "Tom." A member of the Royal Yacht Squadron, he, like Burgess, was in the aviation business. His Sopwith Camel made nearly 1,300 "kills" in World War I—more than any other airplane. Sopwith had purchased Lipton's *Shamrock V* after the old man died in October 1931.

Sopwith later sold *Shamrock V* to Sir Richard Fairey, who was also in the aviation business. Fairey, who seemed to entertain some America's Cup notions of his own, built a wind tunnel and discovered that the double-clewed headsail, or quadrilateral jib, which used a total of four sheets, was very effective. Despite being a business and sailing rival of Sopwith's, Fairey told him about the sail. He either gave Sopwith such a sail, or gave him the data necessary to have one built. The sole understanding was that it not be used until the America's Cup match, so as not to alert the competition. In a race against *Velsheda*, the only J-boat not designed for the America's Cup, *Endeavour* was losing. So Sopwith broke out the quad. The cat was out of the bag. The Americans promptly copied it. The crew of the American defender, *Rainbow*, again skippered by Vanderbilt, dubbed their quadrilateral the "Greta Garbo," because it was so flat.

Endeavour had "rowing winches," where two men seated on deck, facing in opposite directions, would push on four-foot-long horizontal bars. At her masthead she sported the first electric apparent-wind-direction indicator and a windspeed indicator, with both readouts in the cockpit. Both the challenger and the defender had rod rigging—a first in sailing technology.

Sopwith was likely the best amateur helmsman in England, and the boat, designed by Charles Nicholson, was a technical marvel, and beautiful to boot. Sopwith drilled his professional crew, so they were, perhaps, the equal of Vanderbilt's. He had everything going for him;

then, just before departing for America, the professionals went on strike for more money for going "foreign." An attempt at rapprochement failed, so Sopwith fired the lot. He sailed with gentlemen amateurs, who had no big-boat experience.

As bad as the crew was, her "afterguard," a term coined by Vanderbilt, was worse. Her navigator had no racing experience. As Zenas Bliss, the navigator on the defender *Rainbow*, said, "There were times at which we wondered if anyone were navigating for *Endeavour* at all." Another member of the afterguard, Gerald Penny, was there because he was Sopwith's fishing companion. There was Sopwith's wife, who kept time and relayed the position of the defender. Frank Murdoch, an aeronautical engineer who designed much of the rigging on *Endeavour*, was the only competent member of the afterguard, but he was not asked his opinion about tactics. Then, Murdoch was employed by Sopwith in his H. G. Hawker airplane manufacturing and design facility. The company later helped to save England during World War II, and Sopwith was knighted for it.

Nevertheless, *Endeavour* won the first two races in the best-of-seven series. She was particularly fast off the wind, where her huge parachute spinnakers were most ably flown. Prior to this Cup, spinnakers were glorified genoas, but these were huge sails; *Endeavour*'s, for example, measured 150 feet from clew to clew and represented half an acre. It was called an "Annie Oakley," because it was shot full of holes. This was a misguided attempt to release stalled air from the center. The American spinnaker was called a "Mae West," for its bountiful shape. The Americans had considerable trouble flying their chute.

In the third race *Endeavour*, up 2-0, led *Rainbow* at the first mark by an astounding 6 minutes and 39 seconds. "Damned" or not, Vanderbilt was getting ever closer to becoming the first American to lose the America's Cup. He turned the helm over to C. Sherman Hoyt, his light-weather ace. "Perhaps, you can make the darned thing go," Vanderbilt said before retiring below to chew on a sandwich and to contemplate his fate.

Hoyt, who was trained as a naval architect, was a pivotal character in this America's Cup. He was described by writer Scott Hughes as, "a smallish chap (not the 'little runt' he somewhere describes himself), highly charged with some extra special essence of vitality." Hughes had met General Eisenhower and was struck by the similarities between the future American president and Hoyt, describing Hoyt as a "pocket-sized sea-going Eisenhower." Both shared "a look of amiable belligerency, intense tip-toe alertness, and pervading all the impression of power."

Hoyt abandoned the normal course to the finish line. He had often sailed in England and knew of Sopwith's tendency to cover another yacht no matter what. Hoyt sailed high, as if he was not laying the mark, which could not be seen. Sopwith, who was to leeward and ahead, followed, even though he was leading the race and laying the finish line. The likelihood is he did not know his position due to uninspired or nonexistent navigation. Huge Moran tugs, belching black coal smoke and flying the oversized NYYC burgees, were used in those days as mark boats. Bliss, *Rainbow*'s navigator, would take bearings on the tugs as they took up their stations to help pinpoint his navigation.

Sopwith even tacked to get upwind of *Rainbow*, and with the tack he fell into a calm spot and barely crossed the American defender. It took J-Class yachts as long as five minutes to tack.

By this point, Vanderbilt was back on deck. He described the scene, "No one moved on board *Rainbow*, no one spoke, everyone was lying flat on deck along the lee rail. Sherman Hoyt, the only one, except the navigator in his cockpit, in an upright position, was sitting on deck on the lee side, one hand on a wheel spoke. The sea was quiet; the little ripples running along the side were quiet; the rig, the sails, the ship, the wind—all was quiet."

Once upwind of *Rainbow*, Sopwith tacked back. He had so little speed that *Rainbow* broke through *Endeavour*'s lee. *Rainbow* eased sheets and sailed for the finish line and the win by three minutes— making up more than 10 minutes on that last leg.

Sopwith called for a layday and removed 3,600 pounds of ballast from the challenger. Vanderbilt, on the other hand, added two tons of ballast, but more importantly, he sent for Frank Paine, the designer of *Yankee*, who had sailed aboard his creation in the defense trials.

Rainbow had barely beaten *Yankee*, the Boston boat, in the trials; the former won the last race they sailed by one thin second. The selection of *Rainbow* was controversial. It was more a nod to Vanderbilt and his organizational and sailing skills than to the boat. Of course, *Yankee* was again a Boston boat—seemingly anathema to the New Yorkers.

Paine was adept at flying spinnakers. He brought along *Yankee*'s best spinnaker. Help from a defeated boat in the Defender Trials was a singular act of sportsmanship, and one that became something of a tradition in this event.

In the fourth race, there were two protests, the first one at the start. Sopwith luffed *Rainbow* at the start to prevent the American boat from passing to windward. The luff happened under the race committee's gaze. *Rainbow* was apparently in the right, but Vanderbilt had been warned not to protest, if at all possible, to avoid another Dunraven Affair. Thus, he did not protest.

The race committee bent over backwards to be fair, too. It postponed the start of one race because *Endeavour*'s mainsail was not hoisted in the windy and rough conditions. Once his mainsail was up, Sopwith yelled over to the committee boat, "Thank you very much. They would never have done that in England."

Such equanimity was not to last much longer. Had the postponement been granted to the defender, there would have been a worldwide hue and cry.

The second protest in that fourth race happened near the first mark, with *Endeavour* ahead. Sopwith luffed *Rainbow* to prevent the American defender from passing to windward. *Rainbow* did not respond to the luff, and Sopwith fell off to avoid a collision—giving the lead and then the race to the defender. The racing rules required then that the windward boat must alter course if the leeward boat would hit it *forward* of the mast. It was a judgment call that those on the defender and challenger saw differently. If Sopwith had protested only the latter incident, he might well have won the America's Cup; however, he protested the incident at the start and the one near the first mark. In races where more than one protest occurred, they were to be heard in order of occurrence. The race committee, knowing it would have to throw Sopwith out for the first incident at the start, rendering his second protest meaningless, declined to hear both of them on a technicality. It said Sopwith had not displayed his protest flag promptly. The race committee had hoped to avoid controversy but found itself in a firestorm. Said one writer about the incident, "Britannia rules the waves, and America waives the rules."

Sopwith was incensed and, Hoyt believed, his ire compromised his sailing after that. *Rainbow* won the fifth race by a wide margin: 4:01 and then won the sixth and final race due to poor sail selection by the challenger. The final score was 4-2 for the Americans. Had Sopwith not broken out his quad when in England; had he not fired his crew before leaving England; had he engaged a decent navigator—indeed, any navigator; had he not lost his cool after the protests; had he chosen the correct sail in the last race, he might well have regained the Cup for the club that lost it in 1851. Sopwith was no Lipton (or was he?) and he vowed never to return.

ENGLAND AND THE Royal Yacht Squadron challenged again for 1937. Despite his protestations, the challenge was headed and skippered by Tom Sopwith. What mollified Sopwith, interestingly enough, was a visit to England in 1935 by American yachtsman Gerald Lambert and his boats *Yankee*, a J-Class yacht, and the famous *Atlantic*, which set the transatlantic record in 1905. Lambert manufactured Listerine mouthwash; he made a fortune by creating the word "halitosis."

This visit, a "hands-across-the-sea gesture" by a perfect American gentleman and his perfect yachts, was the first time in more than 40 years that first-class American racing yachts crossed the ocean to race in British waters. This was also King George V's Jubilee year. "I look back upon the summer of 1935, as one of the happiest I ever spent yachting," wrote Heckstall-Smith.

Seven Big Class yachts competed, including *Yankee* and *Endeavour*. It was the best of times and a harbinger of the worst of times. Charles Nicholson, who designed such J-Class yachts as *Shamrock V* and *Endeavour*, worried in an after-dinner speech that perhaps they "were experiencing a boom before a crash." Magazine articles began to appear with headlines like "Are J-Class vessels too large?—the racing now at its zenith." A joke circulated that a J-Class skipper put a lighted candle on the deck of his yacht each night. If it was still lit the next morning, there was not enough wind to race; if it blew out there was too much.

As if on cue, the carnage among these boats was extraordinary that summer in England. For example, *Endeavour* lost her mast at the Southend Regatta. That day, a man was lost overboard from *Astra*, and *Shamrock* broke her boom.

By the end of the summer, *Endeavour* had won nine firsts and *Yankee* eight. When the fleet left Dartmouth it was blowing 30 knots. *Yankee* had a commanding lead at the first weather mark.

Lambert described what happened next in his book Yankee *in England*. "Suddenly there was a grinding, crunching noise, such as I had never heard. Mystified, I lifted my eyes from the water and looked aloft. There in that one second I saw *Yankee*'s towering rig, 156 feet of it, steel mast, sails, and gear, go crumpling and falling to leeward in one ghastly mass . . . Then occurred one of the most gracious acts of sportsmanship which I have ever witnessed. *Endeavour*, *Velsheda* and *Shamrock* immediately lowered their mainsails and indicated that, as *Yankee* was in distress, they had no desire to continue the race."

The 1935 season proved so satisfying that Sopwith decided to build a new boat, *Endeavour II*. It was again shaped by Nicholson. They seemed a formidable duo. The new boat was rumored to be faster than its predecessor.

It was obvious a new design was needed to defend. Mike Vanderbilt was chosen by the NYYC to head a new syndicate; but in the waning days of the Depression, the membership was unwilling to ante up much money for the effort. Vanderbilt put up the seed money to fund design if nothing more.

With no one else to turn to, he engaged Starling Burgess again; but he decided to shore up the effort with the addition of 28-year-old Olin Stephens, whose ocean racers, such as *Dorade* and *Stormy Weather*, were by then winning races everywhere. Here Vanderbilt, a man who ran things by the numbers, was seeding the future. History would prove it money well spent.

Stephens was enthusiastic about the collaboration with Burgess, but he recognized that perhaps the older man might have a different view of the arrangement. To protect his reputation, which was tarnished somewhat by *Rainbow*'s performance in 1934, Burgess insisted that who did what be kept secret.

Each designer submitted three models, which were tested at the Stevens Institute of Technology towing tank.[4] While the test tank had first been used in the America's Cup on *Shamrock II*, Lipton's challenger in 1901, this was the most rigorous use of the tank to date. The new models were then compared to models of *Rainbow, Enterprise*, and—amazingly enough—the first *Endeavour*. Nicholson, perhaps for reasons of good sportsmanship or overweening confidence that he could improve upon *Endeavour I* with *Endeavour II*, gave Burgess the lines to what was then unquestionably the fastest J-Class yacht in the world. While Burgess gave Nicholson the lines of *Rainbow*, this was hardly a fair trade.

Sopwith seemed to be more skeptical than Nicholson that *Endeavour II* would be an improvement on *Endeavour I*, because in his challenge he specified that he be allowed to substitute *Endeavour I* for *Endeavour II*, provided that 30 days notice be given. To this the NYYC agreed. It was a much-compromising NYYC, as it further agreed to Sopwith's request that the racing take place in July rather than in September, the traditional time. He believed the winds would blow harder in Newport then.

Sopwith came to America with two yachts, *Endeavour II* and *Endeavour I*, the latter chartered from her new owner, Herman Andreae, for the sum of £1. Sopwith arrived with more than 100 men and two tenders.

The Burgess-Stephens collaboration resulted in the J-Class yacht *Ranger*. She was remarkably ugly, with a flattened stern and snub bow. The latter was designed to reduce weight. She was 87 feet on the water, the longest possible waterline permitted for the Class J, and showed a beam of 21 feet. She drew 21 feet with the centerboard down, 15 feet with it up. She displaced 166 tons, of which 112 tons

---

4. When he died, Edwin Stevens, like his better known brother John Cox Stevens, a member of the *America* syndicate, endowed Stevens Institute of Technology. The campus would be established on the family estate on the New Jersey banks of the Hudson River. Here, many prominent America's Cup yachts would be tank-tested. John Cox Stevens was the first commodore of the NYYC and its founder; his brother Edwin was its third commodore.

Vanderbilt steers Ranger. *Olin Stephens is seen with folded arms. Brother Rod Stephens plays the accordion.* ©MYSTIC SEAPORT MUSEUM, INC., ROSENFELD COLLECTION, MYSTIC CONNECTICUT. ACQUIRED IN HONOR OF FRANZ SCHNEIDER

was lead ballast in the keel. This was a ballast-displacement ratio of 66 percent, the largest ratio of any J-boat ever built.

By autumn of 1936, the design was finished, but Vanderbilt still stood alone against the British. It looked as if there would not be a new design to defend the next America's Cup. Then Bath Iron Works, in Maine, stepped in and said they would build the boat at cost. The designers, Burgess and Stephens, agreed to reduce their fees, and Vanderbilt shouldered the entire burden, about $500,000. The boat was built of welded steel—a first in the America's Cup—with an aluminum mast and Orford cedar deck. Much of her rod rigging came from *Rainbow*, and sails came from that boat, as well as Vanderbilt's first defender, *Enterprise*.

"After sailing *Ranger* for a couple of days," wrote Vanderbilt, "I became convinced that she was totally different from any J-boat I had ever handled. Over a period of years, I had not noticed any very marked difference between *Enterprise, Weetamoe*, and *Rainbow*. They all responded in much the same way and felt about the same. But *Ranger* was totally different." The boat, oddly enough, would "squat down and go." This allowed *Ranger* to use her full length for speed.

When Nicholson saw *Ranger* out of the water, he termed her, "The biggest advance in yacht design for 50 years." *Ranger* had a spinnaker made of 2-ounce Egyptian cotton that was 18,000 square feet—the world's largest. It flew on a pole that was 50 feet long. Her smallest spinnaker was the same size as *Endeavour II*'s largest.

The Vanderbilt boat could not be beaten; she could only be appreciated. *Ranger* slaughtered the other potential defenders during the trials and then annihilated the British and *Endeavour II*. The final tally was 4-0, and in one race *Ranger* won by a margin of 18 minutes. In another she won by 17 minutes. Olin Stephens and his brother, Rod, were in *Ranger*'s afterguard, and Vanderbilt gave Olin and Rod the helm during the fourth race as this unbeatable boat charged for the finish line.

This was Harold S. "Mike" Vanderbilt's third America's Cup win as skipper; with it, he joined Captain Charlie Barr. I would join that select fraternity many years later.

For the entire summer, in different types of racing, *Ranger* won 32 of 34 contests and was never defeated in 12 match races. Interestingly enough, one of the losses was at the hands of *Endeavour I*, skippered by the American C. Sherman Hoyt. Before the Cup matches started, the two *Endeavours, Rainbow*, and the other American J-Class yachts involved in the Cup went on the Eastern Yacht Club Cruise. *Ranger*'s second loss was to *Yankee*, skippered by Lambert, after the America's Cup, which ended August 5. This loss came during the NYYC Cruise.

For years the controversy raged: Was Stephens or Burgess responsible for the lines of *Ranger*—considered the fastest racing boat ever built? After Burgess's death, a leading English journal wrote that Stephens designed the boat. Mike Vanderbilt thought likewise. Respecting Burgess's wish, Stephens remained silent on the matter for 20 years.

In 1956 Vanderbilt wrote in the *New Yorker* magazine that Olin

Stephens was responsible for *Ranger*. Burgess was by now long dead and Stephens was the only man who knew the truth. He felt compelled to answer the question at last. He wrote to the magazine: "Models for tank-testing were drawn up by Burgess and myself, individually, and by draftsmen under close supervision, and the model selected to become *Ranger*, as the result of the tank tests, was a Burgess model."

Nevertheless, Stephens admitted that there was much cross-pollination going on there. "We were both drawing lines and passing them back and forth and were both discussing what we were doing."

AFTER 1937 THE moment in the sun for the J-Class yachts had all but passed. *Weetamoe* was scrapped that year. Two years before, *Whirlwind* and *Enterprise* were similarly recycled. Then *Endeavour II* fell in 1938, and *Vanitie* and *Resolute* (both altered to rate as J-Class yachts), in 1939; *Rainbow*, in 1940, and in 1941, *Yankee* and *Ranger*—the latter the best of the breed. All but one of these (*Endeavour II*) were American yachts, and again it showed the fundamental difference between the American and more sentimental British yachtsman who seemed to love more fully such things.[5] These J-Class yachts were turned into bullets and other armaments used during World War II.

There is a 1937 Morris Rosenfeld photograph of five J-Class yachts sailing together on Buzzards Bay in the Annual Regatta of NYYC. *Ranger*, of course, is in the lead. She is followed by *Rainbow, Endeavour, Endeavour II*, and *Yankee*. All of the boats sport spinnakers. It was Harold S. "Mike" Vanderbilt's favorite photo.

He wrote about it in his book, *On the Wind's Highway*: "I like to think of the 'J' fleet as they are pictured ... With outstretched wings, white as snow, they are flying toward us in formation. *Ranger*, the fastest all-around sailing vessel that has ever been built, heads the cavalcade. Her four older sisters follow in her train. Soaring, a fresh

---

5. At least three of these behemoths not only have survived but are still sailing. They include *Endeavour I* and *Shamrock V*, both owned by Elizabeth E. Meyer, an American. Also sailing is *Velsheda* in England. *Astra*, built as a "Big Class" yacht but converted to a J, was beautifully restored recently.

Vanderbilt's favorite photo shows Ranger *leading her breathren.* ©MYSTIC
SEAPORT MUSEUM, INC., ROSENFELD COLLECTION, MYSTIC, CONNECTICUT. ACQUIRED IN
HONOR OF FRANZ SCHNEIDER

breeze fills the world's largest sails. Presently, their season's work o'er, they will pass by in review. As they have come out of the distance, so shall they go into the distance. The fair wind, their never weary white wings, carry them on—*On the Wind's Highway*, 'homeward bound for orders'—on, to destiny."

CHAPTER 4

1958–1970

THE EARLY 12-METER ERA

FOLLOWING *RANGER'S EASY* victory over the British—indeed, anything afloat—in 1937, there was no America's Cup competition for two decades. Certainly World War II had much to do with the disruption, but there were other factors that contributed to the moribund state of racing for sailing's ultimate prize. As *Reliance* had before her, *Ranger's* perfection discouraged further development of J-Class boats. Also, the cost of building a new J-boat was, in postwar dollars, prohibitively expensive. Finally, the Deed of Gift, which has the weight of law, specified that such behemoths only be used in the America's Cup competition.

In 1956 Henry Sears, Commodore of the New York Yacht Club (NYYC), traveled to England to discuss with Sir Ralph Gore, Commodore of the Royal Yacht Squadron (RYS), whether there was interest in continuing America's Cup racing in boats significantly smaller than J-Class yachts. This discussion between the club that won the trophy in 1851 and the one that lost it resulted in the 12-Meter era.

The 12-Meter, designed to the International Rule, was a logical choice. Since *Heatherbell*, the first 12-Meter, had been built in 1906, some 100 of these boats had been constructed. At least half of them were still sailing in England, including *Heatherbell*, the United States,

Norway, Sweden, Germany, and Italy. The class was impressive when it made its debut, and remained so some 50 years later.

Two rule changes allowed their participation. The Deed of Gift was amended to read, "The competing yachts or vessels, if of one mast, shall be not less than forty-four feet [about the minimum for a 12-Meter] nor more than ninety."[1] Also, waived was the requirement that challengers sail to the competition on their own bottoms. This rule would in due time loose the Australians on the America's Cup world. They would have an impact.

In May 1957 a challenge arrived from the RYS. With it, the NYYC resurrected the America's Cup Committee.

Only *Vim*, a 12-Meter once owned by Harold "Mike" Vanderbilt, was a potential defender. *Vim* was designed by Olin Stephens—a great favorite of Vanderbilt's after *Ranger*. Vanderbilt, a three-time winning skipper of the Cup, campaigned *Vim* in England's Solent, in 1939. This was the final summer before the war. *Vim* won 21 of 27 races against a half-dozen British 12-Meters and never finished worse than third. With World War II, she was brought home to America and left on the blocks in City Island, New York.

In 1951 *Vim* had been purchased by John Matthews, from Oyster Bay, New York. Vanderbilt did not normally sell any of his boats; rather than seeing one of his beloved yachts grow shabby in the hands of less respectful or less financially able owners, he preferred to scrap them. With the best 12-Meter in the world, Matthews decided to enter *Vim* in the America's Cup.

A new defender was called for—or was it? NYYC Commodore Sears announced he was resigning from the America's Cup Committee and forming a syndicate to build a new boat. As he said, "It would have looked awfully damned silly to have sponsored a challenge and then have no boat to defend." For the design of the boat,

---

1. Nothing on a 12-Meter equals 12 meters except by coincidence. The 12-Meter formula is $\dfrac{L + 2d + \sqrt{S} - F}{2.37}$. The result cannot be greater than 12 meters or 39.37 feet. L is the profile length taken above the measured waterline, with other corrections for the fullness of the ends. D is the difference between the skin girth and chain girth. It is a measure of how the maximum beam varies from a standard beam. F is the average of three freeboard stations, and S is rated sail area. Other measurements are fixed arbitrarily.

eventually called *Columbia*, he turned to Olin Stephens, the only man alive in America who had ever designed a 12-Meter.

So Stephens would have his name on two boats: *Vim* and *Columbia*, sailing in the defense trials of the 1958 America's Cup. This would continue a reign that started in the J-Class era and would extend practically unblemished until 1980, when his *Freedom*, which I skippered, defended the Cup.

Olin J. Stephens II was born in 1908 in the Mott Haven section of the Bronx in New York. Growing up in fashionable Scarsdale, New York, Olin was diminutive and studious-looking. In this case, looks were deceiving. He spent much of his class time doodling boats in the margins of his notebooks. While there was no boating tradition in the family, his father bought a 16-foot daysailer in which Olin and his younger brother, Rod, learned to sail. This was eventually replaced by a 26-foot yawl with cruising accommodations. These boats set the course for his life. "I can't really remember a time I didn't want to be designing boats," Olin said.

At his father's insistence, he spent a year at the Massachusetts Institute of Technology (MIT) but dropped out. He described the cause of his departure as some vague psychosomatic illness, from which he convalesced at home. Next, C. Sherman Hoyt, the famous America's Cup sailor and yacht designer, got him a job doing drafting work at the yacht design office of Henry J. Gielow. Then Stephens worked for Phil Rhodes, another well-known yacht designer. He eventually joined forces with Drake Sparkman, a successful yacht broker and insurance agent whom the Stephens family knew from the Larchmont Yacht Club. The firm became known as Sparkman & Stephens (S&S). It is still in existence.

One of Stephens's first designs was *Dorade*, a 52-foot yawl for his father. She sailed the Transatlantic Race in 1931. On Independence Day, 10 yachts set sail from Newport, Rhode Island, for Plymouth, England, including the diminutive *Dorade*.

Almost immediately she split from the fleet, going north when the accepted wisdom was to go south. This wasn't just a roll of the dice. Before the race, Stephens consulted with Casey Baldwin, whom he knew from Rhodes's office. Baldwin had made a fast passage across the Atlantic by the northern route, which was chronicled in William Washburn Nutting's book, *The Track of the* Typhoon. Stephens, who had read the book, knew the northern route tended to be foggy, so he asked Baldwin if there was likely to be wind in the fog. Baldwin thought that to be the case.

Dorade's entire passage to England via the northern route took 17 days. The next boat would not arrive for two days. Not only did *Dorade* win the Transatlantic Race, but she won the prestigious Fastnet Race. It was an extraordinary summer for the 23-year-old designer. When the crew arrived back in New York, they were treated to a ticker-tape parade up Broadway to City Hall—the track of such notables as Admiral Byrd and Charles Lindbergh.

After a 21-year hiatus, the Cup was big news across America. *Life* magazine devoted numerous pages to it. Red Smith, the notable American sportswriter, groused in the *New York Herald Tribune* that it was getting more play than the World Series.

Besides the two Stephens boats, there was *Weatherly*, designed for the 1958 defense by Rhodes, and *Easterner*, designed by Ray Hunt.

John Matthews asked Stephens to design a new keel for *Vim*. Stephens agreed, provided that he be allowed to use information gleaned from the tank test in shaping *Columbia*. Stephens went to work at the Stevens Institute tank in Hoboken to shape a better keel for *Vim* and a better design than *Vim* for the *Columbia* syndicate.

From her long, sharp bow to her revolutionary reverse transom, *Columbia* was awe-inspiring—all-purpose built. That purpose was to win the America's Cup. When Olin's brother, Rod, who worked with him in the design business, was asked about her reverse transom, he explained but half facetiously: "It's slanted to get extra drive from the raindrops."

The *Vim* team represented some of sailing's best and brightest. There was Emil "Bus" Mosbacher, age 36, who would eventually skipper the boat. Mosbacher, a graduate of Dartmouth, won the Season Championship of the International One-Design Class for eight straight summers starting in 1950. It was in this Cup campaign that Mosbacher "invented," at least according to Everett B. Morris, author of *Sailing for the America's Cup*, the now-familiar match-racing maneuver of chasing the other boat away from the line. It was called

Columbia, a 12-Meter designed by Olin Stephens, was the defender in 1958.
©MYSTIC SEAPORT MUSEUM, INC., ROSENFELD COLLECTION, MYSTIC, CONNECTICUT

the "tail-chasing" maneuver because it resembles a dog chasing its tail.[2] If the authorship of that maneuver is in doubt, *Vim* invented the dip-pole jibe, using twin afterguys. This maneuver—as well as the tail-chasing maneuver—remains in vogue today. Mosbacher, who

---

2. The truth is that Captain Charlie Barr, skipper of *Columbia*, used this tactic most effectively against Uriah Rhodes, skipper of *Constitution*, in 1901.

was once Chief of Protocol at President Nixon's State Department, died in 1997.

Another important team member was Frederick "Ted" Hood, then an obscure sailmaker from Marblehead, Massachusetts. Hood had, however, won the Mallory Cup, the men's national championship, in 1956. He beat Mosbacher in the process. Hood brought along some of those new synthetic sails made from Dacron sailcloth that he and his father, "the Professor," were weaving in Marblehead. There also was Dick Bertram, who would soon found Bertram Yachts; Jacob Isbrandtsen, who would later campaign the estimable *Running Tide*; and Buddy Bombard, who worked the foredeck and became the master of this important position. Finally, there were Don and Dick Matthews, the owner's sons. A "crew of owners," they were called.

It was no undistinguished bunch on *Columbia* either. Briggs Cunningham was the skipper; a sports-car racer as well as sailor, his legacy to the sport is the Cunningham hole in the mainsail. Rod Stephens, known as "Tarzan" for his high-wire act on the mast of *Ranger*, worked the bow; Olin Stephens was in the afterguard; Commodore Sears navigated; and Cornelius "Glit" Shields provided much of the muscle. His father, Corny Shields, a legendary 63-year-old sailor, had recently suffered a massive heart attack, but he was there too, watching his son and the crew from *Columbia*'s tender *Chaperone*.

After three days of racing in the Final Trials, *Weatherly* and *Easterner* were excused; the latter boat hadn't won a race that summer. This left *Vim* and *Columbia* to wage war.

As August gave way to September and push came to shove, Corny Shields Sr. replaced Cunningham as starting and upwind helmsman on *Columbia*—this despite his doctor's orders to remain off racing boats. As Carleton Mitchell wrote in his book, *The Summer of the Twelves*, "Now with Corny at the helm for the start and first windward leg, *Columbia* went superbly. It was as dramatic a moment as had ever occurred in any sport, a man risking his life for the things he loved best. The crew seemed revitalized."

The two Stephens boats met on September 4, and *Columbia* won by 4:21. The next day, *Vim* won by 10 seconds. Two days later they raced again, and *Columbia* won by 2:22. The *Vim* crew thought it was over, and there were somber handshakes all around. The only word from the committee was that tomorrow's race would be triangular. According to rumors, Mike Vanderbilt, then age 74, had pressured the America's Cup Committee on which he served, to give *Vim* another chance. He obviously still cared for the old boat. *Vim* won this race, on September 8, by 1:35. This gave each boat two wins and two losses, but the next day, the new boat won by 2:11.

Columbia, with Cunningham again steering, led to the first mark of what was to be the deciding race and rounded with a huge 1:07 lead. In an 18-knot northwesterly, *Vim* responded on the downwind leg with a smaller Hood chute and closed the gap. The old boat rounded the mark only inches ahead. Hardening up for the weather leg, *Columbia* appeared to be pointing higher and footing faster, a potent combination. Near the mark, *Vim*, from behind, initiated a tacking duel and regained the lead, only to relinquish it again at the mark. Behind again, by a boat length, *Vim* had a better spinnaker set and retook the lead. This time, however, *Columbia* set her smaller chute and slowly but surely gained the lead and held it until the committee's cannon boomed, and a cacophony of horns erupted from the spectator fleet. They had witnessed the finest match-race in the annals of the America's Cup. *Columbia*, which won by 12 seconds, would defend.

The America's Cup, between *Columbia* and *Sceptre*, representing the RYS, paled by comparison. *Sceptre*, designed by David Boyd, was "apple-bowed," or carried her maximum beam forward. She was as "wrong"—and for the very same reason—as the British yachts were in 1851, when the schooner *America* ventured to England to win the America's Cup.

When *Sceptre's* navigator asked for a depth sounder, pessimistic management "gaped" at him, wrote Maitland Edey in *Life* magazine. When he asked for a compass, he was told, "You can stay with the other boat." Puzzled, he responded, "You're assuming we'll always be behind?"

It proved a fair assumption. *Columbia*, steered in the match by Cunningham, won all four races by an average margin of eight minutes. The first race was watched by American President Dwight Eisenhower from a destroyer. With the day's racing no longer in doubt he departed early to play golf—his true love. *Vim* would have been more than adequate to defend. *Heatherbell* might have been a more potent challenger.

FOR 1962 THERE came a challenge from Australia. An Australian challenge had been contemplated in 1889, when a Sydney yacht designer visited New York to discuss the possibility. He concluded that since a challenger had to proceed on "its own bottom," this would be impossible. That rule, of course, was waived in 1958, and the Australians challenged for 1962 with *Gretel*, designed by Alan Payne.

The challenge, from the Royal Sydney Yacht Squadron, was led by Sir Frank Packer, a media baron. Packer, in fact, had usurped an English challenge from the Royal Thames Yacht Club. When the New Yorkers accepted the Australian challenge, there were howls of outrage in England. Prince Philip tried to unite efforts in a so-called "Commonwealth Challenge," but Packer demurred. "Maybe we won't do any better [than the British], but every now and again you have to give the young fellow in the family his head."

The NYYC allowed Payne to test models at the Davidson Tank at Stevens Institute of Technology in America. He also used American products, in particular sailcloth from the great American sailmaker Ted Hood. Payne even used Hood sails from *Vim*, a boat the Australians had chartered, and American-made winches. Was the club being sporting or did it believe the challenger needed a more level playing field to keep the competition healthy? The NYYC certainly did not want another *Sceptre* chapter. It wanted a win, not a slaughter.

Payne cleverly designed coffee-grinder winches for *Gretel* that were linked by clutches—a first. This way four men, rather than two, could do the heavy work of tacking the boat.[3]

On the defense side, *Weatherly* was back, this time skippered by Bus Mosbacher, who had shone so brightly in 1958. The boat, orig-

---

3. *Vim*, in 1958, wound headsail sheets around two winch drums, allowing four men to grind the headsail sheet.

inally designed by Rhodes for that Cup, was redesigned by A. E. "Bill" Luders for 1962.

Only one new boat, *Nefertiti*, was built for the defense. Ross Anderson, who owned the big schooner *Lord Jim*, headed the effort. Ted Hood had recently rerigged her, and Anderson asked him to design the boat for a "New England effort"—a tradition that started with Thomas W. Lawson and his *Independence*. Differing from Lawson, Hood was no outsider. Hood's good friend and neighbor, Don MacNamara, was named skipper.

Nefertiti started fast; she won the first series of races against *Weatherly*. Then the exaggerated wetted surface on *Nefertiti* began to take a toll in the softer winds of July. MacNamara, a volatile man, began to show signs of strain. Hood said he fired several crew members, including his brother and the owner's son. There was one particularly grim afternoon when MacNamara demanded that a crew-member be fired for taking an "unauthorized drink of water." Anderson finally had to ask him to take a couple of days off to "calm down." Said Hood, "He just flew off the handle and left. Never came back." Although MacNamara had been an usher at Hood's wedding, that America's Cup summer proved the end of their friendship. They never spoke again. Later, MacNamara, a gifted writer, published a "kiss-and-tell" book, *White Sails, Black Clouds*. Hood was a primary target of his ire.

Mosbacher and *Weatherly* were chosen to defend, and in that order. The defender was not a fast boat, but she was most capably sailed. They met *Gretel*, skippered by Jock Sturrock. He was not named skipper until the eve of the contest. Packer was a man who relished the limelight, and not naming a skipper until the eleventh hour was done, many concluded, to keep the attention focused on himself. Packer also changed navigators on the day of the first race. So the Australian crew that arrived at the starting line on September 15 for the first race in the 1962 America's Cup had never sailed together.

The inaugural race was watched by a huge number of spectators on 2,500 boats. Among them was President John F. Kennedy, who had a summer home in Newport. The race, however, was an anticlimax. *Gretel* was over the line early and had to restart. The first race went to *Weatherly* by 3:46.

Gretel's private wave in 1962. She was the first Australian challenger. ©MYSTIC
SEAPORT MUSEUM, INC., ROSENFELD COLLECTION, MYSTIC, CONNECTICUT

It blew 22–28 knots for the second race. *Gretel* won the start, but
the defender was able to sail through her lee into the lead. Twenty
minutes after the start, a tacking duel ensued. The Australians with
their linked winches got the better of it. After 10 tacks, Mosbacher
knew he was outmanned and curtailed it. *Weatherly* led at the first
mark by 12 seconds. Then came an 8-mile reach where the lead was
unchanged. Both boats jibed for home and the finish. The defender
had trouble setting her spinnaker. Then there arose a huge war
whoop on *Gretel*, sounded by Norm Wright, the mast man. While
under a Hood spinnaker, the challenger had hitched a ride on a huge
Atlantic roller. The wave had *Gretel's* name written all over it. Before
it passed on, *Gretel* had passed *Weatherly*. The defender then hardened up to cross the challenger's stern; with that, the steel guy
snapped and so, too, did her spinnaker pole. *Gretel* won the race by
47 seconds. This was the first time since *Endeavour* beat *Rainbow* in

1934 that a challenger had won a race. There would be further parallels to this contest.

A layday—unbelievably called by the Australians who appeared most potent in heavy winds—returned the wind conditions back to normal. (It was equally windy on the layday.) In 8 knots of breeze, the third race was won by the defender by 8:40.

The fourth race, again in light winds, the defender led on the final leg. However, the Australians were gaining steadily under spinnaker. Mosbacher, taking a page from Sherman Hoyt's book, dropped his yacht's spinnaker and headed up under headsail as if he was not laying the mark. The challenger followed dutifully, as T. O. M. Sopwith had in 1934. Too late, he realized he was being misled. Sturrock fell off for the finish line and set a chute. Mosbacher, to windward, simply bore off on top of him to take the race by a slim 26 seconds. The Americans won the fifth and final race by 3:40 to complete the defense of the Cup.

After the door was slammed on the English in 1960 in favor of the Australians, the NYYC mollified the blow, at least a little, by saying it "might" accept a challenge from them for 1963. England and America are, as everyone knows, "Two countries separated by a common language," and the English, led by Anthony Boyden, a business tycoon, took that "might" to be a "will." While waiting for 1963, Boyden's designer, the same David Boyd who designed the vainglorious *Sceptre*, availed himself of some tank-testing at the Stevens Institute of Technology. The institute was by now a repository of 12-Meter technology. Since it was endowed by Edwin Stevens, a member of the *America* syndicate, this seemed fitting.

An America's Cup in 1963 was not to be. The next Cup, the New Yorkers said, would be in 1964. It was apparent the NYYC was exhausted from mounting the previous defense. Boyden tried to rally public support for his cause but got nowhere. He would have to wait for 1964.

During the breather, the NYYC made American testing facilities and American products, such as sails and winches, *verboten* for challengers. This was accomplished through an interpretation of the Deed of Gift. The NYYC applied a "country-of-origin" rule on the design of a yacht, its designer, as well as its equipment. *America* was "an example of Yankee ship-building," and this returned the competition to its roots.

For 1964 the Americans launched two new boats: *Constellation*, designed by Stephens, and *American Eagle*, designed by Luders, who had redesigned *Weatherly* in 1962. Also, there were Hood's redesigned *Nefertiti* and *Columbia*, sailed by the first West Coast syndicate. It included Bill Ficker, as cohelmsman, and Lowell North, the famous sailmaker. Both men, from Southern California, would play significant roles in future Cups.

The racing, however, starred the two new boats: *Constellation*, steered first by Eric Ridder but eventually by Robert N. Bavier Jr., the advertising manager of *Yachting* magazine, and *American Eagle*, skippered by Bill Cox. At one point, the very red and apparently very fast *American Eagle* defeated *Constellation* in 14 straight races.

In mid-July Ridder asked Bavier to take the helm during a start. *Constellation* did better. This was then extended to the first leg, and eventually to the entire race. Then the syndicate, headed by Pierre S. du Pont, asked Bavier to helm the boat and Ridder to stay aboard as "titular skipper." If technically not a firing, as it was set in motion by Ridder, it was certainly a demotion. With the change, *Constellation* started to beat *American Eagle*. With that, bumper stickers sprouted in Newport saying, "Beat the Bird." The reply came from *American Eagle* supporters on toilet paper that read, "Prevent *Const*ipation."

The trials during the 12-Meter era were usually more interesting than the America's Cup match. In the final trials Bavier and *Constellation* won the first race after a jib-luff wire broke on *American Eagle*. With the loss, the seeds of self-doubt started to grow on *American Eagle*, and gnaw at Cox. Suddenly his helming appeared wooden rather than fluid. Worry seemed etched on his face.

In the second race, *Constellation* took the start. However, Bavier's boat rounded the first mark of the Olympic course two lengths behind.[4] The yachts seemed tied together in this formation for much of the race. On the final leg, however, *Constellation* started a tacking

---

4. This was the first Cup to feature an "Olympic Course"—once around a triangle and then windward-leeward-windward. Prior to this Cup, the races were on a triangular course or else windward-leeward. The length was still 24 miles.

duel. Rod Stephens, her navigator, noticed that she was gaining slightly on each tack, so they kept at it. Before the leg was over, *Eagle* tacked 44 times, *Constellation*, 42—a record. A mile to the finish, *Constellation* took the lead. She won by 1:08. This race, Bavier concluded in his book, *A View from the Cockpit*, "Broke *Eagle*'s heart." The red boat won only one more race that summer. *Constellation* was chosen to defend.

The match was between *Constellation* and *Sovereign*, skippered by Peter Scott, the son of the famous polar explorer Robert Falcon Scott. In 1911–12 the elder Scott lost his most famous race to the South Pole to Roald Amundsen, a Norwegian, by a month. Amundsen favored sled dogs and men trekking on skis, which was considered the modern technique for polar exploration. Scott favored ponies and men pulling sleds—the traditional method. On the long lonely trek back, Scott and his men succumbed to exhaustion, cold, and heartbreak when but 11 miles from a food-and-fuel cache that would have saved their lives. Nevertheless, he died a hero in England—a place where trying seems at least as important as succeeding.

The younger Scott lost his most famous race, too. Early that America's Cup summer he betrayed his lack of experience and asked for an explanation of the circling before the start by the defenders. His crew consisted of rugby players, rather than sailors. One could almost hear the British saying, as they supposedly had said in 1930, "Man power is the right power." *Sovereign* lost all four races; her losing margin in the second race, held on September 17, was 20 minutes.

A boat was the star of 1967. The boat was *Intrepid*, and her designer was Olin Stephens. She was a superyacht, and a giant step forward, in the tradition of *Reliance* and *Ranger*. If these two boats killed off their classes, as both did, *Intrepid* spawned a new generation of 12-Meter yachts. They reached their apotheosis with *Courageous*— another Stephens design that defended the Cup in 1974 and 77.

In designing *Intrepid* for 1967, Stephens looked back. He certainly took a long, hard look at the Cal 40, a Bill Lapworth design that in 1964 crashed the racing circuit with extraordinary success. The Cal 40 was distinguished by a fin keel and a separate spade rudder hung

Intrepid *in 1967. The crew worked the boat mostly from below decks.*
©MYSTIC SEAPORT MUSEUM, INC., ROSENFELD COLLECTION, MYSTIC, CONNECTICUT

well aft.[5] She was comfortable, easy to sail, easy to control even down-wind where the doomsayers expected the rudder to cavitate and lose control. Most important, she was fast. Prior to *Intrepid*, all 12-Meters and most offshore yachts had the rudder affixed to the trailing edge of the keel—an arrangement that tended to make both of them larger

---

5. Lapworth, however, was not the first yacht designer to separate the rudder from the keel. This was likely first done on *Dilemma*, designed by Nathanael Herreshoff in 1891.

than they probably needed to be. It also made the hull's wetted surface greater than it needed to be. As there is friction between a hull and the water, the excessive wetted surface exacts a toll, especially in gentle winds.

In the design process, Stephens considered decreasing the (fore and aft) length of the keel to save further on wetted-surface drag. Each time he did that the model tested faster. The designer worried, however, about a corresponding increase in leeway. It is in upwind sailing that leeway, or sideways slippage, takes the greatest toll, and it is upwind sailing that is emphasized in the America's Cup.

Again Stephens looked to the offshore world for inspiration. There a few yachts had been using a second rudder on the trailing edge of the keel to minimize leeway. Called a "trim tab," the second rudder was oriented to leeward. This reshaping of the keel increased hydrodynamic lift, making the boat closer-winded.

Intrepid's skipper was Bus Mosbacher, making an encore appearance after his successful defense in 1962. He was again helped by Vic Romagna, his crew-boss. In studying the deck layout, they proposed that the coffee-grinder handles and the men grinding the winches be put below deck but the drums be kept on deck. This was not a first— some winches had been down below on *Reliance* and *Enterprise*—but never to this extent.

It was also clever because it circumvented a rule: *Sceptre* in 1958 had a deep and open cockpit that ran nearly to her mast. This lowered crew and mechanical weights—a boon to speed. It also decreased windage. After *Sceptre* the rule-makers declared these openings dangerous and, thus, illegal. Stephens got around this by placing a deck over the crew and winches. Most of the time, *Intrepid* resembled a ghost ship, sailing along with only her skipper, tactician, and two tailers in view. The seven other crew-members had nary a suntan to show for their efforts.

Lastly, Stephens lowered the boom of the mainsail close to the deck to create an "end-plate effect." There is a significant pressure differential on the high-pressure, windward side and the low-pressure, leeward side. The result is a leakage, or spinning, under the boom and in the direction of the low-pressure side. Aerodynamicists term this "induced drag," and it slows a yacht. The low boom allowed less room for leakage.[6] It threatened to decapitate the skipper, however. If little of this was original, Stephens's genius was putting it together in one yacht.

Intrepid's competition in the defense trials was *Constellation* and *Columbia*. It proved to be no contest. Like *Ranger*, the boat could not be beaten—only appreciated.

It was this superboat that the Australians and *Dame Pattie* faced. The challenger was designed by Warwick Hood, then 35, who had worked as a draftsman for Alan Payne, when the latter shaped *Gretel*. *Dame Pattie* was a long boat on the water; she got this exaggerated sailing length in trade for diminished sail area. She was helmed by Jock Sturrock, *Gretel*'s capable skipper.

The Australians, led on shore by Emil Christensen, angered Mosbacher when they bickered over *Intrepid*'s measurement. The night before the first race he paced his bedroom, unable to sleep, muttering over and over, "It's only a game."

The Cup ended with a 4-0 perfect "game" for the defense. *Intrepid* finished the summer with a startling record of 23-1. Mosbacher never raced on a Cup boat again. His two wins in the contest, however, put him in the same league as Captain Henry "Hank" Haff, who defended the Cup in 1887 and 1895. Haff, however, was a professional, Mosbacher, an amateur.

MULTIPLE CHALLENGES BECAME a reality in 1970. This came into being through a December 7, 1962, memorandum issued by the NYYC. It said that in the event it successfully defended the Cup in 1964, and, within thirty days, received more than one challenge for the next match, it would regard the challenges as "received simultaneously." History would prove multiple challenges the greatest gift of all from the defender to the challengers. Before 1970 challengers sailed in a vacuum, while the defender was battle-tested after long trials that involved several boats. Each had different strengths and weaknesses.

6. Preventing induced drag was one reason for the winged keel on *Australia II* (see chapter 8).

In 1970 four countries challenged: Australia, France, Greece, and Great Britain, with the latter two dropping out.

The French, making their debut, were led in grand, if finally ineffectual, style by Baron Marcel Bich, the Bic pen magnate. Bich's boat, *France*, sailed against *Gretel II*, led by Sir Frank Packer and skippered by Jim Hardy. The boat was shaped by Alan Payne, who had designed the first and fast *Gretel*.

In 1970 Olin Stephens was commissioned to design a new boat, which became *Valiant*. The boat was skippered by Bob McCullough, the NYYC Rear Commodore.

With Stephens otherwise engaged, Britton Chance, a young naval architect, was given the opportunity to redesign Stephen's *Intrepid*. This was not Chance's first 12-Meter, as he had designed *Chancegger* for Baron Bich.[7] Not being eligible for Cup competition since Chance was an American and Bich French, *Chancegger* nevertheless became the basis for Bich's *France*.

Olin Stephens was not happy with Chance's redesign of *Intrepid*. He later compared it to one artist reworking another's painting. As he said, "While I think [Chance] is very able, I didn't like somebody else messing with this design."

Asked what he did to improve *Intrepid*, Chance said, "I attempted to improve all-around performance, but you should remember that there was a historical bias in those days to improve heavy-weather performance. I was also competing against Olin doing a new boat and, presumably, he would continue that same trend, which, in fact, he did with *Valiant*."

Stephens took *Valiant* too far to the heavy-weather side of the equation; she was too long on the water, too heavy, and had too little sail area for the venue. Chance's *Intrepid* stopped shorter. Although a redesign, the boat did show some clever touches. Chance hung the rudder beyond the measured waterline. Then he added fairing strips to artificially connect the rudder to the keel. This increased *Intrepid*'s waterline length from 47 feet to 48.5 feet, but the new length was not touched by the measurer's tape, or so the New Yorkers argued.

Intrepid was steered by Bill Ficker, a 42-year-old architect from

---

7. The name came from the designer, Chance, and builder, Herman Egger.

Newport Beach, California. Also entered in the trials was *Heritage*, designed and built by Charlie Morgan, of St. Petersburg, Florida. Morgan also made her sails and skippered her. It was a virtuoso performance but finally counted for naught. *Weatherly* was there, too, ostensibly to round out the competition. Shockingly, she was often competitive with the newer boats, despite the fact that she had been built a dozen years before.

The first-ever challenger trials ended unhappily for the French. Bich did not name a helmsman until the eve of the first race. It was Louis Noverraz, a 67-year-old Olympic silver medalist. Amazingly, he kept *France* ahead of *Gretel II* for five of six legs. At the fifth mark, he hardened up too quickly, and *France* lost speed in light winds. Then she lost the race. Bich named a new helmsman, Poppie Delfour, an aggressive 505 champion. Delfour never led the Australians, and he was summarily replaced the next day by Noverraz, who similarly lost.

In the fourth and final race, Baron Bich fired his two skippers and took the helm himself. He looked resplendent at the wheel in formal yachting attire, including white double-breasted blazer, white hat, and white gloves. However, Bich got lost in the fog and withdrew from the race—citing the danger of racing through the spectator fleet in zero visibility at nine knots. He was furious at the race committee for starting the race and said so, unequivocally. After spending a reported $6 million to challenge, he vowed never to return to Newport. Famous last words, those.

The Australians, who matriculated to the match, were not amused by Chance's rule-beating gambit; they accused *Intrepid* of being 12¼-Meter. Chance was forced to alter his flaps. Similarly, the Australians objected to the head on *Intrepid*, which was not enclosed. This, too, had to be modified.

In the first race the Australians made two mistakes before the start that resulted in protests from both boats. First, they would not allow the "give-way" (port-tacked) *Intrepid* room to keep clear. Next, the Australian boat tacked too close. The NYYC could have, and perhaps should have, disqualified the Australian challenger but opted to disallow both protests, as there was no collision. It wished to be "fair," it said. Knowledgeable observers wondered, however, if the Australians even knew the racing rules.

Once the racing began, the challenger made a mess of a spinnaker set. Then, the foredeck man fell overboard. It took *Gretel II* two full minutes to recover him. Next, a second man fell overboard. *Intrepid* won race one by six minutes. The match appeared over to everyone but Ficker, who now knew for certain he faced a faster boat.

This knowledge caused Ficker to take an awful chance in race two. At the starting line, he tried to squeeze between the committee boat and the Australian challenger. *Gretel*, now started by Martin Visser, headed up to block the way. Just after the starting signal— and *after* was the operative word in those days—*Gretel II* smashed into *Intrepid*'s port side. This seemed a clear-cut violation of the rules that said a yacht cannot sail above a close-hauled course *after* the starting signal has been made. Despite the collision Ficker took the lead. Nevertheless, *Gretel*, now steered by Hardy and appearing clearly faster than the defender, passed *Intrepid* downwind and won the race.

The next morning, however, the Australians were rightly disqualified by the NYYC's race committee. B. Devereux Barker, its Chairman, was astounded by the Australians' lack of knowledge of the racing rules.

"*Gretel* Robbed" screamed the next day's headline in an Australian newspaper. Newspaper columnists in Australia and America, who had but a cursory knowledge of the admittedly baroque racing rules, echoed this sentiment. Even the American Ambassador to Australia sounded a similar refrain. Sir Frank Packer delivered an amusing simile: An Australian skipper "protesting to the New York Yacht Club committee is like a man complaining to his mother-in-law about his wife."

In the face of such negative public opinion, the NYYC considered resailing the race. Bob Bavier, head of the North American Yacht Racing Union, was asked if it would be appropriate to do this. This former winning America's Cup skipper was appalled. "The Australians deserved to win on the race course," he said. "They simply don't know the rules."

A young Australian, John Bertrand, was making his debut in this America's Cup aboard *Gretel II* as a trimmer. Bertrand would later skipper *Australia II*, which won the 1983 America's Cup—the first challenger to do this. He wrote about this incident, "The Australian press went berserk.... But I remember what it was like. I was holding the genoa, and I was the one who had to let it go because we were going above close-hauled and it was back-winding. Then, when we crossed the finish line, Bill Fesq, the navigator, got out the rule book and read the relevant passage. Among the crew there was a thunderous, stunned silence as the full significance became apparent. Our afterguard did not know the rules any better than we had known them in Race 1."

Ficker won the third race, lost the fourth on the last part of the last leg, in very light winds, and won the fifth to take the Cup.

Ficker was good; he was cut from the same cloth as Bus Mosbacher, who was cut from the same cloth as Mike Vanderbilt. The Americans were lucky, and the Australians were blind to the power of the weapon they possessed. The Australians never realized their boat was faster than the defender. Such knowledge might have changed the outcome.

With *Intrepid*'s win, Britton Chance's name was in lights. He told the world he was ready for a blank-paper shot at the master, Olin Stephens.

"Be careful of what you wish for," as the old saying goes.

CHAPTER 5

1974

CHANGING OF THE GUARD

———

YOUTH WAS TO be served in the 1974 America's Cup. The next generation had arrived. The youth movement included Robert E. "Ted" Turner III, Alan Bond, Bob Miller—who later changed his name to Ben Lexcen and wholly changed the fortunes, indeed, the address, of the America's Cup—Britton Chance, and me. All of us would play prominent roles in the America's Cup—if not this time, then soon.

There was, first and last, the *Mariner* crew, skippered by Ted Turner, age 35, from Atlanta, Georgia. Turner was young, brash, loud, southern, smart, a successful—perhaps great—sailor, with a prodigious lust for life. "If I just had some humility, I'd be perfect," he told his able biographer, Roger Vaughan.

The New York Yacht Club (NYYC) apparently viewed him as "Peck's bad boy"—an embarrassment. He was blackballed when he first attempted to join the club. Even without that vote of confidence, he had tried, in 1968, to form his own America's Cup syndicate. Like Thomas W. Lawson, Turner was unsuccessful.

For Turner, 1974 must have been the realization of a lifelong dream. Not only had he been handed the reins of *Mariner* by former NYYC Commodore George Hinman, but he had just been admitted

Turner steers his ocean racer Tenacious *in 1973. Also seen are Bobby Symonette (foreground) and Robbie Doyle, Turner's sailmaker.*
COURTESY MICHAEL LEVITT

to the club's hallowed halls. In no time, however, the dream turned to a nightmare.

Commodore Hinman was in his late sixties. He was in the winter of his life, Turner in the summer. He was as restrained as Turner was uncharted territory; as thoughtful as Turner was loud. We called him "Commodore Hinman," never George. Turner once instructed me that when in doubt about the name of an older gentleman in Newport, you should call him "Commodore." This is because there are so many of them around. Turner was not Commodore Hinman's first choice: Bus Mosbacher was. He wasn't his second either: Buddy Melges was.[1] When both refused, Hinman reluctantly offered *Mariner*'s helm to Turner. He may have been a "bad boy," Hinman learned, but he was a good sailor.

---

1. Melges would skipper *Heart of America* in the 1986–87 America's Cup and be helmsman for Bill Koch in the 1992 America's Cup aboard *America³*. The latter boat was the successful defender that year.

Turner's access to this rarefied world was, primarily, the two Southern Ocean Racing Conferences (SORC) he had won; the first in a Cal 40, *Vamp*, in 1964, and the second in the 12-Meter *American Eagle* in 1970. He had also won the World Ocean Racing Championship in the latter boat—a failed America's Cup yacht turned into a most successful ocean racer—in 1970. He was the Yachtsman of the Year that year. Besides sailing fast, Turner talked faster, more, and probably better than any man in America; indeed, he'd already earned the moniker, the "Mouth of the South." From Turner the world had not heard the half of it yet. He was just getting loosened up. Building an audience.

While born in Cincinnati, Ohio, Turner moved to Atlanta when he was nine. Despite a late start, he became a complete southerner in manners and in accent. Turner attended MacCallie Military School in Chattanooga, Tennessee. He went from being the worst cadet to the best. He was even singled out as the "neatest cadet" in his junior year. The worst and best remain Turner's salient personality traits to this day.

He cried, he said, when he left MacCallie because it was such a perfect place. Turner hoped for an appointment to the Naval Academy at Annapolis, but his father wouldn't allow it. So he attended Brown University, an Ivy League institution, in Providence, Rhode Island.

A good enough sailor by this time, he was offered a summer job to teach sailing at the prestigious Noroton Yacht Club, on the Connecticut shore of Long Island Sound. He would also have the opportunity to compete against other top sailors. The offer came from Bob Bavier, who would skipper the America's Cup–winning *Constellation* in 1964 and, interestingly, *Courageous* in this very (1974) America's Cup. The pay for the summer job was $50. Turner's father vetoed this, insisting his son return to the family billboard business, where his salary was $40. Further, he'd have to pay $25 per week rent to live at home. At this time his parents were making plans to divorce. The unraveling of the family, an on-again, off-again thing, seemed particularly hard on the junior Turner.

To be ordered home was such a disappointment that Turner took a drink and thereby lost the $5,000 his father had promised him if he didn't drink alcohol or smoke until he turned 21. To amortize the costs, he had another drink and then another. In due time, he was expelled from Brown for drinking or invading a nearby women's dormitory. Or both.

He served in the Coast Guard for six months before returning to Brown. He wrote his father about his desire to study classics, said Vaughan, a classmate of Turner's. His father responded, "I am appalled, even horrified, that you have adopted Classics as a Major. As a matter of fact, I almost puked on the way home today...." The letter ended with the words, "You are in the hands of the Philistines, and dammit, I sent you there. I am sorry." Turner gave the letter to the college newspaper, where it was published in its entirety. Turner switched to economics. Caught a second time for having a girl in his dorm room, he was expelled again, never to return.

The Turner in 1974 wasn't the bigger-than-life entrepreneur we see now. Today's Turner is best known for the huge broadcasting empire that bears his name (it was recently sold to Time Warner for $7.5 billion); is owner of the World Series–winning Atlanta Braves and NBA Atlanta Hawks; and is married to Jane Fonda, the Academy Award–winning Best Actress and now exercise guru. The Turner I knew in 1974 ran his deceased father's struggling outdoor advertising business.

Four days before his father took his own life, he liquidated his company for $4 million. The company's accountant, Irwin Mazo, advised young Turner to take the money and go have fun, but the 24-year-old, who had worked in the business for years, wanted it back. Ted Turner eventually worked out a deal to buy it back for $250,000—a sum he didn't have.

Asked by Roger Vaughan why he didn't take the money and run, Turner said, "Well, you know, my father had worked like hell all his life trying to make the big time. That's what he wanted. He went as far as he could, and when he dropped the baton it was for me to pick it up. Plus I am a fighter. I was raised that way. I could never be a dilettante living off the fat of the land. My business is really important to me. I don't know where I would be without it. Off the deep end, I suppose. As Ben Franklin once said, 'For every man that can stand prosperity, there are 10 that prefer adversity.'"

The *Mariner* chapter would sorely test that philosophy.

For 1974 Turner had invited me to sail on his boat in the "cockpit." That was a vague invitation, and I was hesitant, if flattered. Normally, he sailed with a loyal band that changed little.

Knowing the exact role I would play on the boat was important to me. First, the America's Cup in Newport was a long way from my home and life in San Diego. Then, it involved a commitment of several months. Most important, I knew that the best way to become a skipper in the America's Cup was to have been a tactician—the number-two man in the cockpit. As I wrote somewhat naively in my first book, *No Excuse to Lose*, "By being a good number-two man, you can persuade the wealthy people who come back year after year to finance these one-and-a-half-million-dollar yachts that you are a good, safe bet as a skipper. The hardest thing to do in yacht racing is to be selected as skipper of an America's Cup defender. (And one of the easiest things to do is to win the Cup once you've been selected skipper. United States boats have never lost the Cup in twenty-three matches against foreign challengers in 108 years.) So my plan was to go east to show that I could be a team player, learn about 12-Meters, and aim toward getting invited back the next time as skipper."

When pressed about my exact position, Turner told me he wanted me to be his tactician. He must have been unsure of the choice, however, because I later learned he made the same offer to Robbie Doyle, who worked for Ted Hood. Both of us accepted. As it played out, Doyle concentrated on sails and sail trim, and I was tactician.

My invitation to the America's Cup world stemmed primarily from the fact that I had won the Star Worlds in 1971, and the Congressional Cup—then America's premier match-racing series—in 1973. It was at a Congressional Cup, held in Long Beach, California, that I met Ted Turner, who also competed. I'd beaten him there— several times.

I was born in 1942 in San Diego's Point Loma section. If it is a fashionable address, my house and upbringing weren't. My father was a commercial fisherman. He turned from the sea to build airplanes at the General Dynamics plant in San Diego during World War II. There he worked for more than 30 years until he died. As a boy, I drifted down the hill to the San Diego Yacht Club (SDYC) a few blocks away. It was as if this place held a special gravity for me. At some point, the club made me a junior member, likely just to legitimize my hanging around. This opening of the door set the course for my entire life.

From my perspective—fairly parochial at the time—the America's Cup seemed a stretch for a poor boy from San Diego. San Diego is one of the most beautiful spots on earth, at least in my estimation. Nevertheless, San Diegans, isolated by geography, the border, and the long shadow cast by Los Angeles, have something of an inferiority complex. It is practically a cultural ethos. I was no exception to that, particularly back then. In my case, it made me try much harder in whatever I do.

After being allowed to pass through the gates of the SDYC, I crewed first on Starlets—a poor relation to a Star, the boat I coveted—and later Lightnings. Unable to afford a boat, I sailed on other people's boats. One such person was Alan Raffee, who became a mentor to me, but less in sailing than in life. I first met Raffee, who owned a carpet business, through Lightning sailing. I was 19 at the time and attending San Diego State College in somewhat unfocused fashion. Raffee would get into trouble with a rules violation or something, and I'd go over and try to help. He didn't even know how to look things up in the rule book. He was very needy when it came to sailing, but he was a very likable, generous, and truly decent man. He was also a savvy businessman.

In the course of one conversation, he asked me what I was doing for work during the summer off from college. I didn't have the foggiest notion I told him, and he said come and see me. I went, and he said, "What can you do?" I told him I didn't know. Then he asked me how much money I thought I was worth. I told him at least $300 a month. He said, "I'll give you $275, because I have to keep something for myself." That was the first of many lessons he taught me about business.

So there I was, in the carpet business, and soon enough, in management. In truth, Raffee hired me to sail on his boats. In time I dropped out of college to work full time for him; we continued this association until December 1979, when he died in a plane crash.

When it came to sailboat racing, Raffee and I weren't very good, but we were tenacious. He would have me sand every imperfection, every pinprick, from the bottom of his boats. He'd be out there, too, helping me. I can remember one New Year's Day, lying upside down in his carport, sanding the bottom of one of his boats to glossy magnificence. Meanwhile his car, a new Pontiac convertible, was out rusting in the rain. Then he'd inspect the boat with a magnifying glass. Tenacity, gleaned from Raffee as well as others, has become a standard of mine to this day.

Eventually, Raffee bought a Star, my dream boat as a kid. I studied the boat and the class luminaries like other kids of my era studied baseball players. The 22-foot, 8-inch Star, a William Gardner design that dates back to 1911, is one of the sport's oldest one-design classes. It is the oldest Olympic Class, having been used since 1932, with but one exception.[2] Since its introduction, the Star Class has tended to attract the sport's best.

In 1968 Raffee and I needed only to beat Lowell North, the famous sailmaker, and a hero of mine, in the final race of the Olympic trials in the Star Class to make the Olympic team. We were ahead of North, when we ran into a mark. In those days if you hit a mark, you were disqualified. North went on to the Olympics in Acapulco, Mexico, that year and won the Gold Medal.

I purchased Raffee's Star in 1971. With it, I won the Star World Championship, beating North in the process. In 1977 I won all five races in the Star Worlds in Kiel, Germany, which I still consider my foremost accomplishment in the sport.

Despite my lack of an actual college degree, sailing on *Mariner* with Turner was an education in itself. Turner was a redneck, but one with at least part of an Ivy League education. Plus he has a formidable intellect. While steering the boat, he would natter away about complex Civil War campaigns, quote Shakespeare, speak Greek or Latin, or tell dirty jokes in that high-pitched southern accent of his, which seemed drawling yet rapid-fire at the same time. He never shut up, and it only grew worse the worse we got on *Mariner*. On that slow, red boat, there seemed to be no bottom to how bad we could be.

---

2. In 1976 it was replaced by the Tempest (in which I won the Bronze Medal), but the Star returned in 1980.

Britton Chance, the designer of Mariner, *is pictured at Derecktor's boatyard at* Mariner's *ad-hoc launching.* COURTESY MICHAEL LEVITT

Turner also had a ferocious temper and a vicious tongue, should one of the crew make a mistake. He'd bellow things like, "You simple son-of-a-bitch, you piece of dog-meat!"—and that's how he spoke to his best friend, Marty O'Meara, who was sailing on *Mariner*. Nevertheless, he was a born leader who commanded absolute respect on the water. The crew would have walked on water for him; so would I, and I hardly knew him. Plus, I can't even swim—not then, not now. Turner would have made a great Civil War general. Had he lived then, we might all be whistling *Dixie*.

Although on the same team, Britton Chance Jr., *Mariner*'s designer, was made from different stuff. He was then 34, a year younger than Turner. Chance, of Oyster Bay, New York, was all-Brahmin; he had a superior air that was as indelible as a tattoo. He couldn't hide it if he tried. His father, the senior Britton Chance, was an Olympic gold medalist in 1952 in the 5.5 meter class—a 12-Meter writ small. He was a distinguished faculty member of the University of Pennsylvania Medical School. His mother was a noted painter. It was a family of great accomplishment and old money. Like Turner, Chance was no "dilettante living off the fat of the land." That was one of the few things they had in common.

While Turner and I were still hustling—reaching for the proverbial brass ring—Chance had arrived. In 1970, Chance had taken on Olin Stephens, the dean of naval architecture in America, and won. That year Chance's redesign of Stephens's *Intrepid* beat *Gretel II*, the Australian challenger, 4-1. This was fortunate since Stephens's new boat, *Valiant*, was off the pace. Before this, Chance had designed *Chancegger* for Baron Marcel Bich of France. This boat influenced Bich's *France I*, making an encore appearance in this America's Cup.

Chance was a scientist, who studied physics in college. His yacht-design career was based on the scientific approach—not salesmanship. He was a strange mixture of innocence, earnestness, and arrogance, who, while he wasn't well liked, was at least respected.

Chance was unenthusiastic about designing a 12-Meter for Turner. As he told Michael Levitt, my co-author, in an interview conducted in 1984, "I'd sailed a lot of miles with Ted on *American Eagle* and on 5.5s. I've raced against him, and I know what his capabilities are as a skipper. Ted is an excellent skipper, but he's not in the same class as a Dennis Conner, Buddy Melges, or Bill Buchan. I was strongly in favor of Melges skippering the boat, and he seemed fairly willing.

"At that time I tended to deal in absolutes, and so I felt that I had to make everything as good as I could. I was uncomfortable with Ted, and as a result that made me more inclined to do a radical boat. I was afraid the other boat would be better-sailed . . . Ted is good enough to win if he has a boat that will get him out in front, like in 1977 with *Courageous*. That, however, doesn't put him in a class with the good guys. That was proven in 1980 when he went up against the likes of Dennis Conner."

In Chance's mind, "good enough" wasn't good enough for Ted Turner. I got an inkling of this when I arrived at Bob Derecktor's boatyard in Mamaroneck, New York, the day after Thanksgiving 1973, for the first meeting of the *Mariner* crew. I didn't know Chance and barely knew Turner, let alone the crew. After the meeting, Turner, Chance, and I went off for a private chat about the design. It was an odd meeting because I could tell that Chance didn't want us to see the drawings, which he had with him. Then it dawned on me that maybe Chance didn't want *me* to see the drawings. So I excused myself, fully expecting that Chance would ask me to stay. He only grunted, "Okay." There was nothing left for me to do but

The "fastback" stern on Mariner *was an attempt to fool the ocean into thinking she was a longer boat. The ocean was no fool.* COURTESY MICHAEL LEVITT

to shuffle out of the room and wait in my car. Then, after swearing Turner to secrecy, Chance showed him his lines.

Turner came out to the car a couple hours later. A man of unlimited words—keeping secrets is not his strong suit—Turner told me everything. He was both thrilled and terrified, but Chance had convinced him *Mariner* was a "breakthrough." I'm cynical about that word now and was skeptical of it back then. I think people in sailing waste too much time and money worrying about breakthroughs. Just give me competitive equipment, and I'll do okay.

In early May 1974, back at Derecktor's yard for her launching, we saw what Chance had wrought; it was not pretty even to my untutored eye. The very odd *Mariner* had full, U-shaped bow sections, while 12-Meters are usually sharp forward. She had an extremely short keel, while 12-Meter keels are typically long. Then, she had a blunt, truncated after-underbody with steps, like on a hydroplane. *Mariner* also had a hard chine while the typical 12-Meter hull was rounded.

For *Mariner*, Chance's primary focus was quarterwaves—the

waves that form off either back quarter of a boat. If he could keep these waves small, he reasoned, the boat would be fast. To fool the ocean into thinking this was a longer and, thus, faster boat, Chance experimented with keeping the back of the boat artificially full—as Olin Stephens had in 1967 with *Intrepid*. Then he cut it off abruptly where the 12-Meter rule dictated. We called it "the fastback stern," but that was before we sailed it.

There were early indications that *Mariner* was slow—glacially slow. However, it was difficult to tell where our incompetence left off, and bad design started. When, in May, we first left the boatyard, *Mariner* was dragging an inordinate amount of trash behind that "fastback stern." Banana peels would follow us for minutes at a time like seagulls dogging a smelly fishing boat. That was an ominous sign. On the other hand, we couldn't even tack this boat without someone getting hurt. That had nothing to do with yacht design.

In one of the biggest surprises, no—shocks—of that summer, *Valiant*, the syndicate's second boat, was given that "fastback" treatment, too. An also-ran in 1970, *Valiant* was to be skippered by Commodore Hinman, our syndicate head, who had been actively involved in every America's Cup since 1958. According to Vaughan, Chance said that Hinman authorized the changes to *Valiant*; Hinman said he was shocked to see them when he returned from a trip to Florida. Whatever, the damage was done.

When *Mariner* started sailing against *Valiant* in May, we had no way of knowing whether our radical boat was fast or slow. They were, more or less, mirror images. Sadly, both the original and the reflection were terrible, freaks of nature, but only time would tell. Had we known in May what was apparent in June, we might not have missed the July trials.

Mariner and *Courageous*, the other new boat, met over the weekend of June 1–2 in an informal but sobering series sponsored by the NYYC on Long Island Sound. *Mariner* lost both races; on Sunday she lost a 16-mile race by an astounding eight minutes. It was as if she was dragging an anchor. Already Turner was questioning Chance's "fastback" stern in his nonstop patter. Already Chance was questioning Turner's ability.

Soon after this drubbing the entire crew wet-sanded *Mariner*'s bottom. Even Turner and I did this dirty and nasty work. This was a far cry from the more high-class crew of *Courageous*, who had full-time employees to do such dirty deeds. Looking at *Mariner*'s squared-off stern, I asked innocently, "Have you ever seen a dolphin or any fish with a square tail?" Legaré Van Ness, another crew-member, commented, "Even a turd is tapered."

Later, Turner improved upon it. He supposedly asked Chance, "Brit, do you know why there are no fish with square tails? Because all the pointed-tail fish caught them and ate them." At that, Turner walked away in mock disgust, but then he spun around to say, "Brit, even shit is tapered at both ends."

Besides *Courageous, Mariner*'s competition in 1974 was the old *Intrepid*, which won the 1967 and 1970 America's Cup. Both *Intrepid* and *Courageous* were originally designed by Olin Stephens. In *Intrepid*'s case, she was redesigned by Chance for 1970, which she also won, but had since been returned to her original configuration. *Intrepid* was wood, like *Valiant*, while *Courageous, Mariner*, and *Southern Cross*, the eventual challenger from Australia, were aluminum. While commonly used in outsized ocean racers, the International Rule had just sanctioned the material's use in 12-Meters. In fact, this America's Cup had been postponed from 1973, when it was originally scheduled, to 1974, so designers could study the material.

Of course, there was an Arab-Israeli War in 1973, and then an oil embargo (remember gas lines?), which led to a worldwide recession. To at least some members of the NYYC, it seemed unseemly to be burning all that fossil fuel to stage a sailboat race—even, or especially, the America's Cup.

Doubtless, the delay as well as the recession accounted for the fact that while seven challenges were delivered to the NYYC for 1973, only Baron Bich's *France I* and Alan Bond's *Southern Cross* materialized. Had there been more boats and more competition for the Australians, the outcome might have been different. Very different. But the Australians moved from spring training to the World Series and stumbled badly.

Aluminum was supposed to be the miracle material in this league; however, *Intrepid*, skippered by Gerald Driscoll with Bill Buchan as tactician, seemed to be the best boat out there. This had to be painful for Olin Stephens, her original designer, because Stephens's new boat, *Courageous*, wasn't any faster, indeed, she might have been slower. Painful, too, to Britton Chance, as this *Intrepid* was "de-Chanced," as someone uncharitably described it.

Driscoll, *Intrepid*'s skipper, was then 50 years old, and a boatbuilder. He had done the modifications to *Intrepid* at his boatyard. Like me, he was from San Diego, a member of the SDYC, and a Star World champion.

His tactician, Bill Buchan, was also a boatbuilder. A boyhood idol of mine, he was a shining light in the Star Class. As should be apparent, that is high currency with me. Buchan, of Seattle, would win the Star Worlds in 1961, '70, and '85. He would also win an Olympic Gold Medal in that class in 1984.

When I was 15, in 1958, the SDYC hosted the Star Worlds. The club assigned a junior member to each boat to handle lines, wash the boat, and be an errand boy to the crew. As luck would have it, I was assigned to Bill Buchan. His father was crewing for him, but was late arriving, so I got to crew for Buchan while he readied the boat. That is one of the singular memories of my youth.

The *Courageous* syndicate raised money the old-fashioned way— from members of the NYYC. Ushering in a new era, the *Mariner* syndicate, for example, raised tax-deductible money through the Kings Point Fund of the Merchant Marine Academy. This was Commodore Hinman's idea, and a good one it was. *Intrepid* similarly raised money through the Seattle Sailing Foundation. It was tough sledding for *Courageous*, and in January 1974 *The New York Times* reported that her syndicate had given up. With that, her designated skipper, Bill Ficker, who had sailed *Intrepid* so well in 1970, left.

It was not her last breath, however. Soon enough Bob McCullough, Vice Commodore of the NYYC, a member of the America's Cup Selection Committee, and the skipper of the unfruitful *Valiant* in 1970, stepped in to rescue *Courageous*. Her skipper was now the aforementioned Bob Bavier, age 55, then the publisher of *Yachting* magazine.

Mariner sailed in the June trials without much success. She seemed only capable of beating *Valiant*, her poor imitation, which we did in the first race. In the second race, we met *Intrepid*. Turner did

Courageous *sails on Long Island Sound for the first time in the spring of 1973. She would defend that year and again in 1977.* COURTESY MICHAEL LEVITT

a beautiful job at the start, which we won by being even but well to weather of the old wooden boat. He was so overwrought, however, that he was jumping around and shouting orders at everyone. His nonstop noise was making everyone incredibly nervous.

At one point, he shouted at me, "How are we doing?"

"They're pointing a little higher," I told him as calmly as I could after sighting the other boat with a hand-bearing compass. At this bad news, Turner had us trim the sails a bit to see if we could match their sailing angle.

Then he yelled, "Pull up my pants." A crew-member pulled up his foul-weather-gear pants that had somehow slipped to his knees. Again he yelled at me, "How are we doing?"

"They're going a little faster," I said.

A few minutes later, Turner asked the same question. This time I told him, "They're going higher *and* faster." Like good looks and money, that is a formidable combination. *Intrepid* won this race by two minutes and 52 seconds. Clearly, we weren't close to beating a seven-year-old wooden boat. Then the next day we went back to the future and raced the brand-new *Courageous*. She murdered us by nearly 10 minutes.

So woeful was *Mariner* that she departed before the last race of the first round to meet the torch. To be rebuilt. As such, she was the first America's Cup yacht wholly rebuilt during the competition.

The boat, indeed, both boats, as *Valiant* went, too, arrived at Bob Derecktor's yard on June 30. To make it back to the July trials that began on the thirteenth, time was of the essence. On July 1, however, there were no plans from Chance on how to modify the back end of *Mariner*. This was a shock. On July 5, there were still no plans. Then we heard that Chance was apparently working at the Davidson Laboratory Test Tank at Stevens Institute of Technology on a modified fastback concept. He was unwilling to abandon it entirely; the fault, he felt, lay with Turner and the crew, not with his design. The delay caused *Mariner* to miss the entire second round in July.

The *Mariner* afterguard, including Turner and myself, occasionally sailed *Valiant* in this round to keep our skills honed—at the risk of putting too fine a point on it. (The truth is we barely sailed at all that summer.) On July 19, for example, we sailed *Valiant*, which had yet to win a race, against *Intrepid*. In 20 knots of wind, *Intrepid* led *Valiant* at the first mark by only 16 seconds. To us, this was already a moral victory.

A sailhandling error by *Intrepid* at the leeward mark allowed us to get inside. She couldn't tack without fouling us, and Turner herded *Intrepid* to the layline. Indeed, when we tacked for the mark, both boats had overstood. While reaching for it, *Intrepid*, with better speed, started to pass us. Turner indicated that I should share the wheel with him. We had luffing rights, and we exercised them. Without hesitation or mercy. Both Turner and I spun the wheel, and *Intrepid* was unable to respond in time to the luff. Why Driscoll didn't anticipate this, I don't know. What did he expect us to do, roll over and die? The collision resulted in a substantial hole in *Intrepid*'s hide. The wound in *Intrepid* was repaired, but not so in Driscoll. As if we were outlaws, he gave us a wide berth from then on. He probably figured we were crazy, and he had the speed so he could avoid the clinches. This would prove to be telling later.

As the second round ended, *Intrepid* led with a record of 12-5; *Courageous* was 11-6; the missing *Mariner*, 2-3 (with both wins coming from stablemate *Valiant*); and *Valiant* 1-12. Of course, the America's Cup Committee stubbornly maintained that they never kept score. This was a selection process, a beauty pageant. It would select the best boat by a criterion only it knew. If we were beautiful in August, after being such an ugly duckling in June and absent in July, maybe the NYYC would select us. This was, at least, our last hope.

Finally *Mariner* was given a conventional stern by her reluctant designer. Derecktor, who built the boat, wasted no time. A rough and ready man, who was sailing on the boat until he ran afoul of Turner, he took out a Magic Marker and just sketched this huge expanse—the area Chance had worked so hard on. Then his work force took out their Skillsaws and attacked the fastback stern. It fell to the ground with a thunderous crash and was carried away by a forklift, to be thrown out with the next day's trash. It was kind of shocking to see an America's Cup boat—even a very slow, very red one—treated this way.

When the work was completed, *Mariner*'s crew joined Derecktor's employees. We put in 17- and 18-hour days sanding the bottom—doing things like that. Compared to Derecktor's work force, we were rank amateurs, but we did our best. This was not how I imagined the America's Cup. Late one evening, Derecktor came in and saw one of his workers sanding across the boat instead of fore-and-aft. He shouted, "Gabriel! How many times do I have to tell you, sand fore-and-aft, not up and down!"

Now, with Derecktor's work force, English was not typically its first language. In any language, this guy had had enough. He threw down his sanding block and shouted in heavily accented English, "F--- Derecktor!; F--- America!; F--- the America's Cup!" And stormed out of there.

. . .

THERE WERE CALLED "foreign challengers" back then—a name only slightly more cordial than "Mongol horde." The most formidable of the foreign challengers proved to be Alan Bond and his designer, Bob Miller.

Bond, age 36, made his debut in this America's Cup as head of the Southern Cross syndicate of Western Australia. He was actually born in England and raised in London, or, to be perfectly accurate, in Ealing. His father, Frank, moved the family to Fremantle, Western Australia, when Alan was 13. The senior Bond hoped his poor health might improve in a drier clime. Alan Bond found the transition painful; he quit school when he was 14 and got a job as an apprentice sign-painter at Parnell Signs, working for $50 a week. He was not noticeably successful. Only two years into the apprenticeship, he started a similar company, Nu-Sign, to compete directly with his former employer. Bond's company painted signs and eventually did remodeling and painting of houses. It even sold paint.

The company prided itself in taking on jobs no one else wanted, or so Bond said. As he once told a journalist, "It soon dawned on me that there were very few people who really wanted to go out and tackle the difficult work. I found there was money to be made in solving other people's problems."

Around the same time, when Bond was 17, he married the lively, redheaded Eileen Hughes, whose father, Bill, was described by some as the "King of Perth."

For Bond, now married and soon enough a father, it was time to get more serious. For him it was a small move from fixing up property, to buying it, and then developing it. After he'd achieved a modicum of success, Bond favored overblown American cars— "Yank-tanks," he called them. In these ostentatious cars, he would cruise around Perth with his mates. Later, there would be his-and-hers Rolls Royce Corniche convertibles for Alan and Eileen Bond.

Bond made his first million in 1967, at age 29, primarily from property development. One such development was at Kardinya, on the southern edge of Perth. Bond borrowed most, if not all, of the money for the project, and then, as a consummate salesman, sold, sold, sold it. Other people's money, salesmanship, playing the angles, avoiding taxes, "corporate welfare," creative accounting, and nerves of steel were Bond's modus operandi. It took him on perhaps the wildest ride of any Western Australia businessman. These businessmen from Australia's wild, wild west were a high-flying lot. But we get ahead of our story.

Bond's first sailboat was *Panamuna*, taken in trade for a piece of property. His father thought his son needed a hobby to help him relax, and so Bond turned to ocean racing—likely the least relaxing hobby there is. Within two months, Bond had destroyed two masts and learned much about seasickness. *Panamuna* was pretty but not particularly fast, and being the fastest gun in the West, and eventually the world, was very important to Alan Bond. So he turned to Bob Miller for the design of a new boat, *Apollo*, a 58-footer. It would prove a fortuitous choice.

Miller (aka Lexcen) described his first meeting with Bond to writer Jay Broze: "This guy walks up to me, and he's got a suit on and smells like cologne. Where I come from, smelling like cologne meant you were rich, and Bondy looked and acted and smelled as much like a millionaire as anyone could. 'Sure,' I said, 'I'll draw you a boat.'

"Poor *Apollo*. She was built for $40,000 . . . and bloody built in 14 weeks by a motorboat builder who had never done a sailboat in his life . . . The boat leaked like a sieve for her whole career. She was never supposed to get out of the [Swan] river, but Bondy, in his enthusiasm, raced her all over the bloody world."

Bond and Miller brought *Apollo* to America to race. They prepared for the 1970 Bermuda Race at Bob Derecktor's boatyard. It so happened that *Valiant*, our trial horse in 1974, was being built there. It was 6:00 A.M., and Bond, Miller, and other crew-members decided to take a closer look. At that hour, who would know? Bond described the scene this way: "Vic Romagna, who has sailed on many American 12-Meters [in the America's Cup], was there, and he didn't seem to want us around. He felt that the 12-Meter was a big thing, and we should keep our boat and ourselves away—far away. He asked us to leave, immediately, in fairly strong terms."

As Bond told Levitt, Miller, a bear of a man, responded that they weren't interested "in your bloody Cup or boat. If we were we'd come back and win it." Four years later, they were back. Less than 10 years after that, in 1983, they suited deeds to words, by winning it—the first time that had happened in 132 years.

Bond's first Cup challenge in 1974 was linked to Yanchep, Sun City, a Bond development of 20,000 acres, an hour and a half drive north of Perth, on the Indian Ocean. He called it the "Home of the Twelves," as in America's Cup 12-Meter yachts. It offered superb sailing but little else. It was all scrub brush and sand and heat—searing heat. To make it appear something it obviously wasn't in promotional photos, Bond, the former sign-painter, spray-painted a substantial chunk of it green, as in grass. Yanchep was also "Home of the Flies"—pesky flies—that caused it to be called "Yanchep, Fly City," at least behind Bond's back.

John Bertrand, who first sailed for Bond in 1974, and nine years later skippered Bond's *Australia II* to ultimate success, remembers Yanchep with little fondness. As he wrote in his book, *Born to Win*, "The heat and flies were nearly unbearable. One day, I came home and found Rasa [his wife] sitting in the middle of the floor of the living room and crying hysterically...

" 'I can't take it. I can't take it another minute,' she sobbed. 'The flies are driving me crazy.' "

Explaining his run at the America's Cup, Bond said, unapologetically, "Anyone who considers racing for the America's Cup isn't a business proposition is a bloody fool. There can be no other justification for spending $6 million on the Australian challenge unless the return is going to involve something more than just an ornate silver pitcher."

Bond was diminutive and feisty—all rough edges. He said in an unvarnished way what Sir Thomas Lipton, the grocer and perennial challenger from England (1899–1930), or Baron Marcel Bich, the ballpoint pen (Bic) magnate from France, doubtless thought but kept quiet about. It would have been unseemly for Lipton or the stylish Bich to say that.

Bond sailed under the imprimatur of the Royal Perth Yacht Club (RPYC). It is a Victorian-style club where the *Royal* designation is treasured. Like when playing tennis at Wimbledon, white clothes are *de rigueur* when sailing. The club had blackballed Bond when he first applied for membership. Bond was, doubtless, too *nouveau riche*, too ostentatious, for its tastes.

Similar to the NYYC and Turner, the RPYC came aboard—or let Bond through the door—when his challenge proved viable. At the christening of *Southern Cross*, on January 12, 1974, RPYC Commodore Alan Edward welcomed Bond into the fold by saying publicly, "... It gives me great pride that the Royal Perth Yacht Club can count among its members a man of the sporting caliber of Alan Bond." If it welcomed Bond into the fold, it was never a comfortable fit, however.

The club expected to see its proud name on the transom of Bond's mustard yellow *Southern Cross*. He had other ideas, however. He wanted "Yanchep, Sun City, Home of the Twelves." Eventually they compromised with "Fremantle"—the port city for Perth.

The NYYC was scandalized by Bond; so, too, was the press— even the Australian press—who dubbed him "the ugly Australian." Wrote *The New York Times*, "In the aristocratic eyes of the New York Yacht Club, Bond is simply the wrong kind of person to be challenging for a trophy as sacred as the America's Cup. His money is new, made on penny and dollar stocks and later on land speculation, and his manners are terrible. Brash when he arrived here, he is now being described as boorish and uncouth. Worst of all he appears to have come up with an extremely fast 12-Meter."

One might have expected that Bond would tap Alan Payne or Warwick Hood to design his 12-Meter, as both these Australian yacht designers had worthy America's Cup credentials. To Bond, however, they were losers, and he turned to Bob Miller, who had no portfolio in this type of design and was practically unknown outside the Antipodes. Nevertheless, Bond was a man who would go far without formal credentials, and so, too, was Miller. While very different men, in some ways Bond and Miller were kindred spirits. History would prove that among Bond's saving graces were picking and keeping the right people.

. . .

BOB MILLER WAS born in Boggabri, in the Australian outback, in 1936. He described his upbringing this way: "My father and mother were bushwhackers," he said. "Sort of country bumpkins. We lived out in the country, and they weren't very sophisticated people. My father was a restless person; he couldn't keep a job for very long because it was the Depression, and Australia was very hard hit. All I can remember about my childhood is moving about the country and living in tents."

When he was six, the family moved to Newcastle, a coal-mining town about 80 miles north of Sydney on the sea. His father had left home to join the Australian Air Force and never returned. His mother sent him to live with her mother, who was married to a man named Mick Green. Green was an uncommunicative codger, who rarely spoke to the maturing boy. However, when Miller's grandmother died, when he was nine, Green kept him fed and put a roof over his head. Miller first entered school when he was 10 and quit when he was 14. It is interesting that Miller left school at the same age as Alan Bond.

Miller sailed model boats in a man-made pool at the beach; the experience left an imprint on him. "In the pool was a map of the world, with all the continents and the canals: the Suez and Panama Canals. The ocean was about four-feet deep, and the continents stuck up about an inch and a half from the water. It was a geography lesson. That thing was so beautiful, and now it's all covered with sand, and nobody knows it's even there. We used to sail boats in that pool.

"I have a belief that everybody in the world is like a computer card. Everyone has one of those things inside when they're born. Walking around the streets of Newport, there is probably an Albert Einstein. He might be a short-order chef down at the local diner, only he's gone through life and his card has never matched up with the situation. My card made me what I am by my being exposed to that pool and those little toy boats for a minute. The slots fit, and my life was set."

Miller started as an apprentice machinist in a shipyard. In his spare time, he built a 20-foot sailboat in his backyard. Later he became a sailmaker (his sails would be on *Southern Cross*) and soon enough, a yacht designer. Despite the lack of a formal education, he moved easily from one thing to the next. By this time he had won the world championship in the Flying Dutchman Class. A boat he designed won the Australian 18-foot Skiff Class. Miller enjoyed his first notice in yacht design with *Mercedes II*, a 40-foot boat he designed for a friend. The boat was the top finisher in the Admiral's Cup—a considerable achievement. Then he designed *Apollo* for Alan Bond. Thus, began their association.

Bond's challenger, *Southern Cross*, slaughtered the Baron Bich–led French 4-0 in August. Bich's challenges—there would be two more—were grand, if perfunctory, and the Australians had hardly cracked a sweat.

JUST BEFORE THE Defender Finals started in August, I was given the helm of *Valiant* while Turner stayed on *Mariner*, which was now called *Mariner II*. Sadly, only the name had changed. On August 11, we ran practice starts against *Courageous*, while *Mariner* awaited a new rudder. We won five, lost one, and tied one. This couldn't have been a cheery afternoon for Bob Bavier, her skipper. In all sincerity, I offered to go over these starts with him so we might both benefit from the exercise, but the meeting never came off.

Commodore Hinman must have gotten wind of this because shortly thereafter he scheduled a series of short practice races between Turner on *Mariner* and me on *Valiant*. I easily beat Turner at the starting line. In one starting sequence, he fouled us two or three times within five minutes. However, after the starts, the racing was fairly even.

For *Courageous*, going nowhere fast—or at least not as fast as *Intrepid*—help was about to arrive. First came new equipment, and then the cavalry.

Courageous started life with Hood sails, as did we on *Mariner* and *Valiant*. Hood sails, in fact, had been used by every America's Cup defender since 1958—the dawn of the 12-Meter era. *Intrepid*, however, sailed with North sails. North sailmaker John Marshall was in her afterguard. For the August trials, the *Courageous* syndicate followed *Intrepid*'s lead by ordering North sails in hopes that they were the secret of the latter boat's success. They helped, it seemed.

Ted Hood is seen on a Robin *in 1973. Hood, the noted sailmaker and designer, would skipper* Courageous *the next year to victory.* COURTESY MICHAEL LEVITT

Selling North sails to the competition was a tough decision for Marshall. He called Peter Barrett, the managing director of North (Lowell North was out of the country), and asked him what he should do. Barrett, a blunt man, said, "You bet you should make sails for them." Selling North sails to the competition was a tough decision to swallow for the *Intrepid* syndicate, as it felt it diluted its edge. (This would have major importance in 1977.)

Although wearing North sails, *Courageous* soon garnered the help of Ted Hood, the principal of Hood Sails. To see Ted Hood trimming those North sails was a strange juxtaposition.

Hood had had no intention of sailing the America's Cup in 1974. Before Bavier, he had been asked by McCullough to skipper the new boat, but had turned it down. He hadn't liked the design sufficiently to spend a year with it. Instead, he loaded his One Tonner *Robin* on a freighter for England, where he expected to sail the One Ton Cup. The freighter broke down, and the boat never made it. At loose ends that summer, Hood did the NYYC Cruise, which ended in Newport in August.

He was met there by McCullough, who asked him if he'd join *Courageous* "to help out." Hood agreed; he joined Bavier in the afterguard. "It wasn't a tough decision," he told Levitt years later. "It was not like I had to spend the whole year doing it."

Frederick E. "Ted" Hood is tall and stocky in appearance and unpretentious in style. If Yankees are taciturn by nature, Hood is taciturn even for a Yankee. His words seemed measured with a teaspoon. He started into sailmaking in 1950—a propitious time. Sailmaking was going through vast changes then, as a result of new materials perfected during the war years. Cotton sailcloth, first used by *America* in that famous race around the Isle of Wight in 1851, and used for a hundred years thereafter, was replaced by nylon. Then came Orlon and next, in 1954, Dacron. With that latter material Hood would predominate.

In 1952 Hood and his father, Ralph Stedman Hood, nicknamed "the Professor," purchased four pillowcase looms from Pequot Mills and set them up in an improvised sail loft back of Maddie's restaurant in Marblehead, Massachusetts. The Professor experimented with weaving the material—first Orlon, and then Dacron—very tightly. Dacron, invented in 1941 in England by H. R. Whinfield and J. T. Dickson, was a by-product of oil refining. Du Pont purchased the rights to what was then called "Terylene" in 1945; but it would be nearly 10 years before sailcloth was made from it. Dacron is Du Pont's product; polyester is the material's generic name.

Hood and his father did some pioneering work in the weaving and finishing of Dacron. On their pillowcase looms, they wove the cloth in 20-inch sections (commercial cloth typically came in 36-inch sections). This allowed them to move the shuttle less distance and to weave the material tighter than commercial finishers could or, at least, would. The Professor also worked on heat-treating the cloth with hot calenders—this to shrink the cloth down to 18-inch sections—and then he finished the material with "secret chemicals." It was sand, as it turned out; this roughened the fibers to keep them from slipping. Hood Dacron looked different: it had a slightly brown cast to it—

due to the silicate bath. It has been compared to parchment. This brown tint—a good Yankee color—was further highlighted by Hood's signature brown thread at the seams. It also felt different, more like natural cotton than synthetic Dacron.

When the America's Cup competition was renewed in 1958, Bus Mosbacher invited Hood to join the crew of the 12-year-old 12-Meter *Vim* and, of course, to bring along some of his sails. While there were three new American Twelves that year, as you will recall, the stars of the summer were the aged *Vim* and new *Columbia*, both Olin Stephens designs. The defender wasn't named until the second week in September. *Columbia* won the last race by a boat length.

While Hood didn't get to race in the showdown with the British, *Vim* loaned its Hood sails to *Columbia*, which used them. As a result, this quiet man and his sails were a key ingredient in America's Cup success until 1980, when I used North and Sobstad sails on *Freedom*.

August is historically the "cruelest month" in America's Cup annals, as the bottom line looms large. For example, the day before the August trials started, I was given the helm of *Mariner* by Commodore Hinman, and Turner moved to *Valiant*. By any measure, it was a promotion for me but a demotion for him. To Turner's huge credit, when he told his crew he was no longer skippering *Mariner* and would be sailing the second boat, *Valiant*, he urged them to stand behind the effort and to sail with me. He said anyone who quit out of sympathy for him would never sail with him again.

While there was a lot of posturing—a lot of "all for ones"—my relationship with Turner was never the same, and I regret that. He was angry, and not surprisingly, a large measure of that anger spilled over on me. His summer was over; mine, as it turned out, was just beginning.

We won some races with *Mariner* in August and won more starts. It was not enough, and the ax fell for both *Mariner* and *Valiant* on August 20. That afternoon, NYYC Commodore Henry Sturgis Morgan, the 74-year-old grandson of J. P. Morgan, came aboard. He put his hand on Commodore Hinman's shoulder and said, almost tenderly, "Sorry, old man." They looked like two great warriors in the twilight of their lives. Then he thanked us for our participation. For

Turner, at least, it must have had the bittersweet release of a mercy killing. Again, my aspirations for this summer were more modest. I'd done okay. I was just happy to be going home. So was my family.

As my wife, two daughters, and I were packing to return to San Diego, I received a telephone call from Commodore McCullough. He asked me to come out with him on one of the syndicate's boats to watch the next day's racing. Frankly, this was the last thing I wanted to do, but "Commodore," I said, as Turner had instructed me, "I'd love to." Olin Stephens was aboard the boat, too. To me he seemed distant. McCullough and I talked about that day's racing.

Then he invited me for dinner at the crew's house. This was a different slice of life from *Mariner*. Here, dinner was practically formal, with the crew dressed in jackets and ties, and it was served by waiters. Wives, girlfriends, and family members were there, too, so everyone seemed happier.

When my wife, two young daughters, Julie and Shanna, and I had arrived at Conley Hall, the college dorm where the *Mariner* syndicate was housed, I'd learned children weren't welcome. I had to rent a private house in Newport, which was expensive for me, particularly so since it came at a time in my life when I had no money. Further, I was never home, as Turner required my complete support and constant companionship—night and day. Day and night. Turner without listeners is a man lost.

After dinner that night Commodore McCullough invited me into the cockpit of *Courageous* to be starting helmsman. McCullough is a substantial man with a commanding presence. He said, "Young man, I don't want you to feel as though we're putting any undue pressure on you. I don't want you to feel as though you have to dominate *Intrepid* at the start. Just as long as you're comfortably ahead ..."

For a 31-year-old, that was a truly amazing call to arms. Nevertheless, I thought I could do it. After all, I was going up against Driscoll, who seemed scared of me after our collision.

I was to start the boat; Hood was to sail it upwind; and Bavier was to sail it downwind. With only 11 men sailing an America's Cup 12-Meter, we were, of course, top-heavy, and someone would eventually have to go. Who? I wondered. We all wondered, I assume.

Ted Hood didn't want me there. He may be quiet, but he has

an ego. We were hired almost the same day. He was happy, I'm sure, to have his job, and I was happy to have mine. Presumably, there wasn't a lot of conversation between McCullough and Hood about whether I should join the crew or not.

Of all people, Alan Bond didn't want me there either. In a press release, he said, "We are fearful that fouling and striking tactics will be introduced to America's Cup starts. We deplore this approach which is degrading to the dignity and prestige of the America's Cup ... Apart from the unsportsmanlike nature of this approach, there is a definite element of danger to the safety of the crews and boats by adoption of rodeo tactics afloat."

I had to smile at that. I was pleased that he felt so threatened by my presence; that can be an advantage in match-racing.

Had he communicated his concerns to the NYYC? Bond was asked. "Our approach to them is through public opinion," he said. That remark should be viewed through the prism of 1983 where he fought the war, over the legality of *Australia II*'s winged keel, through the press.

Near the end of August, all the races were important. One day, *Courageous* had a comfortable lead over *Intrepid* at the weather mark, and we set the .5-ounce spinnaker. This was the right sail, as the wind was light, and the angle, a broad reach. Halsey Herreshoff, our navigator, noticed that *Intrepid* had up a .75-ounce spinnaker. While all sails were purposely identical in panel layout and color, to discourage imitation, he could tell by the attitude of their sail. Then the wind freshened, and they started gaining on us. As a result, Halsey and I kept trying to encourage Bavier to change to the .75-ounce chute to match them. But he wouldn't. I think that may have been Bavier's ruination. He was off the boat the next day, fired by his boyhood chum Bob McCullough, and Ted Hood was given command. I stayed aboard to start the boat.

Bavier's firing would not be the last. To me, this termination—this public humiliation—spoke clearly of the new seriousness with which the NYYC and its syndicates viewed the Cup: Win or get off the boat. Heads—even those featuring impeccable pedigrees—began to roll.

The score was tied at four when we sailed the final race among defenders on September 2. That day the wind was gusting to 30 knots. Any other day that summer, they would have postponed the race; but time had run out. By the rules, a boat had to be named to meet the Australian challenger, *Southern Cross*. The summer had dwindled to one precious race. The last time things had been this close was back in 1958 when *Vim* battled *Columbia* to the bitter end.

At the starting line, Hood, who had sailed on *Vim* then, took *Courageous*'s wheel, relieving me of duty. He believed, and with good reason, that he was more familiar with the boat in what amounted to survival conditions. He was older and far more experienced racing 12-Meters. I had never sailed on a 12-Meter when it was this rough before.

At the last moment Hood decided to use the Hood sails, not the North ones that we'd been using with greater success in August. Not only was the mainsail his design, but it was a seven-year-old *Intrepid* mainsail and a lightweather (6.8-ounce) sail at that.

When Commodore McCullough saw the Hood mainsail with its distinctive brown thread go up, he grabbed the radio microphone on the tender. I was working the radio, and McCullough said, "Don't you think we ought to be getting the North sail on?" He was trying to be polite and stay calm, despite the pressures of the moment. When I relayed this message to Ted, he said, "I need to look at this sail a little longer." If there was a more incongruous time for a sail check, I didn't know when it could be. McCullough called three more times with the same request. The last time, it wasn't a request; it was a direct order to change to the North main. I relayed it to Ted. He said, "You tell Bob I'm skipper, and I'm going with what we've got up." I'd never heard Hood say more, or anything more forcefully than that. For me, it was a revelation.

Into the radio I said, "This-is-*Courageous*-and-Ted-says-we're-going-to-use-the-sail-we-have-up—*Courageous*-out!" It came out as an eruption as if it were one long word.

The sail choice was the boldest possible move, influenced at least a little by business considerations. Had Hood been wrong he would have been crucified.

During the starting sequence, I knew we were late for the starting line, but I wasn't going to tell Hood that. He had seized the moment.

Intrepid was equally far away. If I had been driving, I would have been going for it, in essence saying to the other boat, "You chase me up there." We were a minute late, as it turned out.

Intrepid could have crossed us on port tack and won the start. However, the ever-conservative or ever-frightened Driscoll elected to tack beneath us, and both boats crossed the line on starboard. It was a misty, rainy day, with limited visibility, as we sailed to the layline without tacking. Normally, it took us 12 minutes to reach the layline at eight knots, as we were traveling. At 10 minutes I asked Halsey, "How much farther to the layline?" He said "a minute." And then, "We're on it!"

Yet there was no impetus to tack immediately to port, because the more we both overstood, the better for us. *Intrepid* would have to sail longer in our wake, where our "dirty"—disturbed—air would hurt her. It is, obviously, twice as much fun to punish the trailing boat for four minutes than for two.

A moment later, I asked Halsey if he was sure. "We're definitely beyond the layline," he said. I said to myself, "If he's wrong, the summer is over." Halsey, the grandson of the famous America's Cup designer and builder, Nathanael Herreshoff, was extremely confident making the biggest call of the summer. I told Ted that I thought it was time to tack. He just shrugged and said, "Ready about!"

We tacked and then *Intrepid* tacked. With the tack they broke a shroud. Later, they blamed this rigging failure for losing the race, but that wasn't the whole story. Despite the mechanical failure, *Intrepid* rounded the mark only 42 seconds behind us. It was still a boat race, in my estimation.

It was so windy that steering was difficult on the reach, but we got ready to set the spinnaker. I waited, however, to see if *Intrepid* set hers. "Fools rush in . . ." I wasn't going to be the first—particularly when steering was so marginal. When *Intrepid* set her star-cut spinnaker, I watched for a moment to see what would happen. It was show time! Her chute filled and then just pressed the mast of this 56,000-pound boat to the water. The spinnaker collapsed, and the boat stood tall, but then the sail filled again. With that it exploded into a thousand pieces of nylon. If nylon spinnaker cloth was made of sterner stuff, someone might have been killed. By delaying the set and sailing high of course for a time we added a few precious seconds to our lead.

Halsey made another brilliant call in this race; this one at the end of the second weather leg. He insisted we do a jibe-set. After the jibe onto port tack and the spinnaker hoist, we didn't drop our jib. In such heavy wind, this triangular sail plus the spinnaker allowed us to sail directly to the downwind mark. Meanwhile, *Intrepid* did a lay-away set and sailed off on starboard for four minutes and, as it turned out, to oblivion. In those conditions, the fastest course to the mark proved a straight line. This is rarely the case in less wind. That night *Courageous* was named the defender.

ON PAPER, THE America's Cup match between *Courageous*, repre-senting the NYYC, and *Southern Cross*, representing Alan Bond, "Yanchep, Sun City—Home of the Twelves," or the RPYC (pick one)—seemed another 4-0 romp for the home team. Up to this point 17 of 22 defenses spanning 104 years had been shutouts. (No wonder so few people cared.) Score aside, it wasn't so easy from my perspec-tive, however.

Southern Cross was skippered in the match by Jim Hardy, a New South Wales wine merchant who skippered *Gretel II* so well in 1970. Before Hardy was given command by Bond, her skipper was John Cuneo, an optometrist and Olympic gold medalist in the Dragon class. Certainly, the challenger from Australia was playing "musical chairs," too.

The first race was sailed in light winds of about 10 knots. Both boats stalled before the line with a long three minutes to go. We were to leeward of *Southern Cross*, closer to the pin end of the line, which was slightly favored. With a minute to go the Australian boat tacked to port, to head for the starboard side of the line. *Courageous* crossed the line three seconds ahead. Then we tacked to port to cover.

It was a long drag race to the layline. Like boxers in the early rounds, we were taking the measure of one another. We seemed to be footing faster than the Australian boat; they seemed to be pointing higher than us. A fair trade. As we neared the layline, it was foggy with visibility of about a half a mile. Thus, we couldn't see the mark.

Then the wind headed both boats, or went right. As the boat to the right, which, in this case, was *Southern Cross*, gains in a shift to the right, the Australian boat appeared ahead.

Southern Cross tacked first to starboard and seemed about to cross us. Before the crossing, however, I suggested that we tack ahead but to leeward of them, in what sailors term the "safe-leeward position." This is a finesse maneuver, and timing is essential. Ted pulled it off, tacking about a boat length to leeward. However, we couldn't make it stick. Again, we seemed to be footing faster; they seemed to be pointing higher.

Now where the mark lay was critical. If we were above the mark (had overstood), we were ahead, but if we were below it, they were. Halsey was unsure where it was, but as luck would have it, I saw it about 12 degrees below us. We were ahead—a little—but being the greedy person I am, I wanted more.

I was certain the Australians didn't know where the mark was yet. So rather than sailing directly for it and tipping our hand, I told the crew to ease sheets and the traveler a little, so as to foot, not point. I told them to do this quietly. This increased our speed. In no time, *Southern Cross* was five or six boat lengths to weather of us with the mark now 20 degrees off our leeward bow. "Let's go for it, boys," I said. At that point, we cracked sheets and unambiguously headed low for the mark. We rounded the first mark 34 seconds in the lead, and won the first race by 4:54. That margin had more to do with the fact that the wind died to about five knots—hurting the trailing boat far more than the leading one—than anything else. In sailing, the expression for that is "the rich get richer." *Southern Cross* seemed a capable boat upwind and could have won this race or at least the important first leg.

At the press conference that night, Alan Bond called me a "cowboy," who used "rodeo tactics." There's always some conversation between match-racing boats, particularly at the start. Some of it's psych, some of it posturing, some of it is defining relationships, like "mast-abeam," that have import on the rules. It's part of the game and is very common in the Congressional Cup—the world series of match-racing.

At the start of the second race, on September 12, both boats had protest flags flying. The incident happened this way: We tailed *Southern Cross* into the spectator fleet with about seven minutes to go. The Australian boat tacked onto port, directly in front of us. With the two boats converging at 8½ knots, Ted Hood was shouting "Staabad! Staabad!" in that nasal Yankee accent of his. Hardy tried to tack back to "Staabad," or starboard, to avoid the collision, but we had to alter course, when but a few feet away, to avoid them. I came quite close to them, however, to make my point. Our bowman, L. J. Edgecomb, came back into the cockpit, with frightened, saucer-sized eyes. He had been certain we were going to cut *Southern Cross* in half. For the NYYC, this contretemps at the start between an American and an Australian yacht must have seemed like shades of 1970, or "*déjà vu* all over again," as that wonderful expression has it.

I was confident we would win the protest, but before that, we had a race to sail. Both boats started on starboard tack with *Courageous* to leeward. The start was about even. This time, Hood squeezed up on them, eventually forcing the Australians to tack to port. We tacked to cover, but *Southern Cross* had gained on us. She tacked and then crossed us. The Australian boat was now ahead. Inexplicably, *Southern Cross* didn't tack back to cover us—the most fundamental maneuver in match-racing. We sailed off on port tack to the favored side of the course; they continued on starboard.

I don't like splitting from the competition even when behind, which we were. What if the wind went left, toward them? They would kill us. What Hood thought of all this I didn't know, because he doesn't talk. I filled the void, just kept talking, telling him what I thought we should do. Then we got a slight header (the wind went right), and I said we should tack. We did. It was a gift from the gods, and there would be more. The wind continued shifting right a total of about 15 degrees. On the right side of the Australians, we continued gaining each time it shifted. Had they covered us when they had the chance, they'd have been ahead. We won the race by a close 1:11.

We'd sailed two races, and the Australians could have won both of them. Had they previously been bloodied in battle, as we were in those titanic battles with *Intrepid*, the result might have been different. But they weren't, and it wasn't.

While we won the race, we couldn't withdraw the protest, as the Australians were protesting us over the same starting line incident. After the protest of 1970, when *Gretel II* fouled *Intrepid* at the start, the Australians accused the NYYC, which provided the juries that heard the protests, of cheating. To avoid such charges, the NYYC used for the first time an International Jury, chaired by Beppe Croce, the President of the International Yacht Racing Union (IYRU), the sport's international authority.

That night at the protest hearing, it wasn't Jim Hardy I faced, or anyone on the Australian boat, but Bond's attorney. That was a first for me. Both protests were disallowed. Even though we won the race, I was shocked that the Australians weren't thrown out for tacking too close at the start. I'd never seen another boat survive that one without a witness to the contrary. Even with the eyes of the world upon them, the Australians had no witnesses to substantiate their case. The decision appeared expedient but unfair, in my opinion, but you can't win one race twice.

For the third race, Bond—who invested $6 million in the Australian challenge, other estimates said $9 million—came unglued. He fired the navigator. Then he fired Hugh Treharne, the tactician. Then he brought back the recently deposed John Cuneo to take Treharne's place.

The Australians lost race three by 5:27, and race four by 7:21. Bond even sailed on the boat in race four, grinding winches. It was not sufficient to inspire the troops, however. The Australians were, on average, 4:40 slower than us.

It seemed the world had seen the last of Alan Bond and Bob Miller. Miller, in fact, contemplated blowing up *Southern Cross* and selling the movie rights. Now that would have been some exit.

History would show that Bond and Miller had just begun to fight. And the legacy of *Mariner*, which created a scientific backlash—at least in my mind—set the stage for their success.

CHAPTER 6

1977

RADIO FREE TURNER

THOSE WHO KNOW me know I always have a plan. As I said about the 1974 America's Cup, "...My plan was to go east to show that I could be a team player, learn about 12-Meters, and aim toward getting invited back the next time as skipper." Sometimes the plan works, and sometimes it doesn't pan out.

I waited in vain for the phone to ring, inviting me to skipper a boat in the 1977 America's Cup. It did ring a few blocks away, however, at the San Diego home of Lowell North. A sailmaker, and by any measure a luminary in the sport and business of sailing, North was invited to skipper *Enterprise*, the new Olin Stephens–designed 12-Meter.

The *Enterprise* syndicate was headed by George "Fritz" Jewett and his wife, Lucy, and Ed du Moulin—all of whom would be so important to me in years to come. It sailed under the banner of the Maritime College at Ft. Schuyler Foundation, Inc.[1] It was set in mo-

---

1. In 1974, when the *Courageous* syndicate nearly foundered, Olin Stephens asked Ed du Moulin if the Maritime College would be interested in establishing a foundation, similar to the Kings Point Fund, for whom *Mariner* sailed. This would allow contributions to the syndicate to be tax deductible. Du Moulin approached Rear Admiral Kinney, who headed the college. The Admiral liked the idea but decided there wasn't sufficient time to establish it for the 1974 Cup. Nevertheless, this laid the groundwork for the Maritime College at Ft. Schuyler Foundation, Inc., that supported the *Enterprise* syndicate in 1977, the *Enterprise-Freedom* syndicate in 1980, and the *Liberty* syndicate in 1983. After

tion by Richard du Moulin, who is Ed's son, and Andy MacGowan, an *Intrepid*-1974 alumnus. The younger du Moulin sailed on *Mariner* and then on the greener pastures of *Intrepid* as navigator in 1974. *Intrepid* had done well with North sails so it seemed prudent to hitch its new wagon, *Enterprise*, to that star. From there, it was a short step to invite Lowell North, the company founder, to skipper the boat.

North was a natural choice. He had just won the 1976 SORC on *Williwaw*, as well as the One Ton Worlds. He had an Olympic Gold and an Olympic Bronze Medal, and had won an incredible four Star World Championships. Probably the only feather he lacked in his cap—both personally and professionally—was skippering and building sails for a winning America's Cup yacht. His firm had come ever so close, first with *Intrepid* and then *Courageous*, in 1974. That was until the final race when Ted Hood, skipper of *Courageous* and North's principal rival in the sailmaking industry, flew his own sails.

North, who began making sails in 1959 in San Diego, is a man of the future. He is tall and thin and positively bubbles with creative fire. By nature and nurture, he fervently believes in the canon of progress—better ideas. Like any self-respecting Californian, he also loves what's new, what's now, and—particularly—what will be. Sailing would have represented a much lower technology without him.

North graduated from the University of California at Berkeley with a degree in civil engineering and a minor in structural engineering. Malin Burnham, another San Diego notable, describes North as an engineer by birth, as opposed to mere education and training. Burnham, himself an engineer by education, said, "Lowell's always fiddling with something in order to improve on it. He and I might have purchased brand-new Stars the same summer. By the end of the summer, he would have 100 holes in the deck. I didn't have any excess holes. I took the boat and went sailing."

After being named skipper, North asked Burnham, a wealthy businessman and community leader, to be his second in command. Burnham, like North—and like me—won the Star Worlds. Malin

---

three campaigns the Maritime College Foundation had assets of more than $1 million to be used to benefit cadets and the institution. The foundation is still active. Beyond that, several of my crew-members came from its ranks: Bill Trenkle, who is still with me and a key player, Scott Vogel, his wife, Dory Street Vogel, and Tom Rich.

won his Star World Championship in 1945, when he was 16. His crew was the 15-year-old Lowell North. As the summer of 1977 played out, Malin would actually steer *Enterprise* upwind. A Star sailor to the core, he used an odd tillerlike arrangement on the wheel. Lowell would start the boat and then focus on boatspeed and tactics. North's lieutenant, John Marshall, then the company's sales manager, would steer downwind.

So, between North and Burnham, San Diego would be well represented in the 1977 America's Cup, but not by me. With no invitation, I focused on the 1976 Olympics in Kingston, Ontario, in the Tempest Class, and the Star Class for the Worlds in Germany the next year.

Enterprise seemed to represent the best and brightest. Besides North, who first sailed in the America's Cup trials in 1964 aboard *Columbia*—the first West Coast effort—there was Olin Stephens, who would be her designer. Stephens, then 69 years old, had co-designed *Ranger* in 1937, the last of the J-Class yachts, and the best of the breed. For 1958, he designed *Columbia*, the 12-Meter, which defended. For 1964, he designed *Constellation*, which defended, as did *Intrepid* in '67, and *Courageous* in '74. Only Bill Luders's redesign of Phil Rhodes's *Weatherly*, which defended in 1962, and young Britton Chance's redesign of Stephens's *Intrepid*, which defended in 1970, had loosened Stephens's hammer hold on America's Cup design laurels.

The *Enterprise* syndicate, not wishing to share what it would fund, signed North Sails, as well as the yacht designer, to exclusive contracts. In other words, North couldn't build sails for the competition, as the company did—however reluctantly—in 1974, by building sails for *Courageous*. The *Enterprise* group earmarked $60,000 specifically for sailmaking. Anything North developed from this research grant would belong to the syndicate, unless or until they were eliminated. Other North designs could be sold to the competition.

Besides North, there was Ted Hood, his principal rival in the sailmaking world, skippering *Independence*, a boat he also designed. North and Hood represented a new breed: industry professionals in the America's Cup. Beginning in 1920, with Charles Francis Adams, skippers of America's Cup defenders had been amateurs.

Hood, of course, had been the skipper of *Courageous*, which defended the 1974 America's Cup. As a result, he was named that year's Yachtsman of the Year. For his sailmaking ability alone, where nary an America's Cup defender went off to battle without Hood sails, the America's Cup seemed practically his birthright.

Oh yes, there was one amateur there: the disgraced Ted Turner—this time sailing *Courageous*. Turner seemed to be showing signs of life on many fronts, however. First, he shut his mouth, at least when sailing. This was perhaps to lick his wounds from the *Mariner* debacle. Then he finished second in Class A in the 1977 SORC on *Tenacious*, the former *Dora IV*, which he'd just purchased. The boat was about the same size and weight of a 12-Meter. That was typical Turner: Get an old proven boat and then sail the dickens out of it. Breaking new ground just wasn't his style. That's one of many reasons why he fared so poorly with *Mariner*. And sailing an old and proven boat was what he was endeavoring to do with *Courageous*.

At that SORC, Turner encountered Britton Chance, *Mariner*'s designer and Turner's *bête noire*, at the bar of the St. Petersburg Yacht Club. Chance had some "strange design" of his out there, said Gary Jobson, who was sailing with Turner. Turner started needling Chance about the design. The designer gave Turner a mild slap across the face and said, "What we really need out there, Teddy, is you steering." At that, Turner hit him. "It wasn't a punch," said Jobson, "but more than a slap to the face."

Next, Turner won that year's Congressional Cup, in his seventh attempt. Among others, he beat Hood and North—his defense rivals—and Pelle Petterson and Noel Robins. The latter two would shortly skipper *Sverige* (Sweden) and *Australia*, respectively, in the impending Cup. That Congressional Cup win should have served as a warning to the world.

More apparent, there were some business successes that couldn't be ignored. In 1970 Turner purchased Channel 17, an unknown and unaffiliated UHF television station in Atlanta. That's the part of the dial that no one could tune in, at least in those precable days. Then, only one in four UHF stations were profitable, and only half of those that were made more than $100,000 per year. He changed the call letters to WTCG—Turner Communications Group. It was the number five station in a five-station market. During the first two years of operation, WTCG lost $500,000 a year. Turner propped up this station and Channel 36, another UHF station he soon purchased in Charlotte, North Carolina, with profits from the billboard business. In 1975 WTCG made its first $1 million profit. In 1976 it made $3.7 million.

That year, Turner purchased the Atlanta Braves baseball team, for $10 million, to have something to put on his television station. Most important, he figured out how to put Channel 17 on the satellite, as HBO had before him. This allowed Channel 17 to become one of cable television's first "Super Stations." This would lead to his CNN (Cable News Network) and dozens of other cable stations, featuring 24-hour news, old movies, long-faded sitcoms, like *Father Knows Best*, even cartoons.

Turner jumped into baseball as he jumps into life—with his mouth running full speed and oblique marketing schemes. On April 10, 1976, for example, he fired the first salvo in baseball's free-agency by signing pitcher Andy Messersmith to a $1 million deal for three years. If this seems paltry by today's standards, where pitcher Pedro Martinez, now of the Boston Red Sox, makes $12.5 million per season, and the average salary in 1997 was $1,383,578, it wasn't back then. The late Charles O. Finley, owner of the Oakland A's, predicted free-agency would ruin major-league baseball. Judgment is still out on that one.

Turner nicknamed Messersmith "Channel" and assigned him number 17. That way, Turner's "Channel 17" appeared on the back of Messersmith's uniform. National League President Chub Feeney was not amused. He told Turner to remove that nickname from Messersmith's uniform and to stop playing poker and showering with his team. Also, he should stop yelling at free agents from the stands—encouraging them to sign with him.

On May 11, 1977, a month before the America's Cup began, Turner decided to manage his baseball team, following a 17-game losing streak. His tenure in the dugout, where he chewed tobacco with the players, lasted but one day. Baseball Commissioner Bowie Kuhn wrote, "Given Mr. Turner's lack of familiarity with game operations, I do not think it is in the best interest of baseball for Mr. Turner to serve in that capacity."

Turner contacted Kuhn to plead his case. Asked why he couldn't be like other owners and remain in the stands, Turner told the commissioner, "Because I'm in last place."

At a cocktail party hosted by the New York Yankees, Turner told Robert Lurie, the San Francisco Giants's co-owner, that he was interested in signing the Giants's hard-hitting outfielder Gary Matthews. No matter what the Giants offered Matthews, Turner promised Lurie he would pay him more. As he was not yet a free agent, this was "tampering"—a violation of the rules of baseball. As a result, Turner was suspended by Kuhn, on January 18, 1977, for one year. During the hearings, Turner threatened an attorney representing the Commissioner with a "knuckle sandwich." Atlanta loved him for it; indeed, a headline in the Atlanta *Constitution* fairly gushed, "Turner, Atlanta Together in a Common Love."

Also in 1977, Turner purchased the Atlanta Hawks, that city's National Basketball Association (NBA) franchise.

This was not a man who was down and out. Turner was reinventing himself into a new and much more powerful form. He would in inexorable fashion become one of the richest and most powerful men in America. For example, in 1985, after failing to buy CBS, Turner purchased the United Artists/MGM entertainment conglomerate before selling off the pieces that didn't suit him. Then, in 1995, his Braves won the World Series. His networks were recently acquired by Time Warner for $7.5 billion, as mentioned, but we get ahead of ourselves.

Before the competition started, in June 1977, Turner was seen as a tarnished skipper, sailing a second-hand boat. To believe in an old boat in the America's Cup is to be anti-progress—the antithesis of the event. Up to this point, only two boats had ever made a successful encore appearance in the America's Cup match: *Columbia* in 1899 and 1901, and *Intrepid* in 1967 and 1970. Could *Courageous* join those ranks? Further, a fired skipper had never staged a successful comeback. Would Turner be different?

Most knowledgeable observers didn't believe so. Don MacNamara, who had sailed aboard *Nefertiti* in 1962, said, "If [Turner] is selected, he will be the first skipper in the history of the Cup to appear on the starting line wearing a muzzle." Another writer said

Ted Turner on Courageous *in 1977. For obvious reasons, "Beat-the-mouth" buttons began to sprout in Newport.* DAN NERNEY

his chances were as remote as the NYYC's America's Cup Committee appearing on the racecourse wearing "skinny-legged blue jeans and motorcycle boots."

How Turner came to control *Courageous* was revealing of the "new improved" version of the man. Hood's *Independence-Courageous* syndicate was managed by Alfred Lee Loomis, a bulky and blustery man. He came from a family of accomplishment and abiding wealth. The young Lee Loomis was given a new 12-Meter, *Northern Light*, by his father after graduating from Harvard Law School. Loomis served in the navy during World War II, eventually serving as a flag officer to an admiral. Loomis worked for Smith-Barney. Then, in 1950, his first oil well struck pay dirt.[2]

The *Independence-Courageous* syndicate had been given *Courageous* for a trial horse. The plan was that Hood would skipper the new boat, *Independence*, which was expected to be faster. If she wasn't, then Hood would skipper *Courageous*. They considered me as a trial-horse skipper for *Courageous*, but Loomis felt I was too aggressive at the starting line for my own good. The truth is, I am aggressive at the starting line; it gets my adrenaline flowing. After that, however, I am conservative, but they didn't know that about me then. More to the point, I had no money at the time to feather the syndicate's nest. Finally, I wasn't interested in being anyone's trial-horse skipper.

Eventually, they offered *Courageous* to Turner. He wasn't interested in being a trial-horse skipper, he told Loomis. He had, however, some conditions that just might make this work. For a substantial contribution to the syndicate, reportedly $350,000, *Courageous* would be entered in the trials, and Turner would be her skipper, no matter how well *Independence* fared. While he could be fired, as he was from *Mariner*'s helm in 1974, he could only be fired if Perry Bass, a wealthy Texan, agreed with the decision. Bass, who often navigated for Turner, was respected by both Loomis and Turner. This was a good idea because while Commodore Hinman, head of *Mariner* in 1974, must have suffered hugely in his firing of Turner, Loomis would not likely lose sleep over it. Incidentally, in this Cup, Commodore Hinman chaired the America's Cup Committee, which would be anoint-

---

2. Loomis's son and namesake was the commodore of the NYYC in 1995–1996.

ing a skipper to defend the Cup. How would Hinman, who had seen Turner at his absolute nadir, view him this time?

There was one other condition to which Turner wouldn't agree. Loomis, who believed utterly in Ted Hood, wanted Turner to use Hood sails exclusively. Turner wanted to be able to use North sails, too. Turner had apparently worked out a deal to purchase state-of-the-art sails from North, or so he thought.

Courageous wasn't the same boat in 1977 as she was in '74, as Hood had redesigned her, too. Yacht design has always fascinated him. He worked, for example, on the redesign of *Vim* in 1958, primarily moving the ballast lower in the bilges and making small refinements to the hardware and the fittings. A year later, he designed and built his first ocean racer, *Robin*, which was influenced by Carleton Mitchell's *Finisterre*, an Olin Stephens design that won a record three consecutive Bermuda Races. For the next America's Cup, in 1962, Hood designed and sailed aboard the aforementioned *Nefertiti* in the defense trials without notable success.

The changes to *Courageous* were expected to be merely skin deep, so as not to invalidate this benchmark for Hood's *Independence*. In 1974 *Courageous* nearly sank in a squall. This didn't exactly please the America's Cup Committee, and the rules were subsequently changed to make these boats more seaworthy. For example, large deck openings became illegal. Also, the volume of the various cockpits was limited to a total of 100 cubic feet, and increased freeboard was required. The mast was beefed up: it could not weigh less than 1,000 pounds, and its balance point was fixed to keep the upper portion from being too light. Finally, in a small effort to make 12-Meters less specialized—to have a life after the America's Cup—the primary winches were brought on deck. Beginning with *Intrepid* in 1967, they had gone below decks, to keep winch and crew weight low in the boats. This measure, however, had turned winch-grinders into something akin to galley slaves.

In doing the cosmetic surgery, Hood discovered a shocking thing: *Courageous* was about 1,800 pounds too light for her length. Instead of weighing 56,000 pounds as specified in a signed statement by Olin Stephens, her designer, *Courageous* weighed 54,200 pounds. The higher figure is the minimum weight for a yacht of her waterline.

To have kept this waterline length, the designer would have had to forsake 84 square feet of sail. This meant that the boat that won the previous America's Cup was not a legal 12-Meter. She was, in effect, a 12½-Meter. Hood told Olin Stephens, her designer, what he discovered. "He didn't believe it," Hood said. "Someone in his office should have known. It was something like 1,500 or 2,000 pounds underweight... I just couldn't believe they'd be that far off."

Neither could Alan Bond, the brash Australian, whose yacht, *Southern Cross*, lost four straight races to her in 1974. Upon learning that *Courageous* was not a legal 12-Meter, he wired the NYYC inquiring when he might expect delivery of the America's Cup. The Cup, not surprisingly, remained with its keeper.

AFTER 1974 THE Australians more or less skulked home to Australia, dispirited by the public flogging they'd suffered in Newport at the hands of the New Yorkers. The Aussies had spoken loudly, as was Bond's style, but carried a little stick. That posture is as abhorrent to an Australian as it was to Theodore Roosevelt.

No one suffered more, however, than designer Bob Miller—or Ben Lexcen, the name he adopted following this Cup. Miller found something salutary in those revelations about *Courageous*. As he told writer Jay Broze years later, "I went for a long boat with low sail area, and that wasn't the right thing, was it? But poor old *Southern Cross*, she wasn't that bad. There were a couple of times when she crossed *Courageous* on the first weather leg, and *Courageous* wasn't even a 12-Meter! ..."

Miller pointed out that to be legal, *Courageous* would have been required to cut two feet from her boom. That would have given her sail area similar to *Southern Cross*. "We might have beat 'em."

But that was then, and this was now. On the foreign-challenger side, Bond was back with a new boat called *Australia*. It was a low-key effort this time. This was necessary for many reasons, not the least of them being that Bond's financial empire was in shambles. Only the good will of his bankers, who couldn't afford to foreclose on him, kept him afloat.

A major problem was Yanchep, Sun City, which was looking like a ghost town in the desert, not the paradise that Bond had promised. There wasn't enough green paint in the world to make a difference. There were no new sales, and those few residents who had bought into Bond's dream were complaining bitterly. There were no schools, no physicians, no jobs, not even bus service to Perth, let alone the monorail that Bond or his sales agents had promised. Times are tough, Bond said, and no one is immune to that.

After the 1974 America's Cup, Miller never returned home to Australia. He wandered about Europe, in what the Australians term a "walkabout," spending more money than he had ever made and separating himself ever further from the America's Cup. While he was at it, he dynamited any number of bridges—even the most important one linking him to Alan Bond, his patron. He also had a falling out with Craig Whitworth, his business partner in the sailmaking concern Miller & Whitworth.

Rather than working, Miller spent much of his time on strange pilgrimages. For example, he once drove his beloved Ferrari a full day out of his way to visit a plant in Molsheim, Alsace, in eastern France, that formerly produced the Bugatti—a classic automobile like his Ferrari. The doors had been shuttered for decades. He merely stared through the dirty windows as if it were a holy shrine.

If he never heard of the America's Cup again, he would be happy, he thought. Nevertheless, he lived in Cowes, England—the epicenter of English yachting, where the America's Cup started in 1851. For the two years he lived there with his wife, Yvonne, he had only one serious design commission. Mostly, he was kept alive by "sympathy jobs from friends."

Then in 1976, Alan Bond turned up in his life again like a good penny. As Miller described it, "I was literally down to my last dollars in Cowes. Yvonne is a very classy lady, and I couldn't tell her that we were broke, so I just went along like everything was fine, but I was bust beans or something, when bloody Alan Bond walks up to me in Cowes. This is Alan Bond of Western Australia, mind you."

The rescue supposedly happened when Miller was eyeing a box of corn flakes in a grocery store, wondering if he could afford it. He described the rescue this way: " 'You're broke!' Bond says. 'You don't have any money.'

" 'How do you know?' I asked.

" 'I can see it in your eyes.'

" 'You're full of s---!'

" 'No I'm not, go get Yvonne, pack your clothes, you're coming back home to design a 12-Meter ... ' "

The next day Bob and Yvonne Miller flew back to Australia to begin designing *Australia* with Johan Valentijn, a Dutch designer who once worked for Olin Stephens at Sparkman & Stephens (S&S). Miller decided he needed a new name, as his old one, in essence, belonged to another: Miller & Whitworth, the sailmaker. Miller claims he had a friend who had access to the *Reader's Digest* subscriber list. He asked this friend to find him a name that nobody had. The friend found six names not taken, and Miller chose Ben Lexcen. "It didn't work," Lexcen said, "I got a call from a guy in Washington, D.C., who said his name was John Lexcen. But there are more: two in California and eight in Minnesota. All his relatives."

Valentijn, who would work for me in 1983, has a different recollection of the Miller-Lexcen name change. He and Miller were about to have their initials carved on the hatch covers of *Australia*. Miller's wife, Yvonne, said if he was going to change his name this was a good time to do it, because if the Australians won the America's Cup, his name would be a household word. They chose Ben Lincoln: Ben after their pet dog, Benji, who had recently died, and Lincoln, for Abraham Lincoln. This seemed an appropriate name for a yacht designer off to America to challenge for the America's Cup. So BL it was. Later, Miller decided he didn't like the name Lincoln, but he needed another last name that began with L, since it was already carved on the hatch covers of *Australia*. Since the hatch covers were made of Lexan, he decided on Lexcen—Ben Lexcen.

Whatever the derivation, Lexcen was affectionately known as "Ben-Bob" in Australia.

The other foreign challengers were *Sverige, France*, and *Gretel II*. *Sverige* represented Sweden's debut in this league. Her helmsman was Pelle Petterson, a Star World champion, like Lowell North and Malin Burnham. Like Burnham, he, too, preferred a tiller to a wheel. *Sverige* had, in fact, two tillers, one for steering and one for the trim tab. The boat also used foot-powered winches—a first, I believe. An industrial designer, Petterson designed the P1800 Volvo, considered a classic in sports-car circles.[3] His father, Helmer, designed the classic Volvo PV444. Pelle received an engineering degree in Sweden and came to the United States, where he studied industrial design at Pratt Institute in Brooklyn, New York, and also learned to speak English like a Yank—or perhaps a Brooklynite. He won a Bronze Medal at the Olympic Games in Japan in 1964, and a Silver Medal in Germany in 1972.

France was another vainglorious Baron Marcel Bich–led challenge. The baron had built a new boat, *France II*, out of wood no less, that proved slower than *France I* (circa 1970). Therefore, they used the old boat.

Equally old was *Gretel II*, skippered by Gordon Ingate, an ocean racer from Australia. She sailed in the America's Cup match in 1970 against *Intrepid*. *Gretel II* was an old boat with a crew of ancient, if America's Cup–experienced, mariners; they averaged 40 years old. When they arrived in America, the crew wore T-shirts that read, "Daughters of America, lock up your mothers."

On the defense side, this America's Cup got off to one of the earliest debuts ever. Likely this was a reaction to *Mariner* and *Courageous*, both of which were slow aborning last time. *Courageous* was practically stillborn; *Mariner* might as well have been.

Independence, built by Minneford on City Island, New York, was launched in August 1976—10 months before the competition began. Then Hood sailed her against *Courageous*, steered alternately by Turner or Robbie Doyle, Hood's Vice President, into December. Testing started again in the spring. Already insiders were saying the new boat, *Independence*, was slower than *Courageous*.

The new *Enterprise*, also built by Minneford, was no Johnny-come-lately, either. She sailed 100 days that 1976–77 winter in San Diego, out of a possible 120 sailing days.

An early start in the America's Cup is something people, including Ted Turner and the late Tom Blackaller, claimed I invented, and something for which I am often blamed. The charge is that I changed

3. Paul Cayard, skipper of *Il Moro*, the challenger from Italy, in 1992, and a helmsman on my boat, the defender, in 1995, married one of Petterson's daughters.

the America's Cup from a summer activity into a year-round pursuit. A business. Excuse me, Ted, but where were you or where was your crew, to be perfectly accurate, during the fall of 1976 and spring of 1977? Gone sailing, I believe.

I saw *Enterprise* in San Diego that winter, and there were more than a few odd things about her. North reasoned that a straight headstay was important to upwind performance. Normally, a headstay sags, and the headsail is cut with luff curve to follow it. One way North straightened the headstay on *Enterprise* was by decreasing the J-measurement, the distance from the forestay to the mast, from 23 feet, 9 inches—which is practically the standard on a 12-Meter—to 21 feet. This also increased the aspect ratio of the headsail. Aerodynamicists know that upwind aspect ratio is key. That's why the longest wing is most efficient—consider the glider. Likewise, the deepest keel is most efficient when sailing upwind.

Straight or not, the result was a slow-tacking boat. The overlap of a 12-Meter genoa is fixed at 16 feet, so North's crew had to move a large, standard-sized sail through a smaller opening, or foretriangle. This difficulty would be exacerbated by Mylar-laminated sails that North would develop, which proved stiffer and harder to tack. Over and over, leads would be blown in tacking duels, where they couldn't turn as well as the competition. Or when *Enterprise* got behind, they couldn't grind the other boat down in a tacking duel. Furthermore, when Burnham had to tack the boat, he had to come off the rail and fold up his mock-tiller affixed to the wheel. Rival crews would know when *Enterprise* was preparing to tack, and, thus, the element of surprise was lost.

That boat also sported a main with an oversized roach, something else with which North experimented. North was right about the benefits of an exaggerated roach but not in this application. The mainsail would load up, even before it was fully sheeted in. That hurt tacking, too. I used *Enterprise* as a trial horse in 1980. Even in a straight line that boat was slow. It would take until 1995 and *Black Magic*, sailed by the Kiwis, for a small J to work.

From the beginning in San Diego, Ed du Moulin wondered about the syndicate's choice for skipper. To du Moulin, North was a perfect gentleman and a skilled sailor, but his priorities seemed wrong. North, he said, appeared more interested in sail-testing than in racing against stablemate *Intrepid*. Du Moulin commented, "All Lowell wanted to do was sail in a straight line, from San Diego to Mexico, testing sails. I'd have to go on the boat periodically to get him to practice racing with *Intrepid*. This was the only way the crew would get a workout."

Lowell seemed the proverbial kid in a candy shop. "An engineer by birth," he gorged himself on the high technology available to him.

He wasn't interested in buying anything off-the-shelf. Richard du Moulin, who was to be navigator on *Enterprise*, and Halsey Herreshoff, likely the most experienced navigator in the history of the Cup, had developed a program for instrumentation, sailing efficiency, and navigation. Such programs are common today. They offered it to Lowell, who wasn't interested, because he had his own ideas. North believes the best way to learn something is to make it yourself. "Just do it!" was an oft-heard imperative at the sail lofts.[4] However, the drive to perfect the instrumentation in this case consumed a major chunk of the syndicate's resources in time, as well as money—two of its most precious commodities. "We never got the instruments working satisfactorily," commented Ed du Moulin.

While du Moulin could have ordered North to take the instrument package, he didn't wish to. This was the syndicate's first conflict, and it seemed important to du Moulin that North win it.

When *Enterprise* did finally race against *Intrepid*, which was again skippered by Gerald Driscoll, of San Diego, she beat her easily. Of course, the winds in San Diego were lighter than would be experienced in Newport, and so, this edge might have been illusory. Also, this *Intrepid* was likely different from the *Intrepid* of 1974. Before being rescued, that two-time winner of the America's Cup was in Hawaii being converted to a centerpiece for a restaurant. Even earlier, she had been rotting away in an asphalt parking lot in the hot desert sun in Phoenix, Arizona. There *Intrepid* was a sideshow to a bank.

So lopsided were their matches, that the syndicate opted not to bring *Intrepid* east. North was against bringing her to Newport, as it would reduce his budget for testing and buying sails. Also, he believed testing against instruments would be of more value.

---

4. This was decades before Nike said it; decades before there was a Nike.

Leaving *Intrepid* on the sidelines displeased the NYYC as well as Driscoll, who had done a good job of restoring her. The club would have preferred to have four boats racing, rather than three. An odd number of boats meant one boat was on the sidelines each race day. But the *Enterprise* syndicate couldn't afford to bring the boat up to 1977 standards, ship it east, and feed and house a crew.

Before the Preliminary Trials started in June, du Moulin received a call from Commodore Hinman to appear before his America's Cup Committee. Hinman told du Moulin that Driscoll, *Intrepid*'s skipper in 1974, had raised all but $32,000 needed to bring *Intrepid* east, and this shortfall could be made up by the America's Cup Committee. Du Moulin was stunned. Driscoll had hatched this plan without informing the *Enterprise* syndicate that owned the boat. "I told the committee, 'There's no way Driscoll can raise enough money,'" du Moulin recalled recently. "'That $32,000 wouldn't mean a thing.' That was the end of that."

TYPICALLY, JUNE ISN'T a serious month in the Defender Trials. The NYYC referred to them without fanfare as the "Preliminary Trials." Nevertheless, Turner was wound tight in June. Part of this was because Loomis treated Turner and his crew like "unworthies"— a motorcycle gang in topsiders. Turner's crew called the camp "Stalag 17." Recalled Jobson, "It was, 'Yes, Mr. Loomis. No, Sir.'" Jackets and ties were *de rigueur* at dinner. One time, Bunky Helfrich, age 40, a crew-member on *Courageous*, came to dinner dressed casually. "He got marched out of there by Loomis," said Jobson. On the other hand, Loomis treated Hood like a favored son.

In every way, Turner and Loomis were worlds apart. Loomis believed the America's Cup was the private domain of the NYYC, and the media be damned. Ted Turner was a media star, if ever there was one, and a media mogul to boot. Loomis once invoked this odd comparison in describing his handling of Turner: "You have to whip a good dog every now and again."

The *Enterprise* camp seemed loose and low-key—like Southern California. This was a stark contrast to "Stalag 17." As Lowell North said after the event, "I don't think I felt I was under pressure. From the very beginning, I felt that unless it was going to be fun, I wouldn't do it. I think the whole crew pretty much felt that way. We never worked around the clock, and we always took time to have fun..."

When East met West, however, there were cultural differences that proved nettlesome. For example, du Moulin, with his impeccable East Coast credentials, grew concerned when he learned a hot tub was on its way from Southern California to the syndicate's home, Seaview Terrace. As he said, "Someone told me that a Jacuzzi was coming from California, but I didn't know what that was. Then I was warned by the conservative members of our syndicate that people bathe in it naked. At that, I grew concerned. The defense trials were a selection process, not necessarily a race-off, and Commodore Hinman, who ran them, was so conservative. I could just see the pictures in the newspapers. It actually saw very little use. At one point, Andy MacGowan stuck a plastic lobster in it to scare people off."

For Turner, the pressure not to repeat 1974 must have been intense—even palpable. Before the first race, he threw up three times, reported his biographer Roger Vaughan.

Nevertheless, in the June Trials, Turner and *Courageous* started strongly, sailing to a 7-1 record. This wasn't necessarily earth-shattering; old boats are often faster in June. With newer boats, it often takes longer to learn the sweet spots. On one day, June 23, he brought his baseball team, the Atlanta Braves, to watch him compete. "I watch them lose, they might as well watch me win," he said. Missing, however, were Andy Messersmith and Gary Matthews—Turner's highly paid free agents. I guess when it comes to baseball players, you can't buy love.

Hank Aaron, who hit a record-setting 715 career home runs, many of them in an Atlanta Braves uniform, was there; he worked for the Braves in management at the time. He professed to being confused by the circling before the start. So, apparently, was Turner, as he opted for the committee-boat (right) side of the line. The wind went left toward *Enterprise*, which sailed into the lead. She won the race by a scant 12 seconds—this was the only race Turner lost in this round. Fortunately, there was a second race that day that Turner won by 20 seconds.

As June ended, Turner was the talk of the town. Not all of it was good. For example, at a party at Newport's most fashionable beach club, Sprouting Rock Beach Association, better known as Bailey's Beach, he commented on the presumed sexual incompatibility of a certain May-December relationship. What she needed, he said unambiguously and loudly, was a younger and better man, and she needed it now.

North's performance in that first round was enigmatic—particularly to outsiders. It was infuriating to insiders. He had a plan: He wished to lose the June Preliminary Trials, so as not to tip his hand too soon. This became known as "sandbagging," which I'm often accused of—even accused of inventing. Then, North planned on winning the July Observation Trials, and slaughtering the competition, Turner and Hood, in the Final Trials in August. The *Enterprise* Committee wasn't happy when North shared his plans with them. "We told him we wanted him to win everything he could, but he proceeded to blow the June trials," said du Moulin.

For example, du Moulin came aboard *Enterprise* one day during a practice sail in the first round to find the cockpit inexplicably filled with water. Lowell said they had a small problem with the cockpit drains or the thru-hull fittings that would be attended to. That wasn't it at all, du Moulin learned later. What was actually preventing the cockpit from draining were "speed-brakes," an idea developed and implemented surreptitiously by North. These were two-inch-thick silicon protrusions that could be lowered some 10 inches into the water to slow the boat purposely.

Even Andy MacGowan, crew-boss on *Enterprise*, who helped design the cockpit drainage system, couldn't tell it had been altered. The crew thought they were merely closing off the drains, at Lowell's behest, not operating the speed brakes. When MacGowan learned about them from Emrys Black, another crew-member who had helped install them in San Diego, it allayed some of his worries about the syndicate that were increasing daily.[5] His experience, which included several years with Sparkman & Stephens (S&S), said *Enterprise* should have been faster than *Courageous*. She tested a minute faster

---

5. For years MacGowan kept one of these plugs in his garage. "I thought it would be a nice souvenir," he said. Recently he donated it to the America's Cup Hall of Fame in Bristol, Rhode Island.

than the first coming of *Courageous* (1974) around the course, and
this version, as modified by Hood, had to be slower.

Lowell's record on *Enterprise* was a spotty 4-6 that first round.
As this round concluded, some important members of the syndicate
thought that North should be fired. Like Nero, who fiddled while
Rome burned, he seemed more interested in testing sails and boat
speed and developing the instrument package than in winning races,
which is the bottom line. One race had to be postponed, for example,
when North's boat was changing sails far from the line when the
preparatory gun went off. The Cup committee, which included five
former America's Cup defenders or contenders, was furious.

Hood's record with *Independence* was a dismal 2-6. How Loomis
and Hood must privately have wished they still had access to *Courageous*; however, in public, hope sprang eternal in that group.

Turner was respectful to Hood, who threatened him not at all;
Peck's bad boy saved his absolute worst for Lowell North. Here,
Turner recognized an appropriate issue and struck directly for the
jugular.

North used the $60,000 grant from the *Enterprise* syndicate to
develop Mylar-laminated sailcloth. He laminated (glued) a Mylar film
to woven polyester. In time—although not this time—there would
prove to be a synergy in this recipe as a Mylar-laminated sail stretches
less than a polyester sail. Also, it weighs significantly less. Low stretch
and light weight are two of the most important qualities in sailmaking. These were the "garbage-bag sails"—as North dubbed them—
as he chose familiar garbage-bag-green Mylar for their color.

The advantages weren't lost on Turner. Citing the deal he had
made with North in Europe at the One Ton Cup the year before,
he demanded that North sell his *Courageous* syndicate the same sails.
The exchange, as North recalled it, was that in the heat of battle
Turner shouted over to him, "Lowell, you're going to sell me some
sails, aren't you?" "Sure, Ted," Lowell supposedly answered. There
was nothing in writing; there wasn't even a handshake.

North is as taciturn as Turner is loquacious. As far as North was
concerned, it was merely a dismissive response to a man who constantly natters away, to a man who would rather breathe words than
air. At that moment, North likely wished to concentrate on the rac-

ing, not the business of selling sails. Turner doesn't have conversations, he's a radio program, or to use the parlance of his business, a "talking head." He has listeners. That exchange was 10 words in the life and times of Radio Free Turner. Nevertheless, those words proved a brutal stick in Turner's hands.

North explained it to *Yachting* magazine. "I knew this was going to be a sticky issue when Turner asked me at the 1976 One Ton Cup if we were going to make sails for him. He figured that the two new boats would be better than his, and that his only advantage would be to have sails from both lofts . . .

"When Turner asked me, I said, 'yes,' because I didn't want to bring up the issue in the middle of a race. I think there was a phone conversation after that, when I asked to postpone my decision. At the Congressional Cup in March we went over it pretty thoroughly. By this time I had talked with the *Enterprise* committee people. The only way we could have made sails for Turner in John's [Marshall] and my lofts was if the NYYC said, 'Okay, make sails for Ted Turner.' Ted and I agreed it was going to be a sticky issue, and that our managers, Ed du Moulin and Lee Loomis, should handle it. It was the only way we could keep our friendship. But when the [America's] Cup committee said that we didn't have to sell him [the speciality] sails, Ted obviously didn't like it."

Turner worried the issue constantly like a tongue to a toothache. To Walter Cronkite, who was filming a segment for *60 Minutes,* he described North as a "lying son-of-a-bitch." MacGowan, who accompanied North to this interview and witnessed a second confrontation immediately after, said, "Lowell, to his credit, never retorted with any animosity, or anger. He was almost saint-like."

Another time, Turner and Gary Jobson, his young tactician, barged into the *Enterprise* compound to confront North. North, Burnham, Turner, and Jobson retired to a small boat for privacy to sort things out. "Ted launched into North," recalled Jobson. "He said, 'You promised me . . . You lied!' Tears welled up in Lowell's eyes. Malin and I just sort of sat there, folding our hands uncomfortably, and staring at the floor."

Ed du Moulin had a breakfast meeting with Turner in Long Beach during the Congressional Cup and tried to explain the syndicate's position but got nowhere. Du Moulin got the strong sense that Turner wasn't even listening to him. To Turner, this was war—a civil war.

Turner was right about the issue, thinks Jobson. "A guy like Ted became a billionaire on handshakes," he said. "He had a clear commitment from North to buy sails. This was a transitional time in the America's Cup, where exclusivity became a priority. Now, of course, it absolutely is a priority."

Du Moulin didn't, and still doesn't, agree. He argues that "it was on the basis of such policy [i.e., exclusivity] that applied also to our designer—Sparkman & Stephens—that we secured the funds to proceed with our design and research."

Jobson now covers sailing on ESPN and is a sought-after lecturer, writer, and corporate spokesman for the sport. Turner, he says, changed his life. They first met in the Interclass Solo Championship in 1972. Turner finished sixth and Jobson and Robbie Doyle, both collegiate all-Americans, finished second and first, respectively. (Doyle, like Jobson, would sail on *Courageous*.) Turner put his arm around both of them and said, "Someday we will do something great together." Turner could deliver lines like that, and you would almost believe him.

About a year before the 1977 Cup, Jobson encountered Turner on an airplane. Turner told him, said Jobson, " 'I could use your help. In return I'll help you in business. You can use my help, even though you don't know that yet.' " For Jobson, it was, in some ways, like a genie coming out of a bottle to do his bidding. However, he had no way of knowing if the genie's magic was real. This was 1976, but two years after Turner nearly self-destructed. His magic proved empty then.

Jobson was then a 26-year-old sailing coach for the Merchant Marine Academy, who made $14,000 a year. It was "cool," he said about the job, "but I was running out of runway"—meaning a future.

Then he sailed with Turner in the SORC, where they finished second, as mentioned, and the Congressional Cup, as tactician, where they finished first. On the water, during the America's Cup, he offered Turner wise counsel; off it, they walked together to the boat every morning and home every evening, where Turner talked. And talked. Jobson, who is as good a listener as Turner is a talker, kept him focused and relatively calm. Jobson listened. And learned.

For Jobson, Turner proved to be a man of his word—a magic genie. So successful did he become in television and business that people called him "JobCo," a nickname that was said with respect. "He truly did help me in business," Jobson said. "Everyday I wake up and say, 'Thank you, Ted. Thank you for helping me.'"

With Turner's success, "Beat-the-Mouth" badges began to be sported by *Enterprise* supporters. On it were Turner's telltale mustache and a mouth opened cavernously. One evening, while having dinner at Castle Hill, Turner spotted such a badge on a man at the next table. He ripped the badge off the man's shirt, tearing it, and said, according to Jobson who was with him, "If you want to beat the Mouth, I'll give you a chance to do it right now if you want to follow me into the parking lot."

It climaxed at the *Enterprise* party, a social event Turner hadn't planned on attending. For the sake of propriety, however, Loomis insisted he go. Turner strolled up to North and threatened to ruin him. Even if it took a lifetime. They stood toe to toe, and Turner, who was clenching and unclenching his fists, seemed about to deliver that famous "knuckle sandwich." North seemed ready, too, when a pretty young woman, totally unaware of what was happening, wandered over to meet North, over whom she gushed. It totally defused the moment—if not the issue.

In July North seemed to be following his personal script. His *Enterprise* posted a 7-6 record, the equal of Turner's. However, *Enterprise* beat *Courageous* five of seven times. More inexplicably, *Independence*, which sailed to a 5-7 record that round, beat *Enterprise* four of six times. What conclusions could be drawn from that? Nevertheless, du Moulin used North's record in July to forestall his firing.

Enterprise wasn't significantly faster than the competition; she might well have been slower. North's tactics weren't particularly inspired either. He did have at least a couple of shining moments, however. In one race against *Independence*, North starboard-tacked Hood, who fell off, to clear *Enterprise*. The moment that Hood turned away from the wind, North tacked on to port, trapping Hood to leeward. In the controlling position, he then herded Hood to the layline. Once on the layline, the leading boat can inflict the most damage. Hood was so surprised he protested, but to no avail. This likely established the "slam-dunk" maneuver, as it would forever be called, as a standard in the America's Cup—in fact, match-racing.

In another race, in July, North drove Turner beyond a mark. Although allowed by the rules, this tactic is rarely used. Turner was so upset, he rammed *Enterprise* repeatedly.

THE FOREIGN CHALLENGERS, the most ever, started racing on August 4. They sailed round-robins to determine a final seeding. This round ended with Bond's *Australia* first, followed by *Sverige, Gretel II*, which dropped out early to make repairs, and *France*. Then, a week later, *Australia* sailed against *France*, and *Sverige* met *Gretel II*. *Australia* beat *France* utterly. In three Cup campaigns, beginning in 1970, Baron Bich's French crews posted a dismal 0-18 record. *Sverige* beat *Gretel II*, but it took her a full seven races and a new mast, to replace one that broke in a windy race, to do it. In the finals, Bond's *Australia*, skippered by Noel Robins, an Australian Soling champion, beat *Sverige* 4-0 to matriculate to the match.

The Final Trials to pick a defender began on August 16. By August 24, *Courageous*'s record was a nearly unblemished 5-1, her only loss coming from Hood's *Independence*. Hood's record was 2-1, *Enterprise*'s, 1-3. For this round, a new, supposedly "miracle" bottom paint had been put on *Enterprise*. It reacted badly to the oil in the water in Newport Harbor, however, and had to be sanded off. This was the only time that the syndicate worked through the night.

Even Mother Nature smiled on Turner. "When we raced *Independence*, supposedly a light-air boat, we got heavy air," said Gary Jobson. "When we raced *Enterprise*, supposedly a heavy-air boat, we got light air."

I was in Kiel, Germany, at the time, preparing for the Star Worlds, after winning a Bronze Medal the year before in the Olympics in the Tempest. A week before the Worlds were to start, I received a telephone call from Ed du Moulin, of the *Enterprise* syndicate asking me if I would be willing to come to Newport and replace Lowell North as skipper. A year before, I would have killed for the job, but now I turned him down as politely as I could. I have great respect for Lowell and for Malin Burnham. I figured if they couldn't beat Turner how could I make a difference? In addition, I remembered how furious Turner was—and probably still is—when I replaced him on *Mariner*. I didn't want Lowell and Malin mad at me, too. They're my friends; we live in the same town, sail at the same club.

It proved a good decision. I went on to win the Star Worlds that year, with five firsts in five races in an 89-boat fleet.

Obviously, push was coming to shove in the *Enterprise* camp. North wasn't covering the competition; indeed, in one race, the crew had to use force to get him to watch the other boat. He'd be off testing sails when the starting sequence was about to start. North once even jibed the boat while under spinnaker without telling the crew. Du Moulin said that John Marshall, North's lieutenant, broke down when he realized his boss, skipper, and friend wasn't going to succeed at this. A man for whom things seemed to come so easily, North didn't have the proper temperament for the America's Cup. Physically, he was showing the strain. "He looked awful," recalled du Moulin.

On August 25 the world learned North had been fired. Rod Davis was the bowman on *Enterprise* at the time. The youngest man on the crew at age 21, he also worked for North, at the Seal Beach loft. When the crew was told that North was off the boat, Davis burst into tears—North could inspire that kind of loyalty.[6] Lowell was replaced by Malin Burnham. Halsey Herreshoff also came aboard as tactician.

The changes didn't make an earthshaking difference. The ax fell first on Hood and *Independence* on August 29. Among those on the America's Cup Committee who thanked Ted Hood for his effort was Bob Bavier, the man Hood replaced as skipper of *Courageous* in 1974. The next day, *Enterprise* was excused. It happened in the midst of a

---

6. Davis, of San Diego, the grandson of an admiral and the son of Whit Davis, former commander of the submarine USS *Razorback*, would go on to sail on *Defender* in 1983, and skipper *Eagle* in the 1986–87 America's Cup, both representing America. He skippered *New Zealand* in the 1992 Cup. An irony—Davis would be fired at the end of 1992, to be replaced by Russell Coutts. Davis was the helmsman on *oneAustralia* in 1995, the year Coutts won it for New Zealand.

colossal thunderstorm. Leaving *Enterprise*, the America's Cup Committee, led by Commodore Hinman, who fired Turner in 1974, made its way to *Courageous* at Bannister's Wharf. Commodore Hinman said, "Captain Turner, I have the honor to inform you and the crew of *Courageous* that you have been selected to defend the America's Cup." At that precise moment, the sun broke through, and the world turned golden—especially for Turner.

Dick Enersen, of Offshore Productions, was filming a documentary of this America's Cup. He was on the dock, shooting the anointing of Turner, when Loomis confronted him and bundled him off the dock. Enersen is a man who matched Loomis in size; he sailed on *Constellation* in 1964. "Christ, Lee," he said. "Can't you be gracious even in victory?"

In an unfortunate swan song, Lowell North commented to a Boston newspaper reporter that, at this point, he had no great love for Ted Turner, and he wouldn't mind seeing the Australians win the Cup. He told the writer he didn't wish to see that in print. The next day the world would read his remarks in the newspaper. It even said that North was going to help the Australians, and had already taken Bond and Dave Forbes, from *Australia*, out sailing on *Enterprise*. The only Australian to sail on *Enterprise* was Gordon Ingate, skipper of *Gretel II*. This happened after the latter boat was eliminated.

Whatever else happened, I think a sad thing for the sport of sailboat racing is that Lowell North never returned to it with the same fire, enthusiasm, and brilliance he had shown before. The sport, I believe, has missed him. I know I have.

Turner, however, wasn't troubled by the havoc he created. As he said, "The highest I ever scored on an IQ test was 128, and I figured that North was about a 148, and since I spotted him 20 points I knew I had to use guile and cunning. I didn't just eliminate Lowell North, I destroyed him. He left here a broken, bitter man. I'm three times the man he is."

So *Courageous*, starring Ted Turner, met *Australia*, starring no one, in the twenty-third America's Cup match. Turner didn't wear "a muzzle"; the America's Cup Committee didn't appear in "skinny-legged blue jeans and motorcycle boots." His record made it all but impossible to select anyone else.

If there were no stars on *Australia*, there was Andy Rose, the tactician, who stuck out like a sore thumb. An American, Rose was hired to coach the Australians. He met the residency requirements and eventually sailed on the boat in this match. And so Rose was probably the first "soldier of fortune" in the afterguard in the so-called "modern" America's Cup. He wouldn't be the last or the most checkered. The aforementioned Rod Davis, "a citizen of the world," probably holds the record in that regard.

The match was, as it often is, no contest. On Sunday, September 18, the Americans were up 3-0. This day, in the course of their walk to the boat, Turner turned to Jobson, whose tactics had been impeccable, and said, "Remember these days. It will never be better than this, no matter what we do..." It ended this day with a 4-0 sweep for the Americans.

On the way in, Turner and the crew toasted their success with champagne that materialized magically. At the dock Loomis was among the first to greet the boat, bearing a bottle of champagne. It was a nice gesture. Then there was beer, aquavit, sent over by the Swedes, and more champagne.

Then came the ritual dunking at Bannister's Wharf, which was crowded to bursting. Starting with Turner, it moved through the ranks to Jobson, Robbie Doyle, the sailmaker, and the rest of the crew. When NYYC Commodore Bob McCullough and Vice Commodore Harry Anderson came by, they were both tossed in. Next came the Australians, including Alan Bond, who met a similar fate. He took it well.

No one pushed Lee Loomis in, however. Loomis jumped in—holding his nose. Enersen's camera was there to film it.

Later Turner, with most, but not all, of his shirt tucked in, staggered to the "winner's circle"—the press center at the Armory on Thames Street. Having trouble with the laws of gravity as well as the laws of the land, he was supported by two smiling if well-armed Newport policemen. It looked like any Saturday night in rollicking Newport, not a very special Sunday afternoon with the absolute star of the show. The toast of the town. At one point, Turner complained they were holding him too tight. The policemen eased their grip, and he sagged dangerously. "You'd better hang on," Turner reconsidered.

On the stage, before hundreds of journalists, Turner placed a bottle of aquavit in front of him. Someone hid it, supposedly to keep it from appearing in the photos, but Turner dove under the table to retrieve it. He reappeared several moments later with a boyish grin and his bottle. "I love the Australians," he bubbled. "I love everybody in this room." Then he began to rub affectionately the very bald pate of Bill Ficker, the moderator, a successful America's Cup skipper himself. Before he could do further damage, Robbie Doyle, Stretch Ryder, and other *Courageous* crew hoisted their skipper to their shoulders and bundled him out of the room. It was some exit.

"Ted Turner," wrote Barbara Lloyd, in the Newport *Daily News*, "rocketed from famous to superstar."

That summer he put the America's Cup on the map. It would never again be "by invitation only"—a private party for the New York Yacht Club.

An era had ended.

CHAPTER 7

1980

READY, WILLING, ABLE

—✺—

AS LUCK WOULD have it, the America's Cup world wasn't done with San Diego, San Diegans, or Dennis Conner. After the 1977 America's Cup, I was asked by Fritz and Lucy Jewett and Ed du Moulin, members of the *Enterprise* syndicate in 1977, to skipper a boat in the 1980 America's Cup. It was to be my debut as a skipper. I was 37 years old and ready.

That said, before accepting I had two conditions. The first was that I couldn't be fired, as Lowell North had been in 1977 and Ted Turner and Bob Bavier were in 1974. We were to swim or sink— God forbid—together. Also, while we eventually decided to build a new boat, which became *Freedom*, I could choose *Freedom* or *Enterprise*, which the syndicate had retained from the Maritime College at Ft. Schuyler Foundation, Inc., under whose aegis we would again sail. The slower boat would be my trial horse, nothing more. This meant I wouldn't be Ted Hood—pushed out of the competition by *Courageous*, ostensibly a boat he designed, and by a skipper, Ted Turner, he approved of, or at least accepted.

Leaving one boat an orphan became an issue—a *cause célèbre*— for Turner, who seems to grow strong worrying such things. At one point, he threatened to boycott the trials if we didn't enter both boats. The New York Yacht Club (NYYC) wasn't happy about an odd number of boats either. While no historian, I did not intend to repeat the mistakes of history. Neither did the *Enterprise-Freedom* group, so off we sailed. Luck was with me; I couldn't have found better "shipmates," better allies, and, as it turned out, better friends than the Jewetts and Ed du Moulin. It proved a potent amalgamation of East and West: the Jewetts and I are from California, Ed du Moulin is from New York, the Maritime College is in New York.

To get to the match, I had to pass through Turner, who was making a return appearance with *Courageous*, which he now owned. For $550,000 total he'd also purchased Ted Hood's unimpressive *Independence*, which would be cannibalized and turned into *Clipper* for Russell Long.

Starting with *American Eagle* in 1968, then *Mariner* in 1974, and *Courageous* in 1977, Turner had more miles and more time in America's Cup 12-Meters than anyone in the world. If I'd steered a 12-Meter more than a dozen times, at that point, it would have surprised me. Thus, I decided to sail to at least close the experience gap with Turner, which was considerable. Before the starting gun first fired in June of 1980, I would log 180 days at sea, in Newport, in San Diego, where Lowell North and Malin Burnham steered *Enterprise*, and then back in Newport, where *Enterprise* was helmed by Tom Whidden and Jack Sutphen.

Sutphen was an interesting choice and a lasting pleasure. When I came aboard *Courageous* in 1974, at the eleventh hour, Jack, a sailmaker from Ratsey, got off the boat. I might not have been so forgiving. He has been with me since 1980 as the driver of my various trial horses and has been a key member of my team. Sutphen, a dyed-in-the-wool New Yorker, complete with a Yankees baseball cap which he affects, moved to the endless-summer world of San Diego where he gets on like a native. It took him 66 years to realize he is a boy of summer.

"No excuse to lose" was my motto in those days; indeed, it was the name of my first book. I would be criticized for my all-out approach by Turner and by Tom Blackaller, a long-time rival, who would be sailing as tactician aboard *Clipper*. Blackaller was nearly as glib, as charismatic, as Turner. As I said then, I certainly don't apologize for working harder than the other guys. In the America's Cup, there is no extra credit for making it look easy—practically the theme of Blackaller's life. The only points go to the first person to cross the finish line. If I had to work harder—to huff and puff to get there—I was willing to expend the time and effort.

We even hired a physical trainer, Arnie Schmeling, to put the crew through its paces. Schmeling's bloodlines were interesting: he is the grandnephew of Max Schmeling, the first boxer to beat Joe Louis. If you think I like that kind of stuff—that huffing and puffing—you're wrong, but I don't ask people to do what I cannot, or will not, do.

In *No Excuse to Lose* I said I'm not the world's best sailor, so I try harder. It's a remark that has long followed me, and one that I've lived to regret. I was attempting to appear modest. Speaking more candidly, I was one of the world's best sailors *and* I tried harder. History would prove that is a difficult combination to beat.

I was a professional in approach, but not in fact. I then ran a wholesale drapery business in San Diego, the business that I'd worked in since college. Sadly, in the winter of 1979, Alan Raffee, my mentor, shipmate, and boss, had died, when a plane he piloted on the way to a ski vacation crashed into a mountain.

In those days, no one, including the skipper, was paid, at least as far as I know. Of course, at least on my two boats, there was an abundance of industry professionals, such as sailmakers John Marshall and Tom Whidden, who might benefit professionally from an association with a winning Cup campaign.

The America's Cup did not do a thing for my drapery business except, probably, hurt it. Therefore, the charge being a professional seemed off-the-mark—gratuitous—to me.

Twelve-Meter design had reached a point of diminishing returns, or so we were told by the press. While yacht designers wouldn't admit it, their 12-Meter boats all came out looking the same. Two-time defender *Courageous* was the benchmark, and "*Courageous* clones" were the result. Like hope, such boats, of varying inspiration and execution, sprang eternal. For example, our new boat, *Freedom*, went right to the source; it was designed by Olin Stephens, who designed *Courageous*, or at least her first coming in 1974. Then there was David Pedrick who designed *Clipper* from the ashes of *Independence*. The old-new *Clipper*, which was launched two months before the first race, featured the keel, rig, sails, and steering gear of *Independence*, but a new hull and deck. Pedrick had worked for Olin Stephens at Sparkman & Stephens (S&S), and on the designs of *Courageous* and *Enterprise*. Similarly, Johan Valentijn, who designed a boat in this Cup for Baron Marcel Bich, of France, also worked for S&S when *Courageous* was shaped. Valentijn was also the co-designer of *Australia*, with Ben Lexcen; this boat would sail again—again for Alan Bond. If a designer hadn't worked at S&S, a boat's "privates" weren't shrouded in those innocent days. Since 1974, all of *Courageous*'s ample charms were there for the world to see. As well as to photograph and to copy.

I was in awe of Olin Stephens when he designed *Freedom* for me. He was, to my mind, the most talented yacht designer. He had the most experience and had designed more winning boats than anyone. He was also the most acceptable from the fund-raising standpoint. The people from New York who, for the most part, funded such things thought he was the master. Any boat he was associated with was the odds-on favorite until proven flawed—was innocent until proven guilty.

That awe, however, never translated to a friendship. I never really got to know Stephens well. He was like a God to me; it was thrilling just to be in his presence. It wasn't Olin and Dennis. He was "Mr. Stephens" to me. This was my debut as skipper; he'd been at this game since 1937. I was poor; he was rich. I was from San Diego; he, from New York. I was young; he was old—almost retired. In every way we were worlds apart.

Freedom was designed with a minimum of tank-testing. The tank had largely been discredited after 1974 and *Mariner*.

Believing there was nothing to be garnered in hull shape, we concentrated on sails—the engine of a sailboat. I started with Hood sails, just to check in, then went with the best of North and, later, the best of Sobstad. By the time the competition ended, I had tested more than 100 sails.

When Robbie Doyle, Vice President of Hood, and a longtime Turner crew-member, agreed in 1979, to sell me Hood sails, Turner,

Olin Stephens designed such defenders as Columbia, *in 58;* Constellation, *64;* Intrepid, *67;* Courageous, *74;* Freedom *in 80, and co-designed* Ranger *in 37.*
DANIEL FORSTER

true to form, was apoplectic. It was the same old beef, just a different year and different sailmaker.

Even here, however, his heart didn't seem in it—an attitude that would characterize his 1980 America's Cup campaign. Turner, of course, was too smart to lean too heavily on his own sailmaker, as he'd done with Lowell North, his rival in 1977. More to the point, that spring Ted Turner's 24-hour Cable News Network (CNN) made its debut.

Understandably, his thoughts were in Atlanta, where his new station was losing a reported $1 million a month. That's a figure that can rivet a person's attention. As his tactician, Gary Jobson said somewhat prophetically, before the 1980 campaign started, "Sailing is not the most important thing in his life right now. His $100 million Cable News Network is infinitely more important to him, as are the Braves, the Hawks, and his other TV stations. Turner has got so much going on that there's no way that he could possibly put it all into sailing."

Experience has taught me that people at the leading edge, like Lowell North, for example, often pay the price more than they reap the rewards. Nevertheless, we used a new generation of Kevlar sails in the 1980 America's Cup on *Freedom*. These sails came directly from the Mylar-laminated sails that Lowell North pioneered for *Enterprise* in 1977. North paid the price; I reaped the rewards.

I've been wrong about this approach, too. For example, I elected not to build *Ganbare*, one of the most successful One Tonners of my generation. In 1973, Doug Peterson, her designer, showed me drawings of a yacht he'd penned, his first. He hoped I would be interested in building and campaigning the boat in the One Ton North Americans. Peterson, from San Diego, proudly spread the drawings out on the hood of my car at the San Diego Yacht Club. It was hard not to laugh. The drawings were ridiculously crude. Further, Peterson was virtually unknown, and his design was a short boat when One Tonners of that day, such as the Ranger 37, were long on the water. "Oh, Doug," I said, "I can't build this."

That boat won the One Ton North Americans in San Diego. After that, he again offered me the boat, for the ridiculously low sum of $20,000. I turned him down. Then Lowell North sailed *Ganbare*

This crossing shot shows *Freedom* ahead of *Australia* in the 1980 Cup.

(DAN NERNEY)

Australia II passes *Liberty* downwind in the seventh and deciding race of the 1983 America's Cup. (DAN NERNEY)

John Bertrand, skipper (left), and Alan Bond, syndicate head,
pose with the Cup. (DAN NERNEY)

Stars and Stripes practices in Hawaii in preparation for the 1986-87 America's Cup. There the big winds blow year-round. (COURTESY DENNIS CONNER SPORTS)

Stars and Stripes '87 is seen under spinnaker at Perth, Western Australia.

(DANIEL FORSTER)

Stars and Stripes '87 blasts upwind in the winds of war. In windy Perth,
the 120-Meter came into its own. (DAN NERNEY)

Conner and crew met President Reagan at the White House.

(DANIEL FORSTER)

The America's Cup went to court in 1988 and stayed there for a prolonged period.

(DAN NERNEY)

David vs. Goliath in the 1988 America's Cup. The sailing and judicial worlds had varying opinions about who was David and who was Goliath. (DAN NERNEY)

The bowsprit of *New Zealand* proved a congenial issue for Paul Cayard, skipper of *Il Moro*, the eventual challenger in the 1992 America's Cup. (DANIEL FORSTER)

America³, the successful defender in 1992, flies her asymmetrical
masthead spinnaker. (DANIEL FORSTER)

The late Raul Gardini (left) and Paul Cayard, owner and skipper, respectively of *Il Moro,* the challenger in the 1992 America's Cup.

(DANIEL FORSTER)

Bill Koch, skipper and prime mover of *America³*, hoists the prize in 1992.

(DANIEL FORSTER)

"We can do it!" was the
motto of the women's
defense syndicate in 1995.
Obviously Merritt Carrey
could, far up the mast of
Mighty Mary. (DANIEL FORSTER)

Black Magic is to weather of *USA 36,* Conner's borrowed defender, in the 1995 America's Cup. (DAN NERNEY)

Peter Blake, syndicate head (left), and Russell Coutts, skipper, celebrate with the America's Cup after New Zealand's win in 1995. (DANIEL FORSTER)

at the One Ton Worlds. They would have won, except for missing a mark. On the basis of this boat, Peterson launched a very significant career in yacht design; he was part of the team of designers who shaped *America³*, the successful defender in 1992 for Bill Koch.

Kevlar is the miracle material used to stop bullets in bullet-proof vests and in tire cord. In a Mylar sail, such as North experimented with in 1977, a Mylar film is laminated to a layer of woven polyester. In these Kevlar sails, the Mylar film is laminated to a woven fabric that features Kevlar fiber in one direction and polyester in the other. If a Mylar sail could be half the weight of a polyester sail—a Kevlar sail could be one-quarter the weight—with the same degree of low stretch.[1]

With Kevlar there were problems gluing the Mylar film to the woven (Kevlar and polyester) substrate. The material would delaminate, or separate. For example, the Kevlar sails on *Freedom* did have problems in this regard. There was our famous Number-10 mainsail, built by North, which was fast, but falling apart. I only used that sail when I really needed some extra speed. It had patches all over it to try to hold it together. That wing went up with a prayer.

We committed to Kevlar sails in 1979, earlier than any group. Learning there would be a shortage of this new material, I purchased enough to satisfy my needs. I saw this as foresight; others saw it in more Machiavellian terms. I "corner[ed] the market," to quote Norris Hoyt, of the *Clipper* syndicate. This was sour grapes, as I see it. The truth, at least according to David Pedrick, *Clipper*'s designer, was that this effort didn't get around to ordering any Kevlar sails until after the June trials. Surprise, surprise, there was no material available.

Another strength Turner had was crew—he is an extraordinary leader. As I said before, if he had been a Civil War general, we might all be whistling *Dixie*. Thus, I tested 120 potential crew-members. I ended up with John Marshall, Halsey Herreshoff, Dennis Durgan, Scott Vogel, Kyle Smith, and Jon Wright, all of whom were famous or would be famous in this or future America's Cups. "My guys," I called them.

Then there was Tom Whidden. A key piece of the America's

---

1. Kevlar sails first appeared in the early 1970s, under the name "Fiber B."

Cup puzzle, I recognized, would be the skipper of the trial horse—the sailing equivalent of a sparring partner in boxing. The best way to improve, I believe, is to sail against another boat, a trial horse that is equally well sailed. Though the skipper of the trial horse is a very important position to me, it isn't the most glamorous job on the waterfront. I had the names of perhaps a half-dozen people who, I thought, might be good in the role. One was Tom Whidden, a young sailmaker from Connecticut, who was a part owner of Sobstad, a small sailmaking concern there. Whidden, I was told, had done a good job with the boats he had, which were fairly ordinary. I also heard he was a good guy and a team player. I was interested because talent and loyalty are what I prize most in people.

I met him at the 1979 Southern Ocean Racing Conference (SORC), which at this stage was in Miami. After introducing myself, I told him I wanted to discuss my plans for the 1980 America's Cup. While he had no objections to such a conversation, he was on his way to the airport to fly home to Connecticut. Would he mind if I came along for the ride? I asked him. At the airport, I wished to continue the conversation so I asked if it would be all right if I flew with him to Connecticut. By now, Whidden was perplexed, if not worried. A casual conversation, at least in his mind, was turning serious. A salesman himself, he knew I wasn't going to leave him alone until I closed this deal. He asked, "What will you do when you get there?" I told him, "I'll go home with you . . ."

On the flight north, I talked him into being skipper of my trial horse. With this out of the way, I got off the airplane in Hartford and flew back to Florida.

Tom Whidden, now CEO of North Sails, the largest sailmaker in the world, has been with me through every America's Cup since 1980. True to his ability to make the most out of whatever he's given, he graduated from the trial horse, *Enterprise*, to sail on *Freedom*, the first-string yacht in 1980. (Then Jack Sutphen took over this role.) In '83, Whidden sailed with me on *Liberty*, as tactician, when we lost the Cup. He has filled that slot ever since. In all this time together—through the wins and the losses—he has become my best friend.

Early on, I threw him a bone, so to speak. I allowed his company to build one sail, a spinnaker, for our program. I had no great expectations for that sail, but it seemed a worthwhile investment. My hope was that we could use it in the America's Cup trials, if not the match, which might help Whidden's business.

True to form, Whidden did a lot with little. When we first hoisted the spinnaker while sailing against *Enterprise*, it was faster—demonstrably faster—than the North spinnakers we had. When I told John Marshall, of North, that Whidden's sail was faster, he just wouldn't believe it. Marshall is so confident, so arrogant. So I proved it to him. Both *Freedom* and *Enterprise* were on port tack, and Marshall was in a powerboat taking pictures. That's typical Marshall—wanting to steal it right away. Whidden obviously didn't like it, but he was just thrilled to have his sail up there. Furthermore, he is too much of a gentleman to say anything about it.

Marshall made us put the sail up and down three times. Knowing Marshall, he probably figured out what made it work the first time, and he wanted it up the next two times so he could take pictures to copy it. That was the first time I've ever seen John Marshall at a loss for words.

With so much riding on sailmaking, we took copious photographs of the sails used each day. As Whidden's company began to play a greater role in sailmaking, Whidden and Marshall would race—even resort to subterfuge—to be first to see that day's pictures. It was comical.

Like "cornering the market," my success in recruiting led to another charge that has long dogged me: that is, I lock up talent. The truth is, I consider it a positive character trait. Why do the best sailors in the world want to sail with me? To ask it another way: Why aren't they sailing with the guys who are complaining about it? I certainly don't have the charisma of a Turner or a Blackaller or the deep, dark pockets of Raul Gardini and Bill Koch, who would play this game in such epic form years later. I bring more of a work ethic and a chance to prove oneself. Most important is my winning record, but at this point there was no overt reason to believe I would be successful here. Turner had the charisma and the money and was the undisputed king of the mountain. He was the favorite, despite his attempts to paint me as such. Ted Turner is Mr. Outside. He gains strength as an underdog. He seemingly gets dizzy at the top of the mountain.

Turner's crew was virtually unchanged from 1977; thus, they were ancient mariners. Their average age was 33 years, and two of his crew were within 10 years of collecting Medicaid. After practicing in the fall of 1979, "Mr. Outside" said, "The main reason we had our practice session was to see if any of our crew had arthritis."

Compare these old men of the sea to the *Clipper* crew, a third defense effort. The median age of that group was 24 years, the age of the skipper, Russell Long, who had recently graduated from Harvard. "I've owned dogs that have lived longer than most of those guys," quipped a *Courageous* crew member. *Clipper* was the TV generation at the America's Cup, there to slay their elders: Turner and me. Their theme song, played loudly as they left the dock, was from "Gilligan's Island," and they called their tender *Minnow*—the "mighty ship" in the theme song. The 40-year-old Tom Blackaller was the senior citizen aboard, there to lend a modicum of maturity.

To the manor born was Russell Long. The manor was in New York City; the year was 1956. Long's father is Summer A. "Huey" Long, a shipping magnate, who long campaigned a series of large ocean-racing yachts called *Ondine*. Russell's mother is an heiress to the Reynolds Aluminum fortune. Russell sailed his first Fastnet Race at the age of seven, aboard his father's 56-foot *Ondine*. He went to prep school in Newport at the prestigious St. George's School, where he met Norris Hoyt, a teacher, sailor, photographer, and writer. "Norrie and I were very very close," said Long. "I spent at least half my time at Norrie's house, talking with him, and meeting all the sailors that passed through there. All the vagabonds." Hoyt would help direct Long's campaign in its salad days.

Selected by Turner, Long was, in essence, to be as Turner was in 1977. He was to be good enough to provide some competition, but not so good as to steal Turner's thunder. Also, like Turner, Long could pay his fair share. History, in fact, repeated itself. As Turner beat Hood in 1977, Long lasted longer than Turner in 1980.

Clipper took her name from Pan Am Airways, a sponsor, which used the name *Clipper* to distinguish its service and equipment. Said

Long, "The future of the America's Cup rests in the hands of corporate sponsors." The event had changed; even the NYYC sold official sponsorships to offset the costs of running the event.

IN THE FIRST race of the defense trials, Turner beat us by 1:25. It was in a northwest breeze that can be substantial in Newport. In this race we used our oldest Dacron sails—they were training sails from 1979. Already Russell Long, who had yet to sail a race, was trumpeting our demise. I wasn't upset; this was part of my plan. I was supremely confident in my sails—they proved a generation ahead of the competitions'. Whenever Turner would build a new sail, I'd just go to a faster one. I had 52 cards—a full deck—he only had 15. We finished the first round with a record of 11-1. We didn't lose another race to Turner that summer.

While willing to engage Turner at sea, I gave him a wide berth ashore. It was like the navy fighting the army; I knew where I was strong. He used the media very well, while I didn't know how to handle them, particularly then. Turner was the star, of course, plus he's very amusing. I enjoyed his sense of humor, as long as it wasn't aimed at me.

I had a plan, however, which is my way. When Turner pushed, I retreated; thus, he couldn't push me. He'd say, "Dennis is a professional." He could make that word *professional* sound like a felony. I'd say, "Thank you very much. Does that mean he thinks I'm doing a very good job?"

If June was bad for Turner, July was downright ugly. It must have been reminiscent of the *Mariner* chapter in his life. In July Turner and *Courageous* did some practice racing with Russell Long and *Clipper*. There was a port-starboard crossing with *Courageous* on starboard tack, with right of way, and *Clipper* on port, the give-way vessel. Long steered *Clipper* down to avoid *Courageous* but then right up again; he obviously wished to cut it close. To send a message. He cut it a little too close, and *Clipper* ended up in the cockpit of *Courageous*. The collision sprung the mast—the second one to fall on *Courageous* that summer. "Ted was upset," said Jobson. "But being Ted, he understood it, too."

Between the two boats, which loosely formed one syndicate, there was one good spare mast. It was an elliptical section designed by Arvel Gentry, the famous aerodynamicist from Boeing. Gentry determined this shape is optimum; it shows less turbulence than a round or D-shaped mast. It was this style of mast that *Courageous* used to win the America's Cup in 1977, and this style of mast had broken. The spare mast belonged to *Clipper*, however. Turner asked for it, but Long refused, despite the fact that the collision was his fault. Long worried that he'd have no spare. Turner tried to allay his fears, by saying he'd give Long the Gentry mast if he needed it, but Long turned him down. Perhaps he worried that Turner might break this mast, too; he'd already broken two. And finally, Long must have pondered privately, why help someone you're trying to beat? "For the good of the defense . . . ," was the knee-jerk response I heard then, and I would hear so often later. I'm all in favor of pooling resources *after* you have been eliminated from the competition, but not before. This is a boxing match, not a team sport.

Jobson said, "We ended up with a piece of junk, and the boat was slow." For Turner and *Courageous*, the show was near to closing.

The NYYC's America's Cup Committee has always frowned on defenders and foreign challengers meeting before the actual match. This reality check might show the challengers where they are, or where they have to go, or how to get there. Despite a military-school background, Turner wasn't big when it came to rules of conduct. In 1970, before he was involved in the America's Cup, he brought his flaming-red *American Eagle* to Newport to act as a trial horse for *Gretel II*, the Australian challenger.

In this Cup, Turner engaged the British yacht *Lionheart* in a scrimmage. The boat, which came to Newport under the leadership of Tony Boyden, who had last campaigned *Sovereign* in 1964, featured a radical, bendy mast that hooked aft several feet at the tip.

The bendy mast gave the boat an extra 100 square feet of *unrated* sail area, but that wasn't all that made it so special. By World War II, the designers of the famous RAF Spitfire airplane determined that the optimum profile, or planform, for a wing is an ellipse—U-shaped. The worst shape for an airfoil is a triangle—a V. It becomes apparent then, that the optimum planform for a sail is as close to an ellipse as possible. This translates to a mainsail with battens—supporting an exaggerated roach (roach is the extra area outside the straight line from head to clew)—set on a mast with considerable aft bend. This is the aerodynamic and nautical version of the hawk's wing.

The tip of a triangular sail isn't very effective. In a wind tunnel it was determined that the luff of a mainsail on a 12-Meter could be reduced at the top by 15 percent without any noticeable effect on performance. The bendy mast, however, provided a four-percent increase in performance. Norris Hoyt, the writer, who early on was associated with *Clipper*, was impressed. He wrote somewhat breathlessly, "*Lionheart*'s extraordinary bendy topmast rig is the greatest performance breakthrough in 12-Meter design."

The mast impressed Turner, too, during that informal scrimmage with *Lionheart*. According to Jobson, he commented that if the Australians got one of those masts, they'd be difficult to beat. Prophetic words, those.

An ad hoc scrimmage with *Lionheart* wasn't Turner's only transgression, at least in the eyes of the NYYC. In the midst of the July trials, he invited an Australian to sail aboard *Courageous*. Adding his muscle to a winch on *Courageous* was none other than Ben Lexcen, the designer of *Australia*. The New York Yacht Club was not amused. They excused Turner and *Courageous* from the remaining two races in July. It must have been akin to his two expulsions from Brown University, or his banishment from baseball. Once again, Ted Turner was Peck's bad boy.

We only lost three races during the trials. This had to demoralize the competition. To provide some motivation for the *Clipper* crew, Tom Blackaller, the tactician, and a North sailmaker in San Francisco, invited Werner Erhard, the founder of the EST movement in Northern California, to conduct one of his Erhard Seminar Training Sessions. Dave Vietor, who sailed aboard *Clipper*, told my co-author Michael Levitt how it went. "We got into this room, and Werner Erhard and his disciples are there. He says to start meditating on your little toe. It's dark; we've cracked a few beers; we'd just lost to Dennis Conner by 10 minutes, and Erhard is going through his patter. He has this really good, mellow voice. So, soon you hear Jack Crane, a grinder, start to snore in the background. Seemingly untroubled by this lack of attention, Erhard says, 'Tell me your deep, dark secrets.' Well, these guys aren't going to say anything; I mean these are tough guys. He isn't getting anywhere. So finally he says, 'Why do you think you guys are losing to Dennis Conner?' And at that point Jack Crane wakes up from his deep slumber and shouts, 'Because he's f------ better than us ...'"

On August 25 Bob McCullough and his America's Cup Committee visited *Courageous*, like the angel of death, and delivered the news, "I have the sad duty to inform you ..." *Courageous* was excused. Turner took it with dignity. Later he was speaking directly to me when he said: "The complexities of mounting a campaign today, with all the thousands of hours of testing that it requires, don't appeal to me. It's too much like working in a science laboratory. It's great to win, and it's not as much fun to lose. But it's not that big a deal. Christ, this is a sailboat race. It's the biggest one there is, but it's still a sailboat race."

It is understandable why Turner would criticize me for doing it my way. When he accused me of ruining the sport with my tenacity, what I think he was really saying was, "Well, look, if I spent the same amount of time as Dennis does, I could beat him." Or, "Make Dennis spend the same time that I do, and then I'll beat him." Turner wanted this to be a contest of skill and sailing ability: a "one-design" contest for sailors. I said, "Come on, now. I don't see that in the rules anywhere. I thought this was a race where the fastest boat, best skipper, sails, crew, and organization wins."

In 1995 Turner's Atlanta Braves finally won baseball's biggest prize: the World Series. Could you imagine him saying, "It's great to win, and it's not as much fun to lose. But it's not that big a deal"? The America's Cup *was* a big deal to Turner—particularly when he was successful at it—and remains a big deal to me. This is the same Turner who told Jobson, in 1977, "Remember these days. It will never be better than this, no matter what we do ..."

Of course, for Turner, life was onward and upward. He sailed seriously only one more time: the SORC of 1981. Turner, as the world would discover, is an eagle. He's married to Jane Fonda. As mentioned, his television networks were sold in 1995 to Time Warner for

$7.5 billion. No one would be surprised if Turner ended up as president of Time Warner, or even president of the United States. Of course, knowing Turner and the vertigo that plagues him at heights, he could crash and burn, too. I remain a fan, if not exactly a friend.

ON THE CHALLENGER side, Alan Bond was back for a third try with his 1977 steed, *Australia*. No longer was Bond the "ugly Australian." To the question why he keeps returning, Bond, then age 42, said, "You get out there and you're as good as the next guy, who might be a Vanderbilt. You get out there, and all you've got is a common element—the wind and the sea—and everyone's equal."

Bond's skipper was Jim Hardy, skipper of *Southern Cross* in 1974 and *Gretel II* in 1970.

Baron Marcel Bich was there also, making his fourth appearance; this time with *France III*, a new boat. Bich's skipper was Bruno Troublé, who would be better known later for his work with Louis Vuitton, the French luggage company. Beginning in 1983, it would sponsor the Louis Vuitton Cup, the challenger elimination series, in grand fashion.

From Britain came *Lionheart*, designed by Ian Howlett, which was also a new boat. Pelle Petterson was back, too, with *Sverige*, representing Sweden.

In the first round, *France III* engaged *Lionheart*, and *Australia* met *Sverige*. *Vive La France*, the French boat beat *Lionheart* in their series. Until then, Baron Bich's boats had never won a race; his record was 0-18. Bendy mast notwithstanding, the British cause wasn't helped by the sacking of its skipper, John Oakeley, on the eve of the competition. Oakeley was replaced by Lawrie Smith. *Australia* beat *Sverige*, but it was no easy win. Hardy's boat was plagued by breakdowns, including a broken mast.

In the finals, the Australians beat the French; however, *France III* won one race, courtesy of a lead-shuffling wind shift. A fine showing for the French, this would be Baron Bich's swan song.

Immediately after seeing *Lionheart*'s mast, the Australians commenced building a bendy mast of their own in secret, in a warehouse near the S.S. Newport Restaurant. They didn't wish to spring it on the world until it was too late for anyone to copy it.

I first learned about the mast from a cook at Handy Lunch, a diner on lower Thames Street I frequented. He told me the Australians were up to something mysterious across the street. I poked around a little and learned what was going on.

Before we raced Australia in the 1980 America's Cup, we had an executive meeting to discuss the bendy mast. The questions were: Do we try to copy it or do we ignore it? It was decided that there was neither the time nor the money to copy it. Basically, the Australians were betting on light air where the extra area would make the most difference. We just hoped and prayed we were good enough to offset that advantage in other winds and in other areas, such as sailmaking.

THE 1980 MATCH, between *Australia* and *Freedom*, began on September 16. With considerable posturing Jim Hardy, the skipper of *Australia*, said on the eve of the contest that he was quite calm. "The poor old defending helmsman, ouch, he's got heaps of fear of defeat."

That "ouch" was a nice touch. No, my fear was light winds.

That was the Australians' public posture. I later would learn from John Bertrand's book, *Born to Win*, that one important link in the chain had collapsed. Wrote Bertrand, "I will admit that I was surprised at the depth of aggression [Ben Lexcen, the co-designer of *Australia*] showed in combat in the 1980 America's Cup against the British, the Swedes, and the French—which is why it was such a poignant and unexpected moment for everyone when Benny, the great iconoclast, was finally silenced and became a puppy instead of a fighter. A big, blue 12-Meter called *Freedom* was the culprit at first sight; it knocked all the bounce and aggression out of our bear. Benny very nearly saluted Dennis Conner as the American slid down to the start of Race 1 . . . I wanted nothing more than to run back for a few seconds and shake him, to shout, 'Come on, Benny! These bastards are just human like us. They're fallible and they can be beaten—but you have to believe we can win.' "

For the first race, on Tuesday, September 16, the wind was light, from the east to southeast—a rare wind direction in Newport. The

Freedom *is ahead of* Australia *in 1980. Note the bendy mast on the challenger.* DAN NERNEY

Australians started to our left. However, the wind went right, to the south, a more familiar avenue—and thus, more of a sure bet—and we led at the first mark by almost a minute. After two reaches, we had doubled that lead. However, nearing the end of the second beat, our steering gear failed. I was able to steer downwind with just the trim tab (a second rudder on the keel), but we recognized that wouldn't be sufficient upwind for the final leg. We wrapped a line around the rudder post and led it to a genoa winch. It was okay for steering straight but tacking was something of a fire drill. While the Australians made up 25 seconds on that last leg, we still won the race by 1:52.

So well did the crew perform on the final leg that I didn't even mention the breakdown after the race at the press conference. I wasn't about to highlight any weaknesses of the defender. Like the smell of blood, a hint of vulnerability can be an edge for the competition. This was only the second breakdown we'd suffered the entire summer, and I was proud of that record. Further, the Australians seemed pleased about the last leg, so why spoil it? As the Machiavelli of the America's Cup, I was pleased by the victory and the time differential.

It wasn't a rout. My thinking was that a badly beaten opponent is a more dangerous one, as he might begin swinging for the fences, to use the baseball cliché.

Alan Bond seemed undeterred by the beating in the first race; indeed, he was upbeat. He bounced aboard *Australia* and announced, "I have decided that we are coming back in 1983 with a major challenge. We'll have the budget and the boat. And we are going to win the America's Cup, right?" Then Alan Bond added, "Ben Lexcen will design the boat, and my skipper and helmsman will be John Bertrand."

It was obviously a huge morale boost to the crew—Bond was saying, "I believe in you"—but I've sometimes wondered about the timing. After one race, the Australians had thrown in the towel—Bond had as much as said so. It proved a close series—closer than the score indicated. The Australians missed a chance; they were already looking ahead to 1983.

In the second race, Thursday, September 18, the Australians sounded a warning, like a shot across the bow, but didn't score a win. They passed us downwind in vacuous conditions. The final leg of 4.5 miles took 2½ hours to sail. Before they could finish, however, the time limit expired. It was all for naught.

The repeat of the second race was delayed while waiting for the wind. If the previous race was any indication, I recognized this race might finish in darkness. Therefore, I got our running lights from the tender. This was an item on our checklist. I did not intend to be protested for an infraction of the rules of the race, not to mention an infraction of the rules of the road.

In very light winds, the Australians found a shift that gave them the lead at the first mark. The boat from the land Down Under held that lead through the next three legs. On the run, however, we got inside of her at the mark rounding. The opening was provided by a poor jibe on the challenger's part. *Freedom* was ahead but not by much. On the last leg, the Australians kept tacking, taking inches and then feet from us.

In darkness, the wind grew even lighter. *Australia* passed us without running lights. I protested her. I would let the NYYC decide if it wished to pursue this matter or not, but I wasn't going to lose the opportunity. It was like buying insurance *after* a disaster—a good deal if you can find someone willing to sell it to you. *Australia* crossed the finish line 28 seconds ahead of us. The last time the Americans lost a race to a challenger was in 1970; the skipper that time, too, was Jim Hardy, known as "Gentleman Jim." He was a popular man here in America.

Later the NYYC's America's Cup Committee arrived at our compound to decide what to do. Otherwise engaged, I sent Ed du Moulin to the press conference, where the conclusion was voiced that I was afraid to face the press. Would we pursue the protest? The press was clamoring to know. Du Moulin didn't know.

The meeting at our compound finally broke up at 9:00 P.M. The NYYC decided to pursue it, and I was in agreement with the decision. Still without dinner, I reported the decision to the Jewetts, du Moulin, Steve Van Dyck, and John Marshall. We continued to discuss the matter until midnight. Du Moulin thought it should be dropped; indeed, he threatened to quit as manager of the syndicate if it wasn't. Marshall, on the other hand, argued we should take the hard line.

Finally, it was decided to sleep on it. Another meeting commenced at 6:00 A.M. Halsey Herreshoff and Jack Sutphen were invited to attend to give their opinions. Men of long experience, they urged us to let it go. Our group went along with that opinion, but now we were at odds with the NYYC. Then the phone rang. It was the America's Cup Committee; they had changed their mind, too. When we communicated the decision to the International Jury, however, they told us that once submitted, a protest couldn't be rescinded. Later, they found a typo in our protest form. Therefore our protest was invalid as written; and we chose not to refile it.

Nevertheless, I'm certain that if we had finished first without lights, and the Australians had finished second with them, they'd have protested. And won. Whatever I thought, the series was now tied at one.

On September 21, we won our second race in winds of 12–16 knots by 53 seconds. It was a race, however, that still gives me nightmares. Our problems began when we selected too light a mainsail. Then, at the start, when we were just about to plant the hook into *Australia,* she wiggled off it. Next, a spinnaker exploded; the head of a headsail blew out; we hoisted the spinnaker under the pole lift; lost a jib overboard; dropped our spinnaker pole in the water; and nearly had a spinnaker wrap around the forestay. It was as if we'd fallen over the edge. Despite all that, we led at every mark. Obviously, in a breeze we couldn't stop this freight train *Freedom*, no matter how hard we tried.

On September 23, we won our third race in winds of 12 knots, by 3:48; and on September 25, we won our fourth, and final, race in winds of 14–17 knots, by 3:38. We used laydays to help nullify the light-air advantage of *Australia*. Also, probably due to the new spar, their sails were uninspired. Four days before the contest, the Australians didn't even have a mainsail that fit the bendy mast.

We won the last race on a gray nasty day. On the way in, I sent the chase boat over to *Australia* to pick up "Gentleman Jim" Hardy, her skipper. He joined us on *Freedom*, which was now overloaded with our supporters as well as sailors. Off the backstay flew a sizable American flag, provided to us by Halsey Herreshoff, our navigator. I gave Hardy the wheel, and he steered *Freedom* into the harbor. At this moment, the America's Cup was "a friendly competition between foreign countries," as the original Deed of Gift promised.

The Australians had sailed well. I was surprised when Bond unceremoniously sold his boat, *Australia*. She would have made a good benchmark for their return in 1983, I thought.

This turning their backs on the past seemed ominous to me.

CHAPTER 8

1983

LOST

———

LEGEND HAS IT that a guest at the New York Yacht Club (NYYC) on Manhattan's West 44th Street was admiring the America's Cup with his host, a member. This trophy was an important part of this club—perhaps *the* most important part—since 1857.[1] The guest wondered, "What will the club replace the America's Cup with when it is finally lost?"

"The head of the man who lost it!" was the stern rejoinder.

Fact or fiction, on Monday, September 26, 1983, my head was on the guillotine. This was the eighty-eighth race for the America's Cup, but more important, it was the seventh and deciding race of the twenty-fifth defense. The score was tied at three for *Liberty*, which I skippered, and *Australia II*, with her winged keel, which John Bertrand, a sailmaker from Melbourne, skippered. This was no ordinary day, as there had never been a seventh race in the 132-year history of this event. Despite breaking fast in the series—I got out to a 3-1 lead—I hadn't won a race in six days.

The ruby-hulled *Liberty* won the start of the seventh race by eight seconds, but *Australia II*'s end of the line was slightly closer to the

---

1. The Cup was won by a syndicate of New York Yacht Club members, including Commodore John Cox Stevens, in 1851. It was officially deeded to the club in 1857.

weather mark. *Liberty* was ahead by 29 seconds at the first mark, 45 seconds at the second, and 23 seconds at the third. At the fourth mark, to windward, *Liberty* led *Australia II* by 57 seconds—nearly a minute. A run and a beat, only 8.8 miles of sailing was all that separated us from a successful defense. What should have been a heady moment wasn't. It felt unambiguously like a death in the family. I knew that the potent white boat from Down Under had gained, on average, a minute on every spinnaker run.

At the weather mark we did a bear-away spinnaker set. *Australia II* did the same 57 seconds later. Her track was slightly to weather of us, as could be expected. Both of us sailed on starboard tack toward the spectator fleet on the right-hand side of the course. Halsey Herreshoff, my navigator, was taking bearings with his hand-bearing compass. The numbers were *decreasing*. The rule is when sighting a boat to your right, as was *Australia II*, if the bearings are decreasing you are falling behind. We'd be behind at the leeward mark. It was like that nightmare when you're running away from an avalanche but not fast enough.

In due time, her wind-shadow started hurting us; it gave me a chill on this otherwise perfect autumn afternoon. So I jibed to port, toward the center of the course. This put us on the inside of the course, which is recommended, as the inside boat has right-of-way at the mark rounding. It also took us away from the sizable spectator fleet, which was roiling the water.

We received a small lift and jibed to starboard—the recommended tactic when sailing in an oscillating breeze. Then we converged with *Australia II*. The Australian boat had enjoyed more breeze on her side of the course and was, in any event, a faster boat. Also, when we had aimed at the spectator fleet, the U.S. Coast Guard moved them away. In essence, we'd done the blocking for the white boat. Two quick jibes and we paralleled her on port jibe. Then, as if using a propeller, or those trick wings on her keel, the boat started sailing lower and faster than we could. In desperation, I tried to match her sailing angle, to keep our wind-shadow on her, but she just sailed lower and gained more. At that point, I turned to the crew and said, "Does anyone here have any ideas?" There was stone-cold silence.

The white boat led at the bottom mark by 21 seconds. She had made up a huge one minute and 18 seconds on this run.

All that was left for us to do was to tack, and tack we did, a total of 47 times. It was a desperation move, but such moves have worked in the America's Cup—most notably in the 1934 America's Cup where *Rainbow*, the American defender, outfoxed the faster *Endeavour*. I hoped desperately for a similar miracle. At one point, I held *Liberty* high in the middle of one of these tacks, to try to break the Australian's momentum. It was, essentially, a tack with a long hold in the center. I hoped the Australians would try to match us, which they did. It wasn't brilliant; I just hoped it was a new maneuver for them, one that might break their rhythm. No such luck, however.

At 5:20 P.M., with the sun dropping toward the horizon on Narragansett Bay, the white boat from Down Under crossed the finish line between the *Black Knight*, the elegant race-committee boat of the New York Yacht Club, and an orange buoy. A lonely gun tolled. History would prove it to be a shot heard 'round the world. And then boat horns erupted everywhere. Whether from Australia, America, or anywhere, the spectator fleet knew full well that history was made this day.

Forty-one seconds later, we followed in our very red, very slow, and very obsolete boat. On *Liberty*, at least, there was profound sadness. After 132 years, the America's Cup belonged to the Australians, and I was the man who had lost it.

There had been ominous signs before. After the 1980 defense, the Alan Bond–led Australians sold *Australia*, designed for 1977 by Ben Lexcen and Johan Valentijn, to the British. It seemed a rash move, as the Australians had in 1980 won one race with this boat and its revolutionary bendy rig.

But John Bertrand, who would become *Australia II*'s skipper, said, "There is no way we can beat Dennis Conner in a conventional 12-Meter in Newport. We're going to have to break new ground. We can't win this thing sailing the same equipment because no matter how good we are, we will at best be equal, and someplace in the chain of necessity we'll be weaker—whether it's in starting skills, tactics, or crew work, or tacking, or sails, or meteorology."

I took the warnings seriously enough to have two naval architects in the program and to build three new boats. After all, competition between sailmakers had worked so well for me in 1980. Also, I had *Freedom*, in which I had defended the Cup in 1980, up and running, if not exactly eligible for an America's Cup campaign.

By 1983, Olin Stephens, the dean of naval architecture, was 76 years old and semiretired, but his firm, Sparkman & Stephens (S&S), now headed by Bill Langan, a young naval architect, penned *Spirit of America* for our *Freedom-Liberty* syndicate. Also for 1983 Johan Valentijn, who had worked for S&S before establishing his own design practice in Newport, drew *Magic* for us. The result was *Spirit* and *Magic*, which never measured up.

Magic, sadly, never measured in. Valentijn was creative but disorganized, and not particularly good with details. Even if his *Magic* had been a competitive 12-Meter, which it wasn't, I couldn't have raced her in the America's Cup. Johan had read the 12-Meter Rule but not the America's Cup Deed of Gift. According to the Deed, "The competing yacht or vessel, if of one mast, shall be not less than forty-four feet nor more than ninety feet on the load waterline." *Magic* was 2.9 inches too short. I was glad no one ever found out about that because we would have looked incredibly stupid. I didn't learn about it until much later. In those days, designers kept their rating certificates secret—even from the skipper, crew, and syndicate that paid their bills.

Further, Johan changed *Freedom*, with which I had defended the Cup in 1980. *Freedom*'s salient design feature was her low freeboard, which lowered her center of gravity, making her more stable. It also presented a smaller target to the wind and waves. After 1980 the rule-makers penalized low freeboard; however, *Freedom* escaped the penalty due to a grandfather clause. That was until Johan moved her rudder and made some other minor structural changes. This nullified her grandfather clause. While Johan and I had discussed the changes, he neglected to tell me they would make the boat obsolete.

When *Spirit* and *Magic* proved glacially slow, and *Freedom* and *Magic* illegal, we decided to build a third boat. The designer would be Johan. First, I liked Johan, and generally I trust my instincts about people. Then, he could give us the time we needed. S&S, as we would hear often, had a business to run. Nevertheless, Langan argued it should be a collaboration. Reluctantly, we agreed; however, when that didn't seem to be working, the tough decision was made to go with Johan alone. Doubtless Langan and Olin Stephens were disappointed, but they'd had their chance—a fair chance. Langan went to work for the competition: John Kolius on *Courageous*.

So Johan designed *Liberty*. Amazingly, the keel on *Liberty* was so far back, we had to load 1,800 pounds of lead three feet from the bow so she would sit on her lines when launched. Eventually, the keel had to be moved a foot forward. From the perspective of design, it was a long, long summer.

FROM THE DOCK of Newport Offshore, it was possible to see—and I mean *see* in all their unfettered glory—seven of eight 12-Meters. That included *Liberty* and *Freedom*, which belonged to my syndicate; *Defender* and *Courageous*, which belonged to a second defense group and included my longtime rival Tom Blackaller and John Kolius. For the challengers, there were *France 3, Azzurra* (Italy), and *Challenge 12* (Australia). Another boat was there, too, *Australia II*; however, she wore her green and blue "modesty skirt," an ugly tarp made of spinnaker cloth that hid her keel and rudder from prying eyes and cameras. It is interesting to note that *Australia II* wasn't the first America's Cup boat so modestly garbed; *Thistle*, designed for James Bell of Scotland for the 1887 America's Cup, was launched wearing a similar skirt.

In *Thistle*'s case it was "much ado about nothing," as she lost the America's Cup 2-0 to the defender, *Volunteer*. No such luck with *Australia II* and her winged keel that lurked behind that tarp. One could say about *Australia II* in 1983 what was said about *America* in 1851. "If she is right, we are all wrong." Well, *Australia II* was, and we were.

"The reason for the keel was twofold," commented syndicate head Alan Bond in 1983 to my co-author, Michael Levitt. "We looked at where we got beat last time, and it was at the starting line. So the theme of the new keel isn't breakaway speed, although we seem to have that; it's maneuverability. The other part was a 'psych.'

Ben Lexcen, a.k.a. Bob Miller, "surfs" his upside-down winged keel on Australia II. This boat ended the longest winning streak in sports. DAN NERNEY

We've kept the keel shrouded because we think Dennis Conner is susceptible to psyching. He looked like he fell apart in 1980 when we beat him in that one race, so a little mystery wasn't going to do us any harm."

On the evening when the Australians finally won the America's Cup, the crowd chanted, "Let's see the keel!" There were thousands of people on the docks of Newport Offshore, on balconies and roofs of nearby buildings, hundreds more on the water in small and large boats, some even swimming. People were responding to it as if this were a miracle—a miracle of yacht design. Even Alan Bond couldn't resist such an entreaty—such joy in the moment—as he responded to the crowd by dropping his boat's modesty skirt.

Later that evening, Ben Lexcen, her designer, said, "The keel? Well, there are about 500 Americans hanging on it at the moment. When we lifted the boat out tonight there were just heaps of them hanging on like leeches when you walk out of a swamp. But I'll try to describe the keel. The keel is somewhat shorter than a regular keel; it's what you could call upside down. It's narrower where it leaves the hull, and long at the bottom. So if you have a regular keel on an ordinary yacht and sawed if off and put it back on upside down, that's something similar to our keel. It doesn't have a bulb like everyone thinks; it just gets a little thicker at the bottom in accordance with its chord. For about half of its length on the bottom it has protrusions [wings] that stick out on each side; they poke down at about 20 degrees, and they are about a meter wide and about two or three meters long. They are made of lead and are very thick and heavy. On the back of the very sloping trailing edge is a somewhat narrow trim tab that is faired in with a plastic, flexible membrane, which gives the lie to it having a double trim tab. It only has a single trim tab, but this plastic fairing bends and fairs the trim tab into a nice smooth curve."

So what did all of this mean to the water? What was the underlying physics of the winged keel? Normally, the fat part of the keel is against the hull, and the keel narrows at the bottom. This is reminiscent of how a wing leaves the fuselage of an airplane and obviously is the easiest attachment to engineer.

Australia II, however, had an upside-down keel. This reverse taper allowed more lead to be packed at the bottom of the keel, increasing the righting arm. Also, by making the wings out of lead, which added three tons at the base of the keel, the vertical center of gravity was lowered a total of 37½ inches (95cm). This made the boat stiffer and a better sail-carrying platform. Then, where the keel joins the hull—called the fillet—is a high-drag area, and making this attachment smaller (i.e., cleaner) decreased drag there. A problem, however, was that this huge tip down low showed an increase in induced drag—that is, water leaking from the high-pressure side of the keel to the low-pressure side. This takes the form of a vortex—an active and speed-sapping spinning. A high-aspect-ratio shape (i.e., deep but short fore and aft) can lessen induced drag. This shape wasn't possible because the International Rule, used to rate a 12-Meter, has a draft limit of 9 feet 2.5 inches for these boats, which is not generous for a 65-foot boat. Also, with the fat part of the keel carried low, a high-aspect shape wasn't possible: a keel can't be fat down low to carry more lead and thin to have a high-aspect shape.

To decrease induced drag—the flow escaping from the high-pressure side of the foil to the low-pressure side—airplanes sometimes have "fences," or more sophisticated "winglets," on their wing tips. Winglets, or fences, are described by aerodynamicists as "multiple-lifting surfaces." Multiple-lifting surfaces can produce lift with less induced drag. The designer, in essence, used this technology on *Australia II*; he affixed "winglets" on the keel to help prevent induced drag. Like the boom on *Intrepid* nearly touching the deck to allow an end-plate effect, or the decksweeper jib, the wings cut off the area where the flow can leak. Also, winglets can produce lift in their own right, making the foil—the keel—even more efficient.

Just as significant, Lexcen made these winglets out of lead, which allowed him to pack even more weight at the bottom of the keel, further increasing the righting arm. Then he angled the wings down. This increased draft when the boat heeled, improving speed to weather. This was a way to get around the limitations of increased draft, under the rule. When the boat was measured upright, the wings didn't extend beyond the measurer's tape, which had to measure 9 feet, 2.5 inches. When the boat heeled under sail, it had a deeper keel, further reducing induced drag and increasing the righting moment. Most observers would say the intent of the rule was for the boat to sail in 9 feet, 2.5 inches of water. *Australia II* could not, but the Australians, led by Alan Bond, syndicate head, and Warren Jones, Executive Director, were better able to make their case for the new keel shape than the NYYC could make its case against it.

Yacht design tends to involve compromises, but *Australia II*'s design was synergistic: The whole was greater than the sum of the parts.

Further, something everyone forgets, the boat was a rocket ship downwind, which had nothing to do with its winged keel. Wings actually hurt a yacht downwind. This was the genius of her sailmaker Tom Schnackenberg, of North Sails, New Zealand, who worked so hard on spinnaker design as well as sailing angles.[2] To me, it is less surprising that we lost to *Australia II* than that we won three of seven races.

---

2. Schnackenberg would get the credit he deserved in 1995 as the design coordinator for Team New Zealand, which beat me in that Cup, too. In addition to directing the designers and the sailmakers in 1995, Schnackenberg sailed aboard the boat.

· · ·

ALTHOUGH WE WON two of every three races, the defense trials that year were a trial for me. The competition was Tom Blackaller, on *Defender*, with Gary Jobson (now the television commentator) as tactician, and John Kolius on the venerable *Courageous*. This was an America's Cup where words spoke louder than actions, and Blackaller and Jobson were clobbering me in the press, if not on the water. Nothing I did seemed acceptable to them.

First, they took me to task for not helping them, not trialing against them. They said this was hurting the American effort. As I saw it, however, we were competitors and were entered in a competition where there would only be one winner. Help them? Help yourselves, guys.

Next, they accused me, as Turner had done in 1980, of sailing too much. All I could say to that was what I said to Ted Turner, "The race is to the swift. There are no points awarded for making it look easy."

Then they discovered that my *Liberty* had been granted multiple rating certificates. This allowed us to remove or add lead ballast and change sail area depending on weather conditions. It was perfectly legal, as long as we complied with the 12-Meter formula. I had taken the idea to the America's Cup Committee in May, before the trials even began. I told them what we had in mind, and they said okay. We were granted three separate rating certificates.

Blackaller and Jobson didn't figure this out until the end of July, and by then they were very frustrated with their new and slow boat, *Defender*. They complained to the press that we had an unfair advantage—although they likely could have done it, too—that I was unethical, and that the rules had been compromised. It was the old argument, "Let's get together for the American effort." If you took that to its logical conclusion, we would have had to share sail shapes, crewmen, computers, skippers, etc.

THEN THERE WAS the challenger, *Australia II*. The questions about *Australia II* revolved around three points: Were the wings legal? If they were legal, was the yacht fairly rated with the wings? And did Ben Lexcen actually design the keel and hull, or were they a product of the Netherlands Aerospace Laboratory and the Netherlands Ship Model Basin where Lexcen worked on the keel for four months?

The rule that addressed the last point could be found in the "Footnotes in Amplification" section of the America's Cup Rule. It read, "A foreign designer—however he is designated—participating in the design of a boat or a sail would violate both the letter and the spirit of the above Resolution, and any boat or sail so designed would be ineligible for use in America's Cup competition . . ."

The man who at least nominally designed this boat, as well as *Challenge 12*, which was, basically, *Australia II* without the winged keel, was Ben Lexcen. While considered a "genius" by those who knew him, he was an intuitive, rather than trained, naval architect with no more than a fourth-grade education. Many wondered if Lexcen had the technical education and expertise to design such a yacht. Said Johan Valentijn, the designer of my *Liberty* in 1983, and who designed *Australia* with Lexcen, for Bond, in 1977, "Ben Lexcen is a nice guy. And I have no doubt that he is a genius, but this stuff is high-tech. It's not something you dream up."

AUSTRALIA II WAS first measured in Australia on March 4, 1983, by Ken McAlpine, an International Yacht Racing Union (IYRU)–appointed measurer from Australia. Her rating certificate was signed by the Australian Yachting Federation (AYF) as a matter of course.

Australia II arrived in Rhode Island in June 1983; she was the last Cup boat on the scene. While being off-loaded from a freighter, she wore her modesty skirt. She was measured at Cove Haven Marina in Barrington, on June 16, by the America's Cup Measurement Committee that included John Savage, an Australian whose son Jack was at the helm of *Challenge 12*; Tony Watts, an Englishman; and Mark Vinbury, an American.

Paul Doppke, of Cove Haven, wrote a letter to Bob McCullough, a former commodore of the NYYC, and head of the America's Cup Committee, describing the secrecy of the measurement. "Please be advised that at the time of the measuring of *Australia II*, I was asked to provide a complete shed with no other boats or work to be done in it for the purpose of complete secrecy.

"After hauling *Australia II*, it was decided that I would be the only person allowed to see the keel since I had to block the hull. They asked me to keep all of my employees out of the shed, and then they supplied two armed guards to make sure that no one would get a look at their keel. The boat was hauled and launched with the shroud in place. When the boat was measured, the shroud was rolled up onto the deck."

It should be mentioned that by the rules, the NYYC and, in fact, any official representing any foreign challenger had the right to be there at the measurement, armed guards notwithstanding. I checked with the NYYC's America's Cup Committee and discovered that while they should have shown up, they hadn't. They were certainly entitled to under the rules that they themselves had created, but they seemed unaware of them. All the secrecy about the winged keel, all the sound and fury that added to the mystique of *Australia II*, could have been dispensed with in June.

Asked about this much later that summer, Commodore Robert McCullough said, "As you remember, the boat was late arriving, and she was the last one measured. Frankly, it was a slipup on our part. We were supposed to have Bill Luders [technical adviser to the America's Cup Committee] there to see it, and we missed the measurement date."

The triumvirate of measurers unanimously agreed that *Australia II* was a legal 12-Meter. Said Mark Vinbury, the American, there was "no question that our committee measured *Australia II*'s keel according to the rule." Apparently, however, Vinbury privately wondered if the keel might be a "peculiarity" of design, as spelled out in the 12-Meter Rating Rule 27 or Rating Rule Measurement Instruction number 7.

Doppke called Johan Valentijn on June 16, the day he participated in the measurement. "Johan," he said, "I've just seen something incredible. *Australia II* has wings on her keel and they're made of lead. It's the damnedest thing I've ever seen. Do you happen to know anything about this?"

"What do you mean 'wings'? " asked Valentijn. "What do you

mean 'lead'? " If an utterance can summarize a summer, like a snapshot, that was it.

Doppke supplied Johan with drawings, which I took immediately to Commodore McCullough. "Commodore," I said, "we have a problem here, and you had better do something about it. *Australia II* has a peculiarity on the bottom of her keel, and we don't think it's legal." It wasn't legal, I told him, because the boat couldn't sail in 9 feet, 2.5 inches of water, which was, I believed, the intent of the rule. He told me to go back to Johan to find out more about this. It wasn't that the club was deaf to all it was being told, it just did not know how to respond effectively.

The technical complexity of *Australia II* wasn't the sole reason we doubted that Lexcen designed it. In May of 1983, before *Australia II* even arrived, Valentijn had an encounter with a stranger who took credit for the design of *Australia II*. This was Joop Slooff, from the Netherlands. Valentijn is Dutch, too, but he lives in America and has a U.S. passport. That made him eligible to design boats for us.

Valentijn was on the dock next to *Liberty* when Slooff approached him. "Are you Mr. Valentijn?" Slooff asked, according to Valentijn.

"Yes," he answered.

"Well, I designed the keel on *Australia II*," Slooff said, now in Dutch, as the conversation continued.

"You what?" asked Valentijn.

"I designed the keel on *Australia II*," Slooff repeated.

Valentijn says that Slooff explained that he was in the United States to attend a seminar on aerodynamics and had decided to stop in Newport. He had heard about Valentijn, his countryman, and had decided to look him up there. Valentijn says he asked Slooff for more details on *Australia II* and about his participation in the project.

"He felt very strongly, and was very proud that he had designed this keel," said Valentijn, who also was experimenting with winged appendages on keels at the time. Valentijn, however, was working with aeronautical engineers at Boeing. When he related the Slooff meeting to a friend at Boeing, he was told, in turn, that Dutch engineers were repeating almost the same story to Boeing employees—that is, that the Dutch designed the keel on *Australia II*, not Lexcen.

This was a clear-cut violation of the rules and this news got the New Yorkers' attention. A plot was hatched asking these same Dutch technicians to design us a boat. In this way, it was hoped, the Dutch would tip their hand. Johan drafted a telex that was sent to Dr. Peter van Oossanen, of the Netherlands Ship Model Basin in Wageningen, Holland, where Lexcen had reportedly worked for four months on keel design. It said, "I understand you and your team are responsible for development and design of the special keel for *Australia II*. We are finally convinced of her potential and would therefore like to build the same design under one of our boats. We will keep this confidential as not to jeopardize your agreement with Alan Bond. However, due to the complexity of problems, we need your maximum input. We can start next week and be ready by August 25."

The telex was sent out under the signature of Ed du Moulin, my good friend and head of our syndicate, who reluctantly signed it. I never saw it. My job was to sail the boat; this the New York Yacht Club kept telling me.

Du Moulin received a telex back that said Lexcen, rather than the Netherlands Ship Model Basin, had done the design of *Australia II*. The telex continued, "As we are contracted to [the Australians] not to test 12-Meter models for any other 12-Meter syndicate until the completion of the 1983 campaign, we have today advised them of your query and requested their permission to undertake work for you. Unfortunately, they have advised us that they are not prepared to allow such dispensation . . ."

On July 25, after *Australia II* began to make her presence felt, Mark Vinbury sent a letter to Tony Watts in England. The subject was whether *Australia II* was fairly rated. Watts, you will recall, was an IYRU measurer who along with Vinbury had been involved in the June measurement of *Australia II*. Vinbury wrote, "I have no question that our committee measured *Australia II*'s keel according to the rule. I am concerned, however, that the rule as it is currently written is not able to assess the unusual shape of this keel and thereby fairly rate the yacht." He asked that the International Yacht Racing Union's Keel Boat Technical Committee (KBTC) address this matter.

On August 3, the New York Yacht Club launched its heaviest missive of the summer. The club posted 34 pages to George Andreadis, Chairman of the KBTC. It described the winged appendages on *Australia II* as "a peculiarity," and asked for redress under Rule 27 and Instruction 7 that addresses such matters. Naval architects such as Bill Luders, Johan Valentijn, and Halsey Herreshoff described the Australian boat as a 12.45-Meter yacht at 20 degrees of heel. They pointed out that the downward-sloping wings gave the yacht added— but unrated—draft. Extra draft makes a yacht faster upwind.

Herreshoff, my navigator, was a yacht designer by training as well as by birth. He is the grandson of Nathanael Herreshoff who designed and built six successful Cup defenders from 1893 to 1920. His uncle was L. Francis Herreshoff, one of Ben Lexcen's yacht-design heroes. This weighty document included Halsey's words: "If the closely guarded peculiar keel design of *Australia II* is allowed to remain in competition, or is allowed to continue to be rated without penalty, the yacht will likely win the foreign trials and will likely win the America's Cup in September."

It was a declaration of war that the NYYC delivered. In response, however, the Australians pointed out that the club, no matter how powerful, was not an entity recognized by the IYRU. At that point, the United States Yacht Racing Union (USYRU)—the forerunner of US Sailing, the sport's national authority—entered the fray. It asked for an immediate ruling by the KBTC.

Warren Jones, who played a worse cop to Bond's bad cop, argued that "no entity and certainly not the NYYC or the USYRU has any right to request that IYRU rerate or comment on the rating of our boat." He also said that Olin Stephens, the Nathanael Herreshoff of his generation, had indicated to the International 12-Meter Association that "in his opinion, *Australia II* was correctly rated and that her designer, Ben Lexcen, should be congratulated for the innovative concept he has employed."

Jones used the occasion to score two other major points: The first, he revealed the existence of du Moulin's telex to the Netherlands Ship Model Basin. "We now feel compelled, however, to make sure that people are aware of the extent to which some Americans have been prepared to go to hold the Cup." Lastly, he demanded to know where the confidential design information that was the basis of the New York Yacht Club's original missive was coming from. "If the NYYC is in receipt of specific information, it can only be through improper means, and we have a right to know who passed it to them and under what conditions..."

The NYYC made an attempt at *détente* on August 7. Commodores McCullough, Robert Stone, and Emil "Bus" Mosbacher, a defending America's Cup skipper, visited Bond's Midcliff mansion, to meet with him and Jones. The meeting disintegrated in no time. Bond allegedly threatened that the NYYC could expect big trouble over this matter if it continued on this course, and that he intended to smear the club, to drag it through the gutter, and to embarrass it in every way he could.

THAT WAS THE private Alan Bond. The public Bond seemed transformed. He had by this time purchased the Swan Brewing Company in Australia—seemingly a bullet-proof investment in that thirsty part of the world. Its black swan emblem—not to mention its product— was everywhere in Newport, even on a spinnaker flown by *Australia II* to or from the races, but not in competition. Other business interests were in oil and gas and, of course, property development.

He had become a collector of fine art. "I built up a large collection of French Impressionists," he told Levitt. "From Renoir, Gauguin, Picasso, Monet to Manet—as well as a big collection of early Australian works." He was particularly proud, he said then, of a recent purchase, an oil painting by Thomas Webber, the botanist who sailed with Captain Cook. Cook discovered, surveyed, and mapped the east coast of Australia in 1769–70.

Bond then funded the game of cricket in Australia, and actively supported that country's equestrian team because of his daughter Susan's interest in the sport. She is one of four children belonging to Alan and Eileen Bond, the spirited redheaded girl he married when she was 17 and he still painting signs. The Bonds mingled easily with Newport society in 1983. Said a Bellevue Avenue matron, "The only trouble with the summer was that I didn't see more of the Bonds . . . As the summer continued, my feelings for the Bond family rose and rose: Stalwart Alan. Gay Eileen." For an emigrant from Ealing, who quit school when he was 14, Bond had come far.

On August 18, the IYRU announced that it would meet on August 30 to consider USYRU's request to rerate *Australia II*. Before that meeting, however, it was learned that the year before, on July 28, 1982, *Victory '83,* the British syndicate, had asked the Keel Boat Technical Committee for a ruling on the legality of wings. "The committee ruled that 'tipwings' are permitted so long as the static draft is not exceeded." This interpretation was given in confidence and ordinarily would not have been made public until November 1983, after the IYRU annual meeting in London.

Finally, on August 26, "Keelgate," as the press dubbed it in the style of Watergate, seemed to end with a whimper. The NYYC wrote in a press release with great cordiality, that it was "pleased to announce that the question relating to the keels of *Australia II* and *Victory 83*, which, too, had tried wings, and the design thereof have been resolved.

"We have received verification from the International Yacht Racing Union that an interpretative ruling respecting the design of the British keel was issued in August of 1982. That ruling under the IYRU regulations is controlling for the 1983 match, and the New York Yacht Club accepts it as such." The press release ended with these cheery words: "With these matters resolved, we can now all focus on the match itself to be settled on the water and may the better yacht win."

Not quite. The issue of who designed *Australia II*, Ben Lexcen or Dutch nationals, wasn't resolved by this ruling. Nor was the NYYC willing to leave it alone, despite its public posture. After the Australians were named challenger, following their march through the first Louis Vuitton Cup with a record of 36-4, James Michael, the attorney for the NYYC's America's Cup Committee, prepared a three-page document. It was a "certification of compliance," that the New Yorkers wanted the Australians to sign. By agreeing to the 10 points delineated in the document, the Australians would have stated publicly—under penalty of perjury—that they had complied with the conditions governing the races.

The first point, for example, read, "*AUSTRALIA II* was designed solely and exclusively by Ben Lexcen, a national of Australia, and no 'foreign consultants' and no 'foreign designer—however he is designated' assisted or participated in the design of *AUSTRALIA II*'s keel, hull, rig or sails." When this was presented to Bond, he refused to sign it.

With two days to go before the first race of the America's Cup, where *Australia II* was to meet *Liberty*, Commodore McCullough went to William Fesq, the former commodore of the Royal Sydney (Australia) Yacht Squadron and Liaison Chairman for all the challengers.[3] He showed Fesq the document Bond refused to sign and said, "Find another challenger!" Fesq refused to do that.

The next day, the day before the first race of the America's Cup, there was a secret meeting aboard *Summertime*, the motor yacht owned by Bus Mosbacher. The theme was simple, if earthshaking. It was whether to proceed with the match or cancel it. Said Vic Romagna, who threw Bond and Lexcen off *Valiant* in 1970—an act which, according to Bond, brought him into the America's Cup fray—"We didn't want to appear to be spoiling it for the sake of spoiling it, but we were convinced the Australians had overlooked nearly every rule.

"We went around the room, and everyone said their piece. Then all of a sudden, the discussion came to a shuddering halt. At that point, if we did vote, it was clear that four members agreed to continue, and five wanted to pull out."

The majority didn't rule, however; this saddened Romagna. "We didn't have the guts to stand up and say we won't race. And so we just folded up our tents and went off into oblivion."

WE DIDN'T WIN the battle on land, but I was determined to win the one that truly counted, at sea.

---

3. Fesq had been the navigator on *Gretel II* in 1970.

We faced an otherworldly machine, and John Bertrand, the competing skipper, seemed formidable. He was then 37 and appeared fully in control—of boat and crew. Plus, he and the crew seemed well insulated by Bond and Jones from the storms that raged ashore. All they had to do was to "sail the boat."

Three years before, when Alan Bond had named him skipper after the first race of the twenty-fourth defense, it came as a complete surprise to Bertrand. Nevertheless, he was a natural for the job. He had sailed on 12-Meters in four campaigns and had experience on ocean racers; he even crewed once for me. He started sailing at age seven, having lived near a beach in Chelsea, a suburb of Melbourne. Although neither of his parents sailed, Bertrand developed a love for it. He won the Australian National Junior Sailing Title in 1964 and was recognized as the best all-round sailor in Australia in 1968.

As mentioned, Bertrand had his first experience on a 12-Meter in 1970 when he sailed as crew on *Gretel II*, the Australian challenger that year from Sydney. He and his wife, Rasa, stayed on in America when the unsuccessful challenge was over in September. He worked on his master's degree in naval architecture at the Massachusetts Institute of Technology. Rasa worked as a nurse in Boston to help pay the bills.

From there, Bertrand's sailing career escalated. He was a member of the 1972 Australian Olympic Sailing Team. After the 1974 America's Cup fiasco with *Southern Cross*, Bertrand elected to stay in the United States again—this time to learn sailmaking at the North Sails loft in Pewaukee, Wisconsin. It was then that he became interested in sailing in the Finn Class. He competed in the 1976 Olympics in Canada, where he won a Bronze Medal. Bertrand returned to Melbourne after that to manage the North Sails loft there. He had planned to compete in the 1980 Olympics in Russia, but instead joined Bond's team when Australia decided to boycott the games, after the Soviets invaded Afghanistan.

ON TUESDAY, SEPTEMBER 13, *Liberty* departed her dock at Williams & Manchester. She was pulled by *Fire Three*, a stately 53-foot Hatteras. As the tow began, our theme song, "Chariots of Fire," blared from speakers on the tender. Next came the theme from "The Empire Strikes Back." It filled the harbor, which was chockablock with boats of all descriptions.

A few minutes later, *Australia II* left her dock at Newport Offshore, pulled by her tender *Black Swan*. Her battle song was performed by Australia's hard-rocking Men at Work. The words of the song go, "I come from a land Down Under. Where women glow and men plunder."

With the 10-minute gun, the wind was from the northwest at eight knots. During the first circle, we tacked, and Bertrand tacked and then bore off inside of us. We were about to jibe to starboard, the typical maneuver, but Bertrand just slid down inside and threw a block at us. "Check!" he might have said, after making only the opening move with his pawn. All we'd heard about *Australia II*'s maneuverability was true; the boat turned on a dime. I decided there would be no prestart circling for me. While I chewed on that bitter pill, the wind shifted 45 degrees to the east, turning the first leg from a beat to a reach. All dressed up and nowhere to go, racing was called off for that day. This doubtless disappointed the largest spectator fleet I've ever seen, estimated at 2,000 boats. Above, there were 15 or 20 helicopters and, perhaps, 50 fixed-wing aircraft. It was scary up there. It was scary down here.

The next day dawned steel gray and promised wind. A cold wind came from the northeast, a foul-weather direction. At 12:10, *Australia II* crossed the starting line first—the wind was now a steady 18 knots. Three seconds later came *Liberty*. This proved to be the first and only start Bertrand won, but, of course, in the America's Cup, it's finishes that matter. The white boat seemed faster upwind than we were, but at least, in so much wind, it was nothing alarming. Next, we decided to engage her in a tacking duel to judge this ability. She was much quicker out of a tack than we were. Thus, we wrote tacking duels off along with prestart circling.

The white boat led at the first mark to weather by eight seconds. This was the first time in modern America's Cup history that the challenger had rounded the first mark of the first race in the lead. The America's Cup course was in those days once around a triangle and then windward-leeward-windward, or 24.3 miles of sailing. *Lib-*

erty was longer on the water than *Australia II* and faster, at least theoretically, on the two reaching legs. This seemed to be the case, but we didn't want Bertrand to know it yet. Coming out of the second mark, with the white boat from Down Under still in the lead, we set a staysail. Bertrand, who must have been very confident of his boatspeed, ignored us. Neither did he cover us, and we simply powered over the top of *Australia II*, rounding the third mark 16 seconds ahead. We still led after the weather leg.

The fifth mark was downwind. Theoretically, at least, we should have been faster, as wings increase a yacht's wetted surface and make it slower downwind. Perhaps Bertrand hadn't read that chapter on yacht design while at MIT, because his boat was a rocket ship. The only thing that kept her from passing us early in the leg was that we were in the mast-abeam controlling position, according to the rules. Blocked by us to weather, *Australia II* simply bore off and sailed lower and faster than we did. I knew, unambiguously, that we were in deep, deep trouble. By sailing down three boat lengths, she broke the overlap. When we reconverged, the Australians were in the controlling position. I'd rarely seen that done.

We sailed side by side for a while, then we got a puff of wind. With our longer waterline, we accelerated. At that instant I jibed *Liberty*, which put us on starboard tack with right-of-way over the Australian boat on port. *Australia II* had but an instant to respond. Opting to take our stern, Bertrand spun the wheel, and, in all that wind, lost steering. With that, she veered into the wind. Checkmate! We won the first race by 1:10.

In Newport the unsettled northeast breeze doesn't last for long—it is more a day-tripper. Soon enough the predominate southwesterly sea breeze begins to blow again. With the sea breeze, summer returns to Aquidneck Island, where Newport is. Race 2, the next day, began in what locals call a "dying nor'easterly." With six minutes to go before the start, the mainsail on *Australia II* fell 18 inches and ripped. A wounded opponent, I knew, was a dangerous one, so I gave the Australians a wide berth at the start, which we won.

Despite ripping their mainsail and losing the start, the Australians led at the first mark by 45 seconds. Even crippled she was faster than we were. On the second beat, it was spotty as the two winds fought for mastery. There were small areas that showed a decent sailing breeze, but large areas without anything. After the first race, the Australians had heard a lot of criticism from the press for not covering us. We thought Hugh Treharne, the tactician on *Australia II*, wouldn't open himself up to more criticism. He would follow the book, chapter and verse. So what we tried to do was to make the conventional response, the wrong one. In essence, I tried to put myself into his head.

This happened on the second beat, on the fourth leg. I had John Marshall, in my afterguard, look for patches of wind on the water; Tom Whidden was looking for changes in wind direction; Halsey Herreshoff was concentrating on where we were in relation to the turning mark; and I concentrated on Treharne and Bertrand.

Australia II was ahead but to leeward, with both boats on starboard tack. Ahead of her we noticed a vacuous hole. Whether Treharne saw it or not I don't know, but *Australia II* couldn't tack to port, because we were on starboard, with right-of-way. She sailed to it and, at first, was headed, which was bad luck for us as the shift went left in her favor. However, more important than the change in wind direction was the fact that the wind died for her more than it died for us. We won the second race by 1:33, to lead 2-0.

On Sunday, September 18, *Australia II* won the third race by 3:14—a huge win and her first. She was faster upwind, but especially downwind. Since the America's Cup turned to class boats, beginning in 1930, this margin was a record win by a challenger. Indeed, it was the greatest margin since 1871—the second defense.[4] The previous record belonged to *Endeavour*, a J-Class yacht, which in 1934 beat *Rainbow*, the defender, by 2:09. The day before, we had tried to sail this race, but the time limit expired with *Australia II* ahead by an astounding 5:57. Sadly for the home team, *Australia II*'s September 18 record win would not last long.

Our last hurrah was on Tuesday, September 20, as summer was giving way to autumn. A skill I have—which serves me well in this

---

4. In 1871 *Livonia*, a challenger from England, beat *Columbia*, a disabled defender, by 15:10. That is the largest margin of victory for a challenger over a defender. This, the second defense, saw the NYYC name four boats to defend: *Columbia, Sappho, Dauntless,* and *Palmer*. It matched its defender to the weather.

arena—is time and distance. It's something I practice all the time. In a boat, car, or even an airplane, I like to challenge friends with small wagers about how long it will take to get somewhere: to the next buoy, for example, in a boat; or to a bridge, in a car.

The most basic rule in yacht racing is that a boat on port tack must stay clear of a boat on starboard. This day, however, I port-tacked *Australia II*, not once but twice, to win the race. The first time happened at the start. We were reaching on port tack toward the pin end of the line. *Australia II* was reaching on starboard tack, with right-of-way. Bertrand looked none too confident at the starting line. He was always hunched over the wheel, looking drained of color, perhaps a little sick to his stomach. This made me bold.

I looked at the Australian boat and more sensed than saw a little bit of daylight. I asked Tom Whidden, "Can we cross their bow?" He doubted it. I took a second look and said, "Hell, we can make it!" That's what we did, and by doing it *Liberty* won the start by a huge six seconds.

John Marshall, who trimmed the main on this boat, recalled it this way. "If anyone is ever going to write about what was the most audacious move in the America's Cup this was it. It was not a move of bravado, mind you, but a calculated, known, brilliant move. Keep in mind that when Dennis made the decision to port-tack *Australia*, both boats were reaching at each other. And the rules permit the starboard-tacked boat to turn toward the line at any time. So Dennis, by knowing in his mind how much he was going to head up [for the line] and looking at the other boat and judging what her course would be when she turned for the line, concluded that we could cross her bow. Dennis was the one person out of 11 on our boat who said with surety, 'We will cross their bow.' "

It wasn't the end, however. On the first leg *Australia II* got ahead, courtesy of her winged keel. The only way we were going to win this race was to tack to port and cross the Australian boat on starboard. I looked over and said, with less certainty this time, "I think we can cross them." Marshall said to me, "Don't expect me to accompany you to the protest room if you tack now." Twenty seconds later, I repeated myself. I knew that if we didn't round the first mark ahead, we'd lose the race. The down side, of course, was if we didn't clear them, we'd lose the race, too; perhaps even end up at the bottom of the deep, blue sea. I held on for another 30 seconds, however, and we got a small shift, a header, which was in our favor. With that we tacked. My heart was in my throat at that crossing. We led at the first mark by 36 seconds. Bertrand sailed that race like a beaten man. He later said, "I'll never endure a humiliation like that again."

We'd sailed a good and aggressive race, yet at the finish only 43 seconds separated us. I was happy for the victory, yet frightened by what it required to win: perfection. The score was now 3-1 for the defenders. Could we defy gravity one more time?

On Wednesday, September 21, with less than an hour to go before the starting sequence, Marshall, my mainsail trimmer, was pumping the mast, trying to make it straighter. The wind was 18 knots, and the seas were lumpy and confused. He wasn't paying attention to what he was doing; he thought he was pumping the starboard jumper but was, in truth, pumping the port. I called for a tack, and with it, the mast ram broke. This was our first significant mechanical failure of the summer.

Tom Rich and Scott Vogel went aloft in punishing conditions to try to fix the mast ram. They needed a replacement part, which, to my utter amazement and disgust, wasn't aboard our tender but ashore. Far, far away. We then asked the Coast Guard to pick the part up with one of its helicopters, but the request was refused. Our chase boat *Rhonda* was sent back to shore to fetch it. When the part arrived, Rich and Vogel worked aloft to repair the mast. Ever closer came the start. Tick-tock! The only direction that was relatively easy on them was to head downwind, but that took us away from the start. Finally, we sailed downwind, but kept the main trimmed on the centerline to slow the boat down. They got the piece in, but it was dissimilar to the first, being a couple inches too long. There was a distinct likelihood it would fail, too.

When Rich and Vogel returned to earth after 50 minutes in the air, they were exhausted—trashed. When the 10-minute gun sounded, we didn't have a headsail on. Immediately, Bertrand engaged us. We turned downwind, and the crew scrambled to get a headsail set, but the luff tape ripped. Finally, we got a headsail up, and I trailed Bertrand toward the pin end of the line. With a substantial push at the end, I drove *Australia II* over the line early. About two feet of her were on the wrong side of the starting line. By the time he made his way back, we led by 37 seconds.

At that moment, the future looked rosy. We were 37 seconds ahead on the first leg, with a 3-1 lead. The wind conditions suited us perfectly; the boat felt good. Then four minutes into the contest, with both boats on port tack, the new mast ram on *Liberty* failed. With the sudden softness of the mast at the tip, numerous adjustments to the mainsail and mast had to be made. *Australia II* gained on *Liberty*. Once she closed enough so our backwind started to hurt her, she tacked away to starboard. I let her go for what ended up being a full 10 minutes. As I explained to the crew, "If we don't round this mark with a substantial lead, we're going to lose the race." My hope was for a shift to the right that never came. *Australia II* led at the first mark by 23 seconds and at the finish by 1:47. The score was now 3-2.

The sixth race was one of the strangest races in thousands of races that I have sailed. It was a great sailing day, with 15 knots of wind from the northwest at the start. A breeze of that strength from that direction tends to be fairly steady in Newport, but this was not the case on this otherwise perfect Indian-summer day.

Liberty won the start by seven seconds. Trailing, *Australia II* tacked to starboard for the left side of the course. We tacked to cover. The Australian boat tacked again to port, and, again, we tacked to cover. Then both of us got lifted on port tack. The Australians tacked back to starboard, presumably to clear their air. Once upwind, she tacked back again to port. In due time, *Australia II* stuck her nose into an entirely different sailing breeze. It was stronger than the breeze we enjoyed, and favorable for her. This was the beginning of a most remarkable 100-degree wind shift from northwest to south, on a day that such things should have been rare. The white boat was gone, winning the race by 3:25—a new record.

Many a day I've wondered about this race. How did the Australians know about that shift? We couldn't see it when we shared a similar vantage point. Also, *Australia II* never even tacked back to consolidate her position. That's the insurance bet should the wind oscillate back in the other direction. They just stuck their nose into it and stayed in it as if God—or someone else—whispered in their ear. Where did that surety come from?

At the press conference after this race I was asked, "John Bertrand has admitted making some mistakes in this series. In your own estimation have you made errors today?" I answered, "I'd like to see the sailor yet that has never made a mistake. I don't think it [not making mistakes] happens very often. Most people can certainly think of something they'd do differently in every race they've sailed, so the answer to your question is yes. We've made mistakes, but I think relative to the potential of our yacht, we've gotten a fair bit out of it in the series, and we're pleased."

The score was now tied at three, and the Australians called for a layday. We used it to reballast our boat—this mode change was the only trick we had left up our sleeve. Lee Davis, our meteorologist, gave us a firm opinion that the wind would be light on Monday, September 26. We removed 1,000 pounds of ballast. This would make *Liberty* fast in light winds, but hopelessly slow in fresh winds. Then we stripped the boat clean. Normally, we sailed with six headsails, six spinnakers, and several staysails. We arrived at the starting line for race seven with two jibs and two spinnakers. Sweaters and boots were left ashore. Dressed for speed, not comfort, the crew wore nothing but T-shirts and shorts.

Then, on the way to the start, the wind was blowing 15 knots. Not only was the boat set up wrong, but it was cold. Just before the start, it died, however, as Davis had predicted. Light or heavy, we lost the seventh race, as related at the opening of the chapter. One point needs to be made, however. Bertrand claims in his book, *Born to Win*, that there was a fistfight on our boat during that downwind leg. There wasn't. When his co-author called to check the story, he was told it never happened. They printed it anyway.

I faced the press alone that evening at the old Armory on Thames Street, on the waterfront. Outside, Newport nearly rioted in happy celebration. Conspicuous by its absence at that final press conference was the New York Yacht Club. Maybe I hadn't done everything right during the summer, but neither had they. I'd built three boats; I'd tried my hardest.

I said to the media as I fought for control of my emotions, "Today, *Australia II* was just a better boat, and they beat us. And we have no excuses. So I'd like to at this point congratulate Alan Bond and *Australia II* on a superb effort over the summer. *Australia II* proved to be an outstanding boat, and today was their day.

"However, I'd like to point out that our guys did a great job of hanging in there in conditions that in the past have proven to be awfully good for *Australia II*, so I'm very proud of them. And I'd like to thank all of you for your support over the summer." I ended it by saying America has nothing to be ashamed of. And then I walked out of the armory with my wife at my side.

Warren Jones, who during the course of the summer had labeled me "big, bad Dennis," saved his best for last. Following me, he said, "All I can say is 'Mate!' That is the very finest Australian saying. And all summer it's been 'Check!' to the New York Yacht Club, to the British, to Dennis, or whatever it was. We were playing chess with them. 'Check, check, check, check.' And today we say 'Mate!' "

The next morning I woke up in Seaview Terrace on Ruggles Avenue, where the *Freedom-Liberty* crew lived in Newport. My head hurt, but it was still where I'd left it the night before. The New York Yacht Club would need some other decoration to replace the trophy we lost.

Later that day the America's Cup was turned over to the Australians on the porch of Marble House. The 52-room mansion, called a "summer cottage" in Newport, was built by William K. Vanderbilt, the father of Harold "Mike" Vanderbilt. The latter skippered three winning America's Cup J-Class yachts in the 1930s. I chose not to attend. The Jewetts and Ed du Moulin were there; Ed presented our battle flag to Bertrand before the America's Cup was given to the Australians.

EVEN AFTER THE America's Cup was carefully packed away and dispatched to its new home Down Under, and Alan Bond, Ben Lexcen, John Bertrand, and the crew returned home as heroes, the issue of who designed *Australia II*—Lexcen or Dutch technicians—continued to burn. In the book *Upset: Australia Wins the America's Cup*, written by my co-author, Michael Levitt, and Barbara Lloyd, now of

The New York Times, Lexcen said of the Dutch technicians, "They were just doing what I told them. Sometimes they'd tell me things back. How the hell can you stop them from telling you things? It's like in a jury—'Well disregard that remark . . . ' You can't disregard that remark. If someone says, 'I think this could be a good idea,' you can't say, 'Well, I didn't hear that.' "

About a year and a half later, Lloyd received a telephone call from the mysterious Joop Slooff, the Dutch technician who supposedly told Johan Valentijn that he designed *Australia II*'s keel. Slooff, head of the Theoretical Aerodynamics Department at the National Aerospace Laboratory, wished to talk about his involvement with Ben Lexcen and *Australia II*. At the time when the yacht was being designed, Slooff was an aerodynamicist who worked as a subcontractor to the Netherlands Ship Model Basin in Wageningen, Holland, where Lexcen worked on the design of *Australia II*. While a cruising sailor who owned a 28-foot sloop, Slooff, then in his early forties, knew nothing about the America's Cup.

That changed, however, in 1981 when he received a telephone call from a casual friend, Peter van Oossanen, who was in charge of the tank-testing program for Ben Lexcen and his patron, Alan Bond. In the late 1970s, van Oossanen and Slooff had served on a Dutch national committee for advanced ship research. Both men were sailors, and over lunch Slooff told him that from his perspective, sailboat keels didn't look right. As he told Lloyd, "If you're an aerodynamicist and you're a sailor at the same time, it's inevitable that you start thinking about those sorts of things. It was in those days that I got the ideas about what a keel should look like."

Van Oossanen asked Slooff if he would be interested in participating. Recalled Slooff, "I didn't know what the America's Cup was . . . [but] I said, 'Oh, why yes; that could be fun. That's something different than airplanes, so why not?' " When Slooff first met Lexcen and van Oossanen they were testing conventional keels, not upside-down winged keels.

Commenting on Lexcen's claim that he was working on upside-down winged keels, Slooff said, "I don't know whether it's true or not. [Lexcen] never showed it to me. It may be that Ben had been thinking about it, but he never told me he was. I think that somebody said we were provided with Lexcen's sketches, or something like that. Well, if we were, then they're still in the mail. I never saw them."

Slooff contributed two ideas that came directly from his training and work as an aerodynamicist. One was that the keel should show a reverse taper: be fatter at the bottom than the top. The second was that it should show winglets, first designed for aircraft by Richard Whitcomb, an aerodynamicist who once worked for NASA. This would cut down induced drag. Slooff said to Lloyd, "When you have a constraint on draft, which you either have because of class rules such as with a 12-Meter, or for practical purposes because you don't want to run aground but want to cruise in shallow waters, these things become very interesting."

Slooff described this shape to Lexcen and van Oossanen. He further commented that a computer program that Netherlands Aerospace Laboratory had been using for a decade could be modified to test keels that work in the water, rather than wings that work in the air. Slooff said that both Lexcen and van Oossanen told him to go ahead with the tests.

The computer testing took about a week; however, it was spread over a three-week period. Slooff produced lines for two keels, one with an inverse taper and one with an inverse taper *and* wings. These shapes were numerically fed into the computer by his staff. The upside-down keel with wings was "significantly" faster than anything Lexcen and van Oossanen had tested. These very lines, Slooff later learned, were used by Alan Bond to patent the upside-down winged keel, something about which Slooff was completely unaware.

Computer testing wasn't enough to convince Lexcen and van Oossanen, however, so 22-foot models were made of the two keels tested in the computer. Slooff helped turn the schematic drawings into models by working with the draftsman and later the model maker. "I witnessed the tank test on one or two occasions. I remember we were getting all excited and jumping all over the carriage that pulls the model along. It wasn't just me; so were Peter and Ben."

Slooff returned to his duties at NLR. However, he did meet on one occasion with Alan Bond, Warren Jones, and John Bertrand to explain "this awkward-looking thing," he said. A year later, Slooff ran into van Oossanen. He asked if they went on to build "that thing." Van Oossanen allowed that they had and promised to keep Slooff apprised about how *Australia II* fared in the America's Cup.

In May of 1983, Slooff gave a lecture in Dayton, Ohio, on aerodynamic methods. As an expert in the field, this is something that he does fairly often. Before returning to Holland, however, he decided to stop in Newport, to get a firsthand look at the America's Cup. He saw such boats as *France, Azzurra*, and *Liberty*. "The moment I saw *Liberty*'s underbody, I knew the America's Cup would be lost," he told Lloyd. It was then he encountered Johan Valentijn. Slooff's version of the conversation went this way. "I don't recall exactly what I said, but as far as I can remember it was something like that he might as well quit right away because they were going to lose the America's Cup. He was quite surprised and quite interested."

Of course, Valentijn's recollection of that conversation was different. He claimed Slooff told him that he designed *Australia II*. The likelihood, Lloyd thinks, is that Slooff was exercising proper scientific decorum when speaking to the press. In Slooff's world, the designer of an airplane is the one with overall design responsibility. That was Lexcen. That doesn't mean, however, that Lexcen originated the concept. Perhaps he was speaking more informally to Valentijn, his countryman.

As the summer of 1983 heated up, van Oossanen asked Slooff to countersign the message to Warren Jones, informing the Australians about the NYYC's interest in the parentage of the winged keel, but he refused to sign it. He was disgusted by the political strife surrounding the matter, and by that message itself, which said in no uncertain terms that Lexcen designed the winged keel. "I would put it differently," Slooff allowed.

While on a sailing holiday with his wife, Lia, in the Frisian Islands, Slooff learned via the BBC that *Australia II* had qualified to sail in the America's Cup match. The Slooffs decided to head to Newport to see the match between *Liberty* and *Australia II*. When they arrived at the *Australia II* crew house on Ruggles Avenue in Newport, van Oossanen introduced the Slooffs as "friends from Holland." In Newport Slooff ran into Lexcen three times, but the designer kept his distance. "...I was so damn mad at what was happening here; that [the Australians] were putting on this act against everybody. But they didn't have to put it up against me. I don't know what the reasoning behind it was. The most frustrating thing for me to find out when I got here was that the Australians pretended, even to me, that I didn't conceive of that configuration; that Ben had thought this up in 1960 or something. . . .

"Anyway, that was one of the most bitter things for me. I would have had no problem at all if they'd said, 'This is the situation, and we would appreciate if you keep quiet,' and that sort of thing. I would have kept quiet. I have kept quiet anyway in spite of everything. This is the first talking that I have done."

CHAPTER 9

1987

FOUND

—◦◦◦—

IT IS A story we apparently never tire of. The character starts with little or nothing; by pluck and, perhaps, luck enjoys some notable success; then loses it all. A winner becomes a loser; the famous become the infamous. It is fodder for *People* magazine and its imitators, TV talk shows, and the tabloids. It is the stuff of clichés: "The bigger they are, the harder they fall." "From the penthouse, to the outhouse."

I was now the first American to lose the America's Cup in 132 years. After that ignoble act, could I make a comeback? Also, did I wish to? Finally, did the world believe my obituary was written and cast in stone? Was it, on the other hand, "a bit premature"—as Mark Twain once observed of his untimely obituary.

In the autumn of 1983, it was time to take stock of my life. I was a $30,000-a-year drapery salesman who had spent an inordinate amount of time racing sailboats, in particular chasing the America's Cup. This was my hobby, not my business. For a hobby, my investment in time in the America's Cup was as impressive as it was distressing. I was hardly your well-rounded guy.

In 1974, for example, with *Mariner*, we'd logged about 500 hours at sea. That boat was so undistinguished, and rebuilt so often, we'd spent as much time sanding her as sailing. My tenure on *Courageous* that long, hot summer added hardly anything to the tally, as I sailed so few hours, being brought aboard in the eleventh hour. In 1980, with the *Freedom* campaign, I spent 3,000 hours on both the East and the West Coasts, learning to sail such boats. Finally, with *Liberty*, I'd spent another 3,000 hours in sailing. That represented at least 6,500 hours of sailing America's Cup 12-Meter yachts.

Could I, I wondered, turn my back on such an investment, hobby though it was? Also, what a story it would be to stage a comeback. On the other hand, I worried that I'd be throwing good time and money after bad. Then, wasn't it time, I wondered, to pay more attention to my family and career?

However, it wasn't until Christmas of 1983, when visiting friends Fritz and Lucy Jewett in Hawaii, that these thoughts crystallized into a course of action. The Jewetts were disappointed with how the New York Yacht Club (NYYC) handled 1983 in general, and me in particular. They said, "Dennis, you form your own group and go get that Cup." Planted by such good friends, the idea began to grow within me.

I returned to San Diego to discuss this with Malin Burnham, whose counsel I value. Burnham, you will recall, is a San Diego banker and successful businessman who sailed with Lowell North in the 1977 America's Cup, before taking over for North.

While agreeing that a trip to Australia to return that Cup to America made perfect sense, Malin counseled that the avenue for it began on New York's West 44th Street—the home of the NYYC. In other words, we should attempt to sail under its auspices. Maybe the club didn't want me as its standard-bearer, but let's not assume that to be the case. In time, I agreed with him. The Cup began at the club—to which Malin and I still belonged—and it should be returned to its rightful home. Since I played a role in losing it—a considerable role some might argue—I should play a part in returning it.

My friend Ed du Moulin, a longtime member of the NYYC, arranged a meeting for me at the club on January 6, 1984. While waiting for the elevator to take me to the Commodore's Room, I purposely avoided looking at the Trophy Room, where that silver ewer, which had launched so many ships, had rested for so long. Was the carpet a different color where its pedestal once stood? Would there be, I wondered, a likeness of my head in its place?

The club, I was told, would be interviewing two other groups. The first—and the one thought to have the inside track—was headed by John Kolius, skipper of *Courageous* in 1983, who would again assume that role in 1986–87, and Chuck Kirsch, the curtain-rod king, who would be the administrator. Kolius, a Texan, came complete with wealthy Texas backers, who had supported Ted Turner through his three runs at the Cup.

Kolius, hired to be a kind of sparring partner for Tom Blackaller on *Defender*, sailed well enough on *Courageous*. He certainly lasted longer than Blackaller and Gary Jobson, his tactician. Just as important, Kolius kept above the fray. In 1983 he appeared clean-cut, talented, and personable. Would he appear less able when the eyes of the America's Cup world were upon him? There is a difference, he would likely discover, going from underdog to top dog.

After outlining my plans to the commodores and describing the syndicate principals—Fritz Jewett would be chairman and Ed du Moulin would help me manage—I spoke briefly about improving the image of the club. In 1983 many Americans ended up rooting for the Australians.

I ended by saying that for me time was of the essence. While I didn't explain it, this was because the Kolius/Kirsch group was already knocking on the doors of potential backers. I knew clearly that he who hesitated was lost.

Two weeks later, I'd received no answer, so on January 20, 1984, I phoned Commodore Bus Mosbacher's office and learned he was out of town. I explained to his secretary that I had hoped for a clarification of my situation. The next day I received a telephone call from the secretary of the NYYC. My presence was requested at a meeting there on January 29, at 4:00 P.M. I was then Commodore of the San Diego Yacht Club (SDYC), and that very day would be hosting a gathering at my house for 200 people, in conjunction with the Manzanillo Race. I suggested that the Commodore call me back, and we'd make arrangements more convenient to both of us. A few hours later, I received a second call. "The Commodore says that in order to accommodate your schedule he has changed the meeting from four P.M. to eleven A.M."

"On what day?" I asked.

"The same day, Mr. Conner."

I knew then this marriage could not be saved.

Fritz Jewett reiterated his suggestion that we go it alone. This time Malin agreed. He even went before the board of the SDYC, for whom we would sail, and said that he would personally be responsible for any debts the syndicate incurred. With friends like that, I headed out into uncharted and, likely, perilous waters. The NYYC went with Kolius, his Texans, and Kirsch.

TO WIN THE America's Cup, you need money *and* design. Like love and marriage in the song, "you can't have one without the other." I went out to beat the bushes for funds, turning primarily to corporate America.

For its first hundred years, 1870 to 1970, or through 21 defenses, the America's Cup defense was funded from the generosity of members of the NYYC, such men as J. P. Morgan and Cornelius "Commodore" Vanderbilt.

The word for men like Morgan and Vanderbilt was *Corinthian*, defined as, "A wealthy amateur sportsman, especially an amateur yachtsman" in *The American Heritage Dictionary of the English Language*.

In 1974, however, a new and different breed came to sail in the America's Cup. These were ordinary men, with ordinary problems and ordinary resources. For example, Ted Turner's father, Robert E. Turner, committed suicide after business reversals; my father was a commercial fisherman who later built airplanes at a plant in San Diego.

Without family money or connections to old money, new methods for raising money had to be found. *Mariner* raised funds through the United States Merchant Marine Academy; *Intrepid* raised funds through the Seattle Sailing Foundation. This gave individual donors a tax deduction for contributions. By 1977 even the NYYC sold corporate sponsorships. Nevertheless, the club never seemed wholly comfortable with corporate largess; its membership must have considered it "uncorinthian," a necessary evil.

Even after 1983, which was a compelling event, at least in my estimation, the America's Cup was no easy sale, as corporate America remained cautious. Until then, the event had received little television exposure. It was acted out in a vacuum, and sponsors, like nature, abhor a vacuum.

Proof that 1983 was different, at least a little, was that *ABC Sports* named *Australia II* the "athlete (sic) of the year." In Australia, where the contest was considered a test of "national virility," as one author put it, 6 million people—or more than one-third of the country— stayed up through the night watching their native sons triumph.

Our first significant corporate contribution for 1986–87 came from Terry Brown of Atlas Hotels in San Diego, who gave us $500,000. Next came Ford Motor Company in the person of Edsel Ford, who became a staunch supporter.

If new at this, I was persistent—a trait I have in selling as well as sailing. At one point, for example, I camped outside Donald Trump's New York office without an appointment. His secretaries tried to shoo me away, to no avail. I told them, "Look, I know he's in there, and I'm not leaving until I see him. You have two choices: You can let me see him, or call the police." He saw me and later he paid for a ticker-tape parade up Fifth Avenue and threw a party for us at the Grand Hyatt Hotel.

Mike Dingman, Chairman of the Henley Group, proved to be one of our earliest and best friends. Not only did the Henley Group come aboard as a sponsor, but Dingman opened any number of corporate doors for us. Mike, who seemed to be on a first-name basis with practically every CEO in America, would get on the phone and say, "Hey, Bill. How's the wife and kids? Great! Great! You're an American, and you must have felt really terrible when we lost the America's Cup. We've got to help these guys win it back."

Patriotism may have opened many a door, but it closed few deals. Often we found the competition already there: Kolius, of the NYYC; David Vietor and Leonard Greene, who purchased *Courageous* for 1986–87; Tom Blackaller, who formed a syndicate through the St. Francis Yacht Club in San Francisco; or Buddy Melges, from the Heart of America syndicate representing the Chicago Yacht Club. If they weren't there, they would be. It was, take a number and move to the rear.

We offered corporations a chance to market their products around our America's Cup effort, as well as an opportunity to reward valued customers and employees with VIP treatment at the races. I also made personal appearances and gave motivational speeches. Our sports-marketing model was the Los Angeles Olympics in 1984, paid for with private, rather than public money. The LA Olympics even showed a significant profit. We met with Peter Ueberroth, the architect of these games, to learn from him.

By the time my syndicate, called Sail America, moved to Australia we had signed on The Henley Group, Allied-Signal, Anheuser-Busch, Atlas Hotels, Ford Motor Company, Merrill Lynch, and Science Applications International Corporation (SAIC).

Call it what you will, I was now in the America's Cup business. At the risk of sounding immodest, I invented it, as Gary Jobson, under the tutelage of Ted Turner, invented the sailing business. All of this sounds commonplace today, but beginning in 1984 we were making it up as we moved along. Now there are people out there—soldiers of fortune who will go anywhere at the drop of a lira or yen, for example—who have used our techniques to make far more money than I ever have or, likely, will. However, I'm an American and would have trouble being anything else. There have been several lucrative proposals made to me by non-Americans that I turned down without much thought. I never say never, but sailing for another country is a decision that I would not make frivolously.

Despite the help of corporate America, there was never a surfeit of money. Yacht design became a hungry beast that absolutely had to be fed. And it was fed, while we, figuratively, starved. We were like a third-world nation trying to fund a space program.

The winged keel of *Australia II* had touched a nerve, and before I even decided to attempt a comeback, I had received several letters from people—dreamers, schemers, and wannabes—with revolutionary keel shapes. One such call came to Malin from Barry Shillito, a member of the SDYC—the home team. Shillito said that he worked for SAIC, a defense contractor. After *Australia II*'s victory, the U.S. Navy took an interest in the winged keel for defense and commercial applications. It commissioned SAIC to study the design.

I was resistant, but Malin bundled me off to SAIC headquarters in La Jolla, a fashionable section of San Diego, to hear Shillito out. We passed through numerous security checks, security guards, strolled down soundproof corridors, and were even sniffed by guard dogs. These were not "man's best friends," believe me. Then, in a conference room, about 15 guys made a presentation. I thought of it as "the-winged-keel-as-brought-to-you-by-the-Department-of-Defense." They had numerical explanations of why *Australia II* could turn so well, sail so high, and foot so fast. It was all very impressive.

All of this work was based on the moment when Alan Bond, after winning the Cup, responded to the crowd's chants of, "Let's See the Keel!" Then and there, the secret keel passed into the public domain; and SAIC, I had no doubt, had a better idea of what its shape and what each curve, span, and varying thicknesses did, than the Australians—if not the Dutch. Had Bond refused to raise his boat's modesty skirt, we might still be marching off to war in Western Australia. Bond's fortunes, which crashed after the 1987 defense, might well have been very different, too. Had he been successful, Bond might well have been too big to bring down (see next chapter).

SAIC wished to work with us on yacht design. They believed the victory of *Australia II* was a black eye for America's scientific and technical community. Specifically, SAIC believed it could bundle yacht design into the computer—change it from an art to a science, a computer science. SAIC also put its money where its mouth was by making a cash contribution. And we were off.

At first I was head of design. In short order, however, I realized I was playing out of my league, and turned to John Marshall, my mainsail-trimmer on *Liberty*, to head the design program. While not a naval architect, Marshall had studied biochemistry at Harvard and attended the prestigious Rockefeller Institute before becoming president of North Sails. Colleges aside, he's the smartest person I know, by a nautical mile.

He wasn't one to pull his punches, either. As Marshall would later describe his marching orders: "Dennis Conner, as much as any other leader in American yachting, was responsible for the anti-intellectual, anti-technological attitude that made real design progress impossible from 1980 through 1983. He experienced firsthand on *Mariner* what a disaster could be produced by the technical approach

gone off course, and he also had seen the sterility of tank-test refinements from *Intrepid* to *Courageous* to *Enterprise* to *Freedom*. Dennis,
however, faced his error squarely, recognizing he had been beaten by
what he derided and that only by embracing a design-intensive approach could we win."

Beginning in 1982, I'd heard over and over that designers can't
work well in competition. That was why Sparkman & Stephens (S&S)
and Johan Valentijn couldn't design boats together. Nevertheless, I
had always placed sailmakers in competition and believed this stim-
ulated them to do their best. If designers can't work together, that's
their problem, I concluded. So rather than naming two of them for
1986–87, I named three: Bruce Nelson, David Pedrick, and Britton
Chance. Chance may have been a problem for Ted Turner but he
wasn't for me. I welcomed his intelligence and could ignore his dearth
of charisma.

Nelson, a recent graduate of the University of Michigan, had
never designed a 12-Meter; however, he was making a name for
himself in the design of offshore yachts. When he worked for S&S,
Pedrick had participated in the design of *Courageous* in 1974, which
was successful, and *Enterprise* in 77, which wasn't. Working on his
own, he was the designer of *Clipper* in 1980 and *Defender* in 1983,
neither of which made it to the match. Chance redesigned *Intrepid*
for 1970, and designed the god-awful *Mariner* in 1974. An interesting
triumvirate: Pedrick is a choirboy in looks and character; Chance is
more the tortured artist; Nelson is all-California cool. There he ended
up hanging out his shingle despite being born and raised on Long
Island's gold coast and educated in Ann Arbor.

However, I left it to Marshall to sort things out. I wasn't looking
for congenial dinner companions but good, no—great—yacht design.
Now I was the challenger, and this time decided to swing from my
heels for the fences, as the Australians had done in 1983, and the
Americans had first done in 1851.

In Perth, Western Australia, the new venue of the America's Cup,
the wind is worthy of a name: the "Fremantle Doctor." In the summer, the desert air of Western Australia heats up in the sun. As the
temperature rises, so does the air. Then cooler and moister air off the

Indian Ocean roars ashore, like a freight train, to replace it. This is the fabled Fremantle Doctor. It makes a daily "house call," providing relief from the heat and flies. During the Australian summer months of December, January, and February, the Doctor averages about 18 knots and often blows considerably more.

I visited Perth in April 1984 to line up crew accommodations and a staging area for our boats, as well as to lobby to be Challenger of Record.[1] On the way home I stopped in Hawaii. Here, following my conversation with the Jewetts, my America's Cup journey to Western Australia began.

Then it dawned on me—I would plant my syndicate here, in Oahu, before moving to faraway Australia. The logic seemed impeccable, and why it never occurred to anyone else, I couldn't imagine. While Western Australia enjoys the Fremantle Doctor only during the summer months, when the America's Cup would be held, Hawaii enjoys such winds year-round. The seas may be different: long in Hawaii, shorter and choppier in Fremantle, but the wind strength is the same. So every day for a year and a half, we were slugging it out in the winds of war off Diamond Head, and when we finally arrived in Western Australia, we were ready. The other teams weren't as adept at handling boats in heavy weather. Besides, in Hawaii, we were out of their sight. That suited me fine. We weren't out of mind, however, which ended up suiting me fine, too.

While waiting for the designers to return to earth from their ivory towers, we tested boats and crew. We had *Liberty*, designed by Valentijn, and *Spirit of America*, designed by S&S, left over from 1983. So we modified *Spirit* and kept *Liberty* untouched, to serve as a benchmark. Bill Trenkle, who has been with me since 1980, cut off the bottom of *Spirit* a few feet above the waterline. Then he changed her underbody, added structure to support a winged keel, and next affixed such a keel. All these changes came from our designers. It was, in some ways, a dress rehearsal. Thus, *Spirit* became *Stars & Stripes '83* and, as it turned out, a wolf in sheep's garb. *Stars & Stripes '83* proved considerably faster than *Liberty* and, by extension, faster,

---

1. The Yacht Club Costa Smeralda, on Sardinia, was named Challenger of Record for 1986–87.

we believed, than *Australia II*. Our first step in a journey of a "thousand miles," or more accurately 11,737 miles—the distance from Newport to Western Australia—seemed in the proper direction.

Stars & Stripes '85, our first new boat, was built at Bob Derecktor's boatyard in Mamaroneck, New York. Her salient feature was her exaggerated sailing length—the amount of boat at the waterline in touch with the water.

There is a direct relationship between waterline length and hull speed. A tradeoff, however, is maneuverability. Another is speed in light winds. Nevertheless, we wanted a drag racer, not a slalom skier. Then, too, we placed our bet on heavy winds; if we were wrong we'd be home for Christmas. *Stars & Stripes '85*, affectionately dubbed the "cruise-liner" by the crew, was three feet longer on the water than any 12-Meter in 1983. She was also fast from the word *go*.

The designers warned me, however, that there was nothing leading edge about her—they had merely polished the apple—and there was no reason to believe that other groups couldn't come up with something as good if not better. So, the designers beavered away on *Stars & Stripes '86*, a boat I hoped would be the last word on the subject.

When that boat was launched, she had a radical bow section, so as to fool the ocean into thinking it was a longer boat. (Where had I heard those words before?) She was also long, like her predecessor. Differing from her predecessor, she was slow. Marshall described her as a "valuable learning tool." Perhaps, but I'd heard that sorry refrain before, and wasn't happy to be funding Ph.D. programs for "wayward boys." What little faith I had in yacht designers and yacht design was rapidly ebbing with the money we didn't have.

Our budget was $15 million—of which we'd amassed $10 million. Nevertheless, hope sprang eternal, for the designers if not for me, and they kept at it.

We decided not to attend the 12-Meter Worlds, held in Perth in February 1986. It didn't seem worthwhile to break stride from our steady progress in Hawaii. Then, too, I didn't have a lot of money to transfer boats and crew to Australia and then bring them back. I worried, too, as is my way, that I'd be giving more than I'd be getting. Nevertheless, we were described as "in Elba"—in exile. The "popular wisdom," espoused by the press, had it that we were afraid to show the world that we were slow. Of course, the flip side of that coin was just as viable: Perhaps, we were afraid to show the world we were fast. The press might have paid more attention to us because we weren't there than they likely would have had we come. It proved an effective ploy.

Bond's group won the regatta with his new *Australia III*, skippered by Colin Beashel. Chris Dickson, sailing for New Zealand, making his and his country's debut in this rarefied world, finished an astounding second.

Dickson, who was 24 and, as such, 20 years my junior, did it in a fiberglass 12-Meter—the material's debut in this league. Since 1974, nearly all 12-Meters had been made of aluminum; before that, venerable wood.

The New Zealand syndicate was headed by Michael Fay, a 37-year-old merchant banker from Auckland, about whom the world would learn a lot more soon enough.

The New Zealand challenge actually started with Marcel Fachler, a silver and gold trader. When he faltered, Aussie Malcolm, the former New Zealand National Cabinet Minister, gathered the reins. Malcolm similarly lost his way, and Fay entered the fray. His conversion to the America's Cup was a recent thing: He became interested in it when he saw what it did for Australia. And for Alan Bond. He commented to ESPN that he wished to bring "the America's Cup industry" to New Zealand.

Fay recognized, and would exploit, another quality of fiberglass that would help him do so well in the America's Cup trials that followed: the ease with which a molded fiberglass structure can be duplicated. He built two identical fiberglass boats. This way he had a practically perfect trial horse. If something worked on one boat, it would work on the other. It wasn't invalidated by a nuance, or peculiarity, of design. This way, he put design progress on a superhighway, as opposed to the bumpy dirt road that most of us traveled.

In third place came John Kolius and *America II*, representing the NYYC. Right behind the New Yorkers came Bond's *Australia II*, by this time a dowager duchess, and a stranger in a strange land. *Australia II* was designed for the lighter winds of Newport.

The series raised serious doubts about the New Yorkers, particularly from the perspective of leadership and design. They had spent the better part of two years tuning two new 12-Meters in Western Australia and in Newport, and had a third new boat about to be delivered. At the Worlds, a crew-member fell overboard; the boat suffered from a broken topping lift and a ripped mainsail. The syndicate with the most—boats, practice time in Perth, and money— had stumbled badly.

Many wondered: Did the emperor have no clothes? Sure, they sailed the Worlds in the syndicate's first boat, *USA 42*, but *USA 44*, its second boat, was rumored to be even slower. Indeed, *42* had beaten *44* in the Cadillac Cup—an internecine battle played out before supporters and sponsors in Newport, much to the chagrin of yacht club members.

All boats were designed by S&S, in the person of Bill Langan. It was Langan who, for 1983, designed the undistinguished *Spirit* for us. Later, he and his firm attempted to collaborate with Johan Valentijn on the design of *Liberty*. Eventually, Langan went to work on John Kolius's *Courageous*, which began life for 1974 in his shop. This became the basis of a strong friendship between Kolius and Langan.

From the beginning the New Yorkers wanted two designers in the program: S&S and German Frers, the talented Argentinean yacht designer who had made a name for himself in maxi boats. Syndicate head Chuck Kirsch, who owned a Frers design, had promised this would be the case. NYYC members worked hard to get Frers a "green card," or work permit, for a foreigner. This would make this Argentinean eligible to design boats for the Americans. The syndicate was apparently most unhappy with *USA 42* and *44* and wanted Frers, not S&S, to design the third boat.

Kolius, it was said, stood firmly behind Langan, who was striving to rebound from the firm's failure in 1983 and, perhaps, to escape personally from the long shadow cast by Olin Stephens, who had all but retired.

A member of the syndicate said Kirsch "was like the girl in the song who couldn't say no." He was saying "yes" to the New Yorkers about getting Frers to design the third boat and "yes" to Kolius that Langan would design the third boat. Speaking from both sides of your mouth is difficult to sustain indefinitely. When the decision was made not to use Frers, Kirsch departed. He was replaced by Arthur Santry, the next NYYC commodore.

Commodore Santry, Chairman of the Board of Combustion Engineering, was cut from sterner stuff. Rather than competing designers, he began to talk about competing helmsmen. This must have been distressing to Kolius. In due time, if for a brief time, he quit; that act proved to be brinkmanship, however.

In a hardly edifying press conference he called in Newport, Kolius said that management had created an "imbalance" in the many facets needed to run a campaign, including finances, technology, public relations, and the team itself. "My entire sailing career has been based on one premise, and that is that the closest and strongest team wins. The players get more than their share of attention, but the team includes all the other ingredients as well. The problems with the America II Challenge are not insurmountable as long as each element is judged under the same light."

He took no questions and departed from the prepared text only once to say, "I wish I could explain fully the hurt that accompanied this decision. I've put everything I've had into this campaign, and I seem to have failed it, or it has failed me, depending upon your viewpoint..." At this point, he could barely hold back the tears. It was heartfelt, but it shed little, if any, light on what was going on behind closed doors.

If Kolius wouldn't explain, others would. Beyond yacht design and competing skippers, sailmaking apparently became an issue. In 1983, Kolius was a young sailmaker from Texas, building sails under the Ulmer logo. After the America's Cup that year, Butch Ulmer, the firm's principal, gave him a substantial chunk of the business, and half the name: the firm became known as Ulmer-Kolius (UK). Likely a strong impetus for this union was Ulmer's desire to crack the lucrative America's Cup market. The America II syndicate, however, had agreements with North and Sobstad to build sails. Asked to sign an agreement that he wouldn't build sails, merely sail the boat, the 33-year-old Kolius refused.

When Kolius walked, a top-secret meeting was held at La Guardia Airport, in New York. Lee Smith and O. L. Pitts, two wealthy

Texans, and generous contributors to the syndicate, flew in for the meeting. Commodore Santry was there, too. Apparently Smith and Pitts had put up a substantial amount of the syndicate's money. The NYYC was given an ultimatum: Give us back our $3 million, and you run the show. Or step aside.

In due time Kolius returned to the fold. A new executive board was formed, with the NYYC holding but two of 11 seats. It was the NYYC's syndicate in name only.

Once the syndicate's train jumped the tracks, it never recovered. They'd be home for Christmas of 1986—not even making it to the semifinals.

Blackaller and Jobson were right: I don't feel obliged to help the competition. If we gave nothing to the 12-Meter Worlds in Perth in 1986 or to the America's Cup world, we got something back. Several of my people were on the scene and reported back that *Stars & Stripes '85*, some three feet longer on the water than the 1983 crop of Twelves, also was about three feet longer than the 1986 crop. This had tremendous import on the design of our third new boat. The question was: How far out on the waterline limb did we wish to go? At this point, I wasn't sure I needed a third new boat, three feet shorter or not, and I was very sure I couldn't afford one.

Despite our lack of funds and, certainly, my enthusiasm, two designs continued to intrigue the design team: an evolutionary one, Model 30, and a revolutionary one, Model 32.

To build or not to build was the question we pondered for about 10 days. Finally, we concluded that we'd come this far, we might as well go the distance. Whether that was to success or oblivion—to the penthouse or the outhouse—I had no clear idea at this point. The decision was made to build Model 32, the radical one.

The boat took three months to build in New York, and then several weeks to ship to Hawaii. It would have to prove fast, right out of the box. If it wasn't, there would be no time to optimize the design. It would be written off as another "valuable learning tool." The boat, which became *Stars & Stripes '87*, proved competitive with the well-tuned and liked '85. If two feet shorter than '85 and '86, she was a foot longer on the water than what the competition was showing. So off we went to Western Australia with *Stars & Stripes '87* to see what lay ahead.

Common wisdom had it that there would be little interest in an America's Cup so far from America. If Australia is on the other side of the earth, which it is—depending on your perspective, of course— then Perth is on the other side of Australia. The population of Australia then was about 16 million. The population of Perth was 1.6 million. That is but a drop in the bucket for the world's corporations that nearly all of us were depending on at this point. So much for common wisdom. Originally there were 24 challengers from six nations who anted up the not-inconsiderable entrance fee. Of those, 13 made it to the starting line—the largest armada ever—as did four defense groups.

The Australian defenders first: It was all for none Down Under. Kevin Parry was a Western Australia multimillionaire and business rival of Alan Bond's. A landlubber, Parry had attended a luncheon where Bond, who by this time was practically the King of Australia, as his father-in-law was once the King of Perth, was discussing the importance of support from the business community for the America's Cup. Caught up in the moment, Parry volunteered his help, but Bond, for his own reasons, snubbed him.

Parry said, "The hell with you. I'll go it alone." He formed the *Kookaburra* syndicate—after Australia's native bird, with its distinctive cry that fills Australia's forests. The call, which sounds like a laugh, has given the Kookaburra the nickname the "laughing jackass." His syndicate started with a $7 million budget, but by the time it was over, it cost Parry $28 million. Apparently, there's nothing like a grudge match between Western Australia's self-made millionaires to loosen the dollars.

Parry's anointed skipper, Iain Murray, had a similar, and similarly unsatisfactory, run-in with Alan Bond. In the 1983 America's Cup, the 25-year-old Murray had skippered the vainglorious *Advance* with dignity if a singular lack of success. A more apt name for the boat might have been *Retreat*. Nevertheless, after *Advance* was excused, Murray and his cohorts, all as keen as Murray was, were invited by countryman Alan Bond to sail *Challenge 12* to help Bond's

Australia II tune up for the Cup. Apparently, by this point, the *Challenge 12* crew had had a bellyful of Bond and the *Australia II* crew, and vice versa. Murray loved it. "It was an eye-opener in terms of boat development; an eye-opener in the way they campaigned that boat, the way they fought the New York Yacht Club—a lot of very positive things there."

After being a sparring partner in 1983, Murray offered his services to Bond for 1986–87. Bond snubbed him, too. Apparently the Bond without the Cup was a better judge of character than the one with it, because Murray and Parry proved Bond's undoing.

Murray was born in 1958 in Sydney. He played soccer and rugby at school and grew physically large and dependable. Today, he is called "the Big Fella." He started sailing when he was 10 at the public school he attended. Murray enjoyed early success in the Cherub Class; eventually winning the Australian National Championship three times.

He gravitated to the high-performance, if lawless, Sydney Harbour 18-foot Skiff Class. "There really aren't any rules," said Murray. "The size limit is 18 feet, the boats can't be any narrower than six feet at one point, and the start's at 2:30."

Any number of antipodean sailing notables have made their way through the "Eyedeens," as the Australians pronounce it, before going onto other things, including Ben Lexcen and Bruce Farr. The latter was part of the team that designed the very successful Kiwi boats in this America's Cup.

Murray began looking for sponsorship in 18-footers when he was 17. He found it from Channel 7, in Australia, and his boats were called *Color 7*. He didn't drive a car and wasn't able to sign checks—his mother had to do that—but Murray was fully sponsored. Soon he was designing his own 18-footers. He won the class championship six years in a row, and later, the Etchells World Championship in 1984. He was named Australian Yachtsman of the Year in 1985.

Beyond skippering the *Kookaburras*—there would be three of them—Murray, then age 27, headed the design team that consisted of John Swarbrick and Alan Payne. When the first *Kookaburra* was launched, in all her yellow glory, bumper stickers mysteriously appeared in Perth saying, "Stuff the yellow bird." This wasn't an attempt at humor. From the word *go* there was tremendous animosity between this group and Bond's.

Even before the defender elimination series began it was a civil war. For example, John Bertrand, Bond's skipper in 1983, had gone on to fame and fortune in Australia. He was expected to play but a limited role in Bond's camp in 1986–87. Then Bertrand's book, *Born to Win*, came out. The book, which was co-authored with Patrick Robinson, a British writer and publisher, took the slant that *Australia II* wasn't that fast after all. It would not have mattered, said Bertrand, whether his team sailed *Challenge 12* or *Australia II*. Bertrand credited his own "mental toughness" for winning the America's Cup.

Ben Lexcen, Bond's designer then, and again in 1986–87, was reportedly incensed by the claims. He supposedly gave Bond an ultimatum: "Either he goes, or I do." Bertrand departed.

Then, when *Australia II* trialed with *South Australia*, another defense group, *Kookaburra* was purposely and forcibly excluded. Imagine that! Bond's group didn't wish to help a rival—particularly a dangerous one—get up to speed. However, Bond's boats trialed against us, a challenger. Such fraternization between the "enemy" was never countenanced during the NYYC's watch. It was shocking how slow Bond's boats were. Even *Australia IV*—Lexcen's and, indeed, Bond's last word on the subject. We couldn't imagine this boat beating *Kookaburra*. Bond's boats were designed by only one man: Ben Lexcen. The *Kookaburras* were designed by three, as were our boats and the Kiwis' boats.

Iain Murray, however, forced his way into a race between *Australia II* and *South Australia*. *Kookaburra*, claimed Murray and other observers, seemed to be sailing higher and faster than the duo. At the end of a 2.5-mile upwind leg, *Kookaburra* was, Murray claimed, an astonishing 10 boat lengths ahead. This made Warren Jones, Bond's Doberman, and John Longley, Bond's crew-boss, furious. The root of all this evil was, of course, money. Any defender that could show a clear superiority in the early going could expect to reap the benefits of what little corporate support there was in Australia for the America's Cup.

It got so bad that Dr. Stan Reed, Chairman of the Royal Perth Yacht Club's America's Cup Committee, was forced to issue a Memorandum to Defenders. It laid down six rules, and unambiguously told defenders to behave. Or else.

Before the defender elimination series was over, there would be about 45 protests; sometimes there would be four, or even five, in one race. The first time *Australia IV* and *Kookaburra III* raced, the jury disqualified *both* of them despite the fact that both completed the course and *Kookaburra III* won. I'd never heard of that happening before. There were no on-the-water umpires in this Cup series, as there wouldn't be until 1988, and protests lasted late into the night. The majority of these protests were leveled by the two *Kookaburra*s that sailed in the defense trials. As a result, Warren Jones publicly described them as "howling like dingoes"—an oath of utmost contempt in Australia.

From their perspective, it had to be ugly; from ours, it was sublime. The Australians seemed bent on self-destruction.

On our side of the fence, three challengers worried us: Tom Blackaller, sailing for the St. Francis Yacht Club in San Francisco; Chris Dickson, sailing for the Royal New Zealand Yacht Squadron; and, of course, Kolius and the NYYC.

Blackaller, who had been nipping at my heels for 20 years, came to Perth with a trick 12-Meter, *USA*. Rather than giving the boat a keel to provide lift *and* carry ballast at the same time, the designers, Gary Mull and Alberto Calderon, separated the functions. The "keel" only carried ballast to balance the sailplan; it was a huge bulb of lead on a single strut. Lift and steering were handled by twin rudders, one at the very bow of the boat and one at the stern. These high-aspect-ratio rudders produced lift with less of a penalty in drag. It could have been a breakthrough, and Blackaller was talented enough to win the Cup even without one.

While Blackaller, I'm sure, considered himself a better sailor than I, the record didn't bear that out. He sailed Stars 15 years before I did, but I won the Worlds before he did. Blackaller never won the Congressional Cup, the SORC, or an Olympic medal, all of which I did. Twice before Perth, he'd been in the America's Cup but never made it into the match, let alone won it. In Perth, Blackaller was joined by his talented prodigy Paul Cayard, who would skipper *Il Moro* for the Italians in 1992.

Dickson worried us, too, because of his success in the Worlds and his youth. With the change of venue, was this, members of the press speculated, a game for younger men? Also, Dickson's boats were made of fiberglass, which was an unknown quality in the America's Cup. Indeed, it might prove as radical as Blackaller's *USA*.

Finally, what I'd seen and heard about Kolius and the NYYC hadn't impressed me. Nevertheless, the yacht club had a 135-year history with the Cup that couldn't—and shouldn't—be dismissed.

In the fifth race in Round 1, in October 1986, we met Blackaller for the first time. With 1:15 until the start, my *Stars & Stripes* chased his *USA* to the line, both of us on port tack. He was to weather of us, and as such, the give-way boat. I began to push him up—closer into the wind. "Coming up!" we shouted. Amazingly, he ignored us. "Coming up, damn it!" I yelled. I could have fouled him out then and there, but you win some and lose some in the protest room. I wasn't eager to try my luck there. In danger of hitting the committee boat, I opted to tack to starboard rather than jibe. Wrong! We trailed them by 34 seconds at the start. At the first mark, *USA* led us by 50 seconds.

The course was different in Perth than Newport. There were two extra legs, and each was shorter, although the distance was about the same (24.5 miles).[2] The second leg was a run, and the third another beat. On the latter leg, we sailed well and narrowed his lead. We approached the mark on the port-tack layline. Laylines are dangerous places, and a wind shift, a lift, meant we had overstood the windward mark.

Blackaller, while ahead, came at us on starboard tack. With the unwanted lift, we cracked sheets and sailed well deep of the layline, giving Blackaller the misconception that we had overstood the mark by a country mile. Actually, while we'd overstood, we hadn't overstood that much. Not wanting to make the same mistake—overstand the mark—he tacked before the layline. Thus, he was barely able to make it. We came up and sailed to the mark in fresh air, when we

---

2. The course in Perth was 8 legs: windward-leeward-windward; then two reaching legs; then windward-leeward-windward. The Olympic course in Newport was 6 legs: windward-reach-reach-windward-leeward-windward.

should have been asphyxiated. This maneuver cut his lead in half, to about 140 yards, and it must have shaken his confidence. It was an embarrassment that would have shaken mine. But Blackaller was, if anything, a warrior.

By the end of the second reach, we were only 34 seconds behind. On the final beat, we decided to engage him in a tacking duel. I'd noticed during the prestart dance that *USA*, with its "canard" rudder forward, as it was called, was slow to turn. Once we got halfway up the leg and into the center of the course, we started tacking. Seven tacks later, his lead was diminishing, so he broke it off before it was totally erased.

Blackaller approached the port end of the finish line on port tack. The wind was stronger there. He tacked to starboard a bit short of the layline and, thus, was in the controlling position. As the give-way boat, we'd have to duck him. With the duck it would be game, set, and match. However, I saw the smallest of openings and took it. I decided to cross him on port. I went to the leeward side and watched it. He came up to block us. I noticed, however, that his jib went light—luffed. I called him for changing course, which as the right-of-way boat he was not supposed to do in such proximity. Once cleanly across him, I started breathing again.

I tacked to starboard; he tacked to port. I crossed him. Then both of us luffed for the line. We had barely more momentum than he did and crossed the line 3 feet ahead, to the roar of the gun. It was a huge win for us, if not that significant in the score. Races this early only counted for one point. It was the type of race that you never forget if you win, and can't forget if you lose.

"Plastic Fantastic" was one of the many nicknames *Kiwi Magic* was dubbed. She was, as I've said, the first fiberglass (i.e., plastic) 12-Meter. Theoretically, this construction method could allow a boat to be lighter and stiffer—meaning less likely to bend—than an aluminum boat. In seas, an aluminum boat bends just a little but a little more than a glass boat. That lessens the tension in the forestay and the backstays. Each time the boat, and then the rig flexes, it spills just a bit of wind. This can add up, and the loss of speed is more pronounced in the aluminum boat than a fiberglass one.

Lloyd's Registry of Shipping was supposed to establish building standards (weight, rigidity, length, girth, scantlings) to be sure that the fiberglass boats didn't have an edge. However, when we were measured in Perth, I noticed that two points were omitted that we considered important: the calculation of the exact lengthwise weight distribution and the vertical center of gravity. We were afraid that the New Zealand boat was light in the ends. While the weight of the entire boat might meet specifications, if that weight was packed in the middle, leaving the bow and stern lighter than aluminum 12-Meters, the Kiwis would enjoy an enormous and illegal advantage. Anyone acquainted with fiberglass boatbuilding knows that it is impossible to verify density and weight distribution in a glass hull without taking core samples.

The day after we were measured—and this was before the racing even started—Malin Burnham sent a letter to Commandante Gianfranco Alberini of the Yacht Club Costa Smeralda, the Challenger of Record, saying in part, "We request that Lloyd's surveyor take core samples of all composite-construction yachts to ensure that the laminate meets the 'as built' Lloyd's specifications."

The press dubbed this "glassgate," and I was the spoilsport. Again. After all, I'd whined about the winged keel in 1983, and now I was whining about the glass 12-Meter. This was being discussed endlessly. Then, in one of my more unfortunate moments, I said at a press conference, "The last 78 12-Meters built around the world have been built in aluminum so why would you build one in fiberglass unless you wanted to cheat?"

When we raced Dickson in the first round, we beat him by 49 seconds. (Of course, perhaps he was sandbagging, to defuse the issue. As it played out, this was the only blemish on Dickson's record until the Louis Vuitton Final a couple of months later.) After the victory, there was a press conference where I was asked for my impressions of the race, which I gave. Then Dickson took the microphone and said, "It was painful enough losing the race and just as painful to listen to it all over again. Actually, I thought *Stars & Stripes* looked a bit light in the ends."

When the laughter subsided, I piped up, "We'll take core samples." I was impressed by Dickson at that moment.

Round-robin I ended with *America II, Kiwi Magic,* and *Stars &*

Stripes at the head of the class, tied with 11-1 records. The New Yorkers had beaten us, which showed clearly how vulnerable we were downwind.

Round-robin II started badly for us. In short order, we lost to *New Zealand* and then *USA*. By the time it was over, we'd also lost to *Canada II* and *White Crusader*, from England. Of 11 races we'd sailed that month, only five of them were in our conditions: heavy air. We were lucky to finish this round in third place; behind *New Zealand* and *America II*.

New Zealand, with a record of 33-1, won Round-robin III in December to advance into the semifinals. We finished second with a score of 27-7. My arch rival Tom Blackaller and *USA* finished third, meaning we would face him in the semifinals. *French Kiss*, sailed by Marc Pajot, finished fourth and would sail against *New Zealand*. Gone was the NYYC after being in America's Cup matches for 135 years. Gone, too, of course, was John Kolius, its standard-bearer. In this round, where each win counted for 12 points, they'd lost to each of the four semifinalists, and also to also-ran *Heart of America*, steered by Buddy Melges.

The semifinals proved anticlimactic for both *Stars & Stripes* and *Kiwi Magic*. The Kiwis beat the French 4-0, and we beat Blackaller by the same score. That was satisfying for a number of reasons, not the least of them because Blackaller had beaten us two of three times before the semis. It appeared as if we were peaking at the proper time. My hope was that the Kiwis had peaked too early.

One of the stranger moments in the semifinals occurred after the third race, when both *Kiwi Magic* and *Stars & Stripes* were told to report to the measurer's pen for a spot check. I asked Ken McAlpine, the Australian measurer, if we were allowed to send a representative to see *Kiwi Magic* being measured. He said that we were. At the last moment, I substituted my name for Robert Hopkins's, who worked for our group. The Kiwis seemed shocked when I arrived there in a rubber boat. I found Chris Dickson and congratulated him on his win over the French, then offered him a cold Budweiser—a sponsor of ours. When I left, I noticed the beer was untouched.

When it was our turn to be measured, Dickson's father returned the favor and represented them. He seemed determined that the measurer should take a hard line with us. While trying to appear calm, I really wasn't. We'd just sailed a tough and wet race with *USA*, and the boat sat deep in the water, due to waterlogged sails. *Stars & Stripes* was likely floating lower in the water than she otherwise might, which could invalidate her measurement. The rules, however, allow you to replace wet sails with dry ones of the same number before the measurement.

In the midst of the measurement, Tony Watts, the measurer, fell head over heels into the chilly harbor water. Everyone tried not to laugh as it isn't a good idea to offend the measurer, but poor Tony looked like a drowned rat. It was about 6:00 P.M. and quite chilly. Perhaps this is why we passed so easily.

At the onset of the Louis Vuitton Finals, on January 13, 1987, the Kiwis' record was 37-1. Their record was the best in the history of the Cup; it would not be equaled until 1995 by another group of New Zealanders. We were 31-7, primarily for having lost to the Kiwis two of three times, and to Blackaller two of three times.

After we dispatched Blackaller home to the States, I recklessly predicted to a friend that only eight races separated us from regaining the America's Cup. That meant I believed we'd sweep the Kiwis and sweep the defender. Some friend! Somehow, the press got wind of that prediction, and Chris Dickson was asked what he thought of my remarks at a press conference. He said, "There is no possible way *Stars & Stripes* is going to beat the Kiwis 4-0. I'd like to think she is not going to beat the Kiwis at all. All we can go on is the history of the racing in this America's Cup. The Cup is all about winning yacht races, and the simple fact is that one boat has a better track record than the other."

As it played out, Chris Dickson was right; we didn't beat the Kiwis 4-0. We beat them 4-1. And so, rather than eight races having separated us from regaining the Cup, nine had.

The third race with the Kiwis, on January 16, was one of the most interesting of the series. The score at this point was 2-0 in favor of *Stars & Stripes*. We won the start, however slightly, and rounded the first mark in front by 21 seconds. *America II* had generously loaned us a .75-ounce spinnaker that we hoisted on the second, or downwind, leg. (No such offer came from Tom Blackaller, however, and *USA*.) Ten seconds later, the snap shackle, affixing it to the halyard, opened up. Down the spinnaker floated in a sickening heap.

The crew rushed forward to rectify it. While some of them pulled the fallen spinnaker out of the water, the rest hoisted a new one. It took them only 91 seconds, and we still held the lead. However, in our haste, we had fouled a halyard. Scotty Vogel had to be hoisted to the top of the mast to clear it. I held a higher course to prevent the Kiwis from passing us to windward. We jibed to starboard, but Dickson held onto port tack. However, when he turned more downwind, to sail by the lee, his wind-shadow slowed us. When he jibed onto starboard, he tucked his bow under our stern, so he was riding our stern wave, like a surfer. This maneuver helped him get up to speed more quickly.

Dickson demanded room at the mark, as he had an overlap, he claimed. Sometimes he did, and sometimes he didn't. Nevertheless, if you deny a boat room at a mark, you must prove the lack of an overlap, so reluctantly, I let him round ahead of us.

For two hours, we chased them. On the second beat we tacked 35 times. On the third beat we tacked 24 times. At the seventh mark, we'd narrowed the gap to 14 seconds. Then on the beat to the finish, I told the crew, "Get ready, we're going to kick their butts and grind them down."

With that I began tacking. The wind was roaring by this time, and the seas were steep and overlaid by a three-foot chop. We tacked 55 times over the 3.25-mile leg—an America's Cup record. It was akin to combat. At the end, *New Zealand* beat us by 38 seconds, and she deserved the win. Nevertheless, so pumped up were my guys, they were glad-handing one another. While they won and we lost, there were no real losers this day.

We won race four after the Kiwis suffered a breakdown. The score was now 3-1; the press was only too happy to remind me that I led the Australians 3-1 in 1983. Like that's something I'll ever forget.

On January 19, we sailed the fifth race. The wind blew 31 knots true on one leg of the course. We led at the first mark by 42 seconds. On the second beat, however, our jib exploded. As the crew worked feverishly to replace it, I asked for the traveler on the main to be eased. There is an optimum boatspeed for every windspeed, and even without a headsail, I just sailed lower to keep our speed at the target. Unfortunately, this happened when we were near the layline, so I had to tack, without a headsail, and with the guys wrestling on the foredeck. This put us on port tack, with no rights, and with the New Zealanders coming at us on starboard with all rights and the speed of a freight train.

If we couldn't cross them, we'd lose. Just as in the fourth race against *Australia II* in 1983, I went for it. As the two boats came together, one from America and one from New Zealand, I felt surprisingly calm. A moment before disaster struck, the crew got the new jib up. I had them! Because they couldn't cross us, the Kiwis tacked to leeward of us. Our lead was cut from 48 seconds to 14, but we still led.

The Kiwis threatened again on the first reaching leg, with a gennaker, a specialty, reaching, asymmetrical spinnaker that began to appear in this Cup. They nearly caught us; had the leg been longer they would have passed us. After the wing mark, however, that sail proved wrong. Besides, *Stars & Stripes*, traveling at 13 knots, threw up a huge quarterwave that the Kiwis couldn't cross. They tried to change the gennaker to a symmetrical, running spinnaker but made a mess of it and ended up having to drop both sails. In spite of the fire drill, Dickson didn't give up. The race wasn't decided until he hit the seventh mark and had to reround. There and then, *Kiwi Magic* turned into Kiwi Tragic. We'd won the Louis Vuitton Cup.

ESPN showed the Louis Vuitton Finals, and later the America's Cup match, live on television in America; the racing began at 1:00 A.M. on the East Coast. I wanted people to see the "tree fall in the woods," as I've said, and consented to have the cameras aboard *Stars & Stripes* for them to see it. This was much to the displeasure of my crew. ESPN did a spectacular job—in pictures and in words, too, it told the America's Cup story more lucidly than it has ever been told. We continued to hear how sailors, armchair sailors, and just suddenly interested people stayed up through the night to watch. It was most gratifying. Few would have believed it, but America's Cup racing, particularly in Perth, seemed made for TV.

After we won the Louis Vuitton Cup, Malin Burnham had received a visit in our compound from Arthur Santry, then Commodore of the NYYC. Santry's message was to the point. According to Burnham, Santry said, "Since you people have a good shot at winning the Cup, I just want you to know, it still belongs to the New York Yacht Club."

IT WOULD HAVE been great to have a rematch of 1983. However, the winner of the Defender Trials was Iain Murray and *Kookaburra III*. Alan Bond had been in this game since 1974, and thus, it was a tribute to the Murray-Parry group—a first-time effort—to best so much experience. In the finals *Kookaburra III* beat *Australia IV* 5-0.

After *Kookaburra III* was named defender, Bond told the press, with a lack of equanimity, "Kevin [Parry] has an awesome responsibility." Then he addressed Parry directly, "We won it for Australia, now don't you lose it." Then he spoke to the media again. "If Kevin doesn't defend it, we'll go and get it back for him."

Parry responded, "We were very sincere in what we set out to do—to give them [Bond's group] the best competition possible or to help them achieve their greatest effort in defending the Cup they brought to Australia.

"However, I will not put up with any spite or nonsense. We are dedicated to our efforts to keep the Cup in Australia, and we're entitled to do this by superior technology, superior teamwork, and superior excellence."

Then Parry told Bond, "The fact that you were not good enough in the rundown is just a fact of life . . . We are out there to do our best, and we are not prepared to put up with any needling or spite."

During one of the early meetings of the challengers, it was unanimously decided that we would stick together to defeat the Australians. The Kiwis, in the person of Aussie Malcolm, had been a party to this verbal, if not written, agreement. However, once we eliminated Michael Fay's New Zealand syndicate, they decided to help the Australians. They claimed it had to do with the close cultural and sporting ties between their two nations.

Or maybe, the Kiwis weren't interested in traveling halfway around the world, to San Diego, to challenge for the next Cup. Australia is next door. Perhaps, too, it was pay-back for my intemperate remarks. Come next July, there would be an even greater price to pay for them.

Whatever the reason, this alliance between the Kiwis and the Australian defender was as threatening as a kiss-and-tell book. By this time the Kiwis knew the good, the bad, and the ugly about us.

It backfired, however, because the New Zealand boat proved faster than *Kookaburra*, and in no time the waterfront knew all about it. It was as simple as a syllogism: *Stars & Stripes* was faster than *Kiwi Magic*. *Kiwi Magic* was faster than *Kookaburra III*. Therefore, *Stars & Stripes* is faster than *Kookaburra III*. It was logic I couldn't argue with. I'm dangerous when I'm confident, and at this point, I was very confident.

January 31, 1987, was the first race of the America's Cup. It had been 40 months since I lost the Cup in Newport. To say it was a heady moment is an understatement.

The animosity between Kevin Parry and Alan Bond on the race course, in the protest room, and behind the scenes, had turned many Australians off. Furthermore, the Australians are an exuberant people, and they expect their athletes to be visible, personable, and open. Certainly, the *Kookaburra* crowd was nothing of the sort; they were businesslike, not likable. For them, there were no theme songs, no battle flags, no fanfare. No fun.

On this January morning, however, they lightened up a little and passed out Australian flags to the crowd, who staged an impromptu parade past our compound. I decided to join them; however, I waved the Stars and Stripes. They seemed to enjoy having "big, bad Dennis," as I was known in Australia, in their midst. I know I enjoyed it.

Our tenure in Australia is likely the highlight of my sailing career. Perth was truly "the Home of the Twelves," as Alan Bond once so glibly described his nearby development, Yanchep, Sun City. This ponderous yacht, the 12-Meter, was much better suited to windy Perth than to Newport.

The Aussies were wonderful hosts. I'd hear over and over again, "Good luck, Dennis." I now understood and appreciated for the first time the warm feelings Americans had shown to the Australians in this competition, beginning in 1962. It's a wonderful rivalry, in the best sense of that word. Once, I stopped on the street and bought a newspaper from an Australian kid who recognized me—and wished me well. I asked him if he'd like a ride on *Stars & Stripes*. He showed up the next day, and I gave him a ride.

The only sad part of our stay Down Under was that I received a death threat before the America's Cup match started. Thus, I was forced to hire a bodyguard. He tried to get me to wear a bullet-proof vest, but I refused. My parading with the Australians, waving an American flag, gave him fits.

We departed the dock for the first race of the America's Cup match at 9:40, to the strains of Jimmy Buffett's song "Take It Back." He had written it for us: "Call it pillage, call it plunder, we're takin' it from the boys Down Under."

"It," of course, was the America's Cup.

The only thing that worried me this fine summer day was that the wind was from the east, rather than the west, the latter being the direction whence the Doctor came a-calling. It was a hot wind, off the desert, like the Santa Ana wind in Southern California. Light winds were not our strong suit; in them, our long boat, with its abundance of wetted surface, seemed glued to the ocean.

On *Kookaburra III*, we faced the dynamic duo of Iain Murray and Peter "Crash" Gilmour, as he was now called for his aggressive tactics. Gilmour, who had skippered *Kookaburra II*, would start *Kookaburra III*, and Murray would drive it the rest of the way. This was the same arrangement I had with Ted Hood in 1974. Alan Bond as much as called me "Crash" Conner in that long-ago America's Cup.

Despite Gilmour's cock-of-the-walk reputation, we won the start. It was, however, the shortest line I'd ever seen in any of the previous 17 America's Cup races I'd been in. Like overwatering a football field to nullify a swift back, it was done, I believe, to play to "Crash" Gilmour's strengths. The short line meant he had us and our drag racer, *Stars & Stripes*, on a short leash. There was no place for us to run, no place to hide. When I complained about it, I was told, in essence, what you see is what you get.

At the gun, we were on the left-hand side of *Kookaburra III*, which we wanted. We got the first shift, to the left, and were gone. The winning margin was 1:41. There was the silence of death at the finish. The second race wasn't a whole lot more complicated; with the Doctor in residence, we won by 1:10.

The third race was the most interesting. On the first leg, we escaped a slam-dunk attempt by *Kookaburra*, as the Australian defender couldn't quite get her nose in front of us. Eventually we sailed into a lee-bow position, forcing her to tack away. No boat, Murray would later explain, had broken through its lee, as we did, during the entire campaign. Before the broken slam-dunk, we successfully clamped on two lee-bow maneuvers. It was as potent a leg as I've ever sailed. We won the race by 1:46.

On the final leg, I noticed their chase boat approaching *Kookaburra*, but couldn't figure out what was going on, as this was a violation of the rules. That night at the press conference, after I described the race, Murray addressed the visit. "Dennis explained today's race pretty well, but he missed out the bit on the last leg when our rubber boat came alongside and told us we had a bomb on board. They asked us what we wanted to do. We checked our options list and our immediate response was: 'So what's the bad news?'"

The final race was on February 4. We won it by 1:59, our biggest margin. As we crossed the line, and the gun sounded, I exploded in joy and relief, "Damn, we did it! We did it, guys!"

With this win, I went from the outhouse, to the White House, to the covers of *Sports Illustrated* and *Time* magazine.

Before that, however, there was the trophy presentation at the well-starched Royal Perth Yacht Club. Bob Hawke, the Australian Prime Minister, recalled what Perth was like 40 months before when Alan Bond, Ben Lexcen, John Bertrand, Warren Jones, and others appropriated the Cup. It was, he said, one of the most memorable moments of his life.

There was another memory he had, he said, of that day, "... of a very remarkable American, Dennis Conner," who had just received "a fairly hefty kick in the gut.

"What we remember of that day was the courage and the grace with which you took that blow. It's very difficult for any of us to understand how you felt that day. I offer you and your crew our admiration and our respect and more than that, our deep affection.

On behalf of all the people of Australia, I offer you our unqualified congratulations on a magnificent achievement."

Prime Minister Hawke handed me his Australian hat and asked me to deliver it to President Reagan. The hat sat on the top of the America's Cup, which was strapped in by a seat belt, in first class on the Continental Airways jet that flew the team and me home. The DC-10 was flown in especially for us, and chartered jointly by Continental and Pepsi Cola. I presented the hat to the President. And the America's Cup to the San Diego Yacht Club.

It is, as I've said, a story we apparently never tire of.

CHAPTER 10

1988

THE MOUTH THAT ROARED

—◁∂∅▷—

THE 12-METER WORLDS were sailed in Sardinia in June 1987—
some five months after the Cup competition ended in Perth. This
Italian event—more beauty show than title bout—was won by Michael Fay's New Zealand team, which finished second to us in the
Louis Vuitton Cup (LVC) in Western Australia. If the racing was
low-key, Fay's team proved that Perth was no fluke. I have no doubt
that in the absence of *Stars & Stripes*, the Kiwis would have won the
America's Cup in their debut. That honor, however, would have to
wait for Bill Koch in 1992.

A meeting of the 12-Meter Owners' Association was convened
during the Worlds. Fay had a number of ideas on how to market
the next America's Cup and about the 12–Meter Class. Meanwhile,
he had to be planning his incredible backdoor assault on the America's Cup. Fay shrewdly kept everyone off guard.

After Sardinia, Fay and Andrew Johns, his redheaded attorney,
flew to San Diego. He phoned Dr. Frederick A. Frye, Commodore
of the San Diego Yacht Club (SDYC), who invited both men to lunch
there on July 17. Frye, a busy pediatrician, was late. In his stead, Fay
and Johns were entertained by Doug Alford, the Vice Commodore.
Unable to contain himself, Fay told Alford that the Mercury Bay
Boating Club, his club, was going to challenge San Diego one-on-one

for the America's Cup. The boat would be 90 feet on the water—twice the size of a 12-Meter. Alford, caught unawares, uttered, "I guess we can respond with a 90-foot catamaran." With no disrespect meant to Alford: "From the mouths of babes . . ."

When Frye arrived they had lunch—a pleasant one it was according to all concerned. Then, over coffee, the New Zealanders told Frye that they were looking forward to another tilt at the Cup. Frye said that San Diego would be delighted to see the Kiwis, this time in 1991. "No," Fay corrected him. They'd be coming much sooner than that, in a boat 90 feet on the water. Then Fay and Johns expanded on the challenge. The boat would show a load waterline length of 90 feet—the maximum for a one-masted vessel under the Deed of Gift, the document governing the contest. Its draft would be 21 feet; beam waterline, 14 feet; and show a maximum beam of 26 feet. Racing would commence in 10 months, according to the timing specified in the Deed. With that, the clock started ticking.

Thus, Michael Fay grabbed the America's Cup world by the throat. He became "the Mouse That Roared"—to borrow the book and movie title—or more accurately, the Mouth That Roared. Gone forever were 12-Meters—the boat used since 1958. They were banished to the scrap heap. And gone, at least for this time, were multiple challengers. If the America's Cup is sports most contentious contest, that had to be its singular most combative act.

Unsure of his ground, Frye responded somewhat shakily, "We'll be in touch." Surer of his ground, Fay didn't wait for an answer. By August, if not well before, he commenced building his superboat.

The yacht club was not amused. Malin Burnham, head of my *Stars & Stripes* syndicate, which had been folded into Sail America, just wished the whole sorry affair would go away.

The SDYC didn't formally respond to Fay until August 8. On this day, it, and the America's Cup Committee, rejected the terms of the New Zealand challenge. On August 31, 1987, Fay filed a brief with the New York State courts. For the first time in the then 136-year history of the oldest trophy in sports, the America's Cup entered the legal system, where it would remain for an unhappy and prolonged period.

At this point San Diego had three options: fight, roll over and die, or build a boat to meet Fay. Of course, where the money would come from if we chose to do the latter, no one knew. We were still paying off debts from the 1987 campaign and, so, had no money. Also, we had no community or corporate support at the time.

It was all so clever. Fay had a head start in design; San Diego would be forced to explore new technology on the edge of yacht design and construction, with a clock ticking rapidly to the 10-month deadline. *New Zealand*, the boat Fay ended up building, was 90 feet on the water and 132 feet, 8 inches overall. Its mast was 153 feet above the water, and it sported 17,300 square feet of sail—that is 700 square feet more than *Reliance*. It had wings on the sides to allow the 36-man crew to hike. Forget about the J-Class boats in the thirties, there hadn't been a boat like this in the America's Cup since the Great Sloop era, which reached its climax in 1903 with *Reliance. New Zealand* was a 133-foot skiff—designed by Bruce Farr, a New Zealander living in America. He was one of three designers who worked for Fay in 1986–87. Maybe Fay could afford to design, build, and campaign such a boat in the allotted time, but we couldn't.

I'm not a rich man; the San Diego Yacht Club isn't the New York Yacht Club at the turn of this century. Neither is the New York Yacht Club the New York Yacht Club at the turn of this century.

It takes time to muster corporate support. Typically, budgets for sports promotions are set a year, or even two, in advance. I'm sure Fay, a man who cut his eyeteeth in corporate takeovers, knew this.

Then, I was tired—bone weary. Fay's challenge came only five months after we'd recaptured the Cup in Perth. I'd been chasing the America's Cup practically nonstop since I lost it in 1983—that was almost four years. Before that, I had put in the better part of six years preparing for a successful defense in 1980, and then trying to defend it in 1983. I'd neglected my family, friends, and business. Doubtless Fay counted on my lack of energy and enthusiasm. Then, too, Michael Fay's challenge would keep his name in lights, something he seems not to mind.

The very next day, September 1, the court issued a restraining order, preventing the America's Cup Committee from naming the venue and the dates of the next defense. This restraining order was lifted on September 9. Two days later, the committee selected San Diego as the site for a "normal," multi-challenger America's Cup regatta in 12-Meter yachts in May 1991. San Diego Mayor Maureen O'Connor said the city pledged its full support for the event.

Fay's right to mount his challenge was argued before Justice Carmen Beauchamp Ciparick, of the New York Supreme Court. In addition to arguing against the legality of Fay's challenge, the SDYC wanted the judge to amend the Deed of Gift, to give the defender the right to determine the type of boats to be used and the dates of the next competition.

Arguing against SDYC's petition for the change to the Deed of Gift was the New York Yacht Club (NYYC). Strange bedfellows were New York and New Zealand. This, thinks Malin Burnham, could have been the manifestation of Commodore Santry's warning in Perth that the America's Cup "still belongs to the New York Yacht Club."[1]

Eleven weeks later, on the day before Thanksgiving, Judge Ciparick announced her decision: "... Mercury Bay Boating Club has tendered a valid challenge and that San Diego Yacht Club must treat it as such in accordance with the terms of the Deed."

I was in Australia at the time, on business. Accepting the decision of the umpire, I flew to Auckland, where Fay runs Fay, Richwhite & Company, a merchant-banking business, to congratulate him. He seized the moment and called a press conference. The least I could do was to offer my congratulations. While I didn't know Michael Fay well, he acted like the Donald Trump of New Zealand. Perhaps he is. Nevertheless, he seemed appreciative of my appearance—like the cat given permission to eat the canary. With the canary home-delivered on a silver platter.

On Thanksgiving Day, a half-world away, there was a meeting in San Diego. Tom Ehman, Chief Operating Officer of Sail America, reviewed the judge's decision with Malin Burnham and Commodore Frye. A letter was drafted by Ehman and faxed to Fay. It said, in part,

---

1. Was this, I've since wondered, the start of a friendship between New Zealand and New York that culminated in the latter being named the Challenger of Record for the match in 2000, to be held in New Zealand?

"All design and construction elements, including such items as [the] number of hulls and particulars of rigging, shall be our choosing . . ."

Ehman, whose glib manner masks a keen mind, commented, "We told Fay, 'Here it is. We're playing by the Deed. We might defend in a monohull, a multihull . . . or a windsurfer . . .' Fay said we mentioned everything but a hot-air balloon. We were hoping he would see that his challenge had overlooked a few things; that if we pressed our attack he might back off. It's like SDI (Strategic Defense Initiative). You don't get the Soviets to the table unless you start from a position of strength."

In a December 15, 1987, meeting, three weeks after the judge's decision, Burnham tried to negotiate a compromise. According to Burnham, he told Fay that he should torch his plans; the SDYC would torch its plans, and they would start with a blank sheet of paper. The competing vessel would be a boat bigger than a 12-Meter but smaller than a 90-footer, and the competition would be open to all nations.

"It was obvious during that meeting, I wasn't persuading him," said Burnham, "so in a last-ditch effort, I leaned across the table. I said, 'Michael, I want to tell you one last thing. In this country, we don't take very kindly to sneak attacks . . . If you insist on going through with this challenge, we will use every method not just to beat you but to sink you.' There was no response. He just kind of stares at you."

As warned, San Diego commenced building two catamarans. It was thought that this type of boat was fast enough to beat whatever Fay was building; also, it could be built in the limited time remaining. Further, San Diego believed it was legal under the Deed of Gift— certainly as legal as Fay's 90 footer.[2]

Fay returned to court, where he sought contempt charges against

---

2. Malin Burnham, Chairman of our Sail America syndicate and a former commodore of the SDYC, asked Ed du Moulin, of the New York Yacht Club (NYYC), if a friend of our family, to form a committee to study whether under the Deed of Gift, SDYC could defend in a catamaran. Also on the committee were Harman Hawkins, a lawyer who is also knowledgeable about yachting and the America's Cup, and Joanne Fishman, the yachting writer for *The New York Times*. After 300 hours of study, it was concluded that SDYC could defend under the Deed of Gift in a catamaran with a waterline length between 44 and 90 feet. Bruce Kirby, the yacht designer, pointed out that SDYC could even defend in a vessel 114 feet on the water if it had two masts. This provision is still in the Deed of Gift. "Unfortunately, Joanne could not separate the legality from the morality," said du Moulin, "and she departed."

San Diego for its decision to race a catamaran. On July 25, 1988, Judge Ciparick's court said that such a ruling was premature. She said, in essence, "Go race and come back later." The judge warned, however, that in no way was this an endorsement of the catamaran; San Diego should proceed at its own peril.

The America's Cup is based on "mutual consent," between the challenger and the defender. Recognizing that this isn't always possible, the Deed reads, "In case the parties cannot mutually agree upon the terms of the match, then three races shall be sailed, and the winner of two of such races shall be entitled to the Cup." On September 7 and 9, 1988, Fay's monohull, *New Zealand*, met our catamaran, *Stars & Stripes '88*. I was at her helm. We were very fortunate in having corporate sponsors Marlboro, Merrill Lynch & Co., Inc., and Pepsi Cola USA on our side. It was David versus Goliath, but the America's Cup world had varying opinions on who was David and who was Goliath. The much smaller catamaran won both races easily; the first by 18:15, and the second by 21:10.

WHILE WE WON on the water, there were no real winners in the twenty-seventh defense of the America's Cup. There was blame enough for all. Unquestionably, we'd left the back door ajar, but who knew there was a thief in our midst? Fay is a merchant banker, and his challenge was handled with all the heavy-handedness of a corporate raid on the America's Cup.

Who is Michael Fay—The Mouth That Roared? Fay was just 38 when he challenged for the second time. He hails from New Zealand, an island nation of 3 million people and 60 million sheep. New Zealand is so small and so isolated that New Zealanders consider Australia the "Big Apple." Fay's step-grandfather, a chief justice, described him as "some kind of con man."

Fay was educated to be a barrister, or attorney. His legal career lasted but five months, when he turned to merchant banking. After a year and a half at a firm, he was fired for being a "disruptive influence." He opened his own firm in 1974. It was at this point that his step-grandfather described him so uncharitably. In 1987, when he challenged for the second time, Fay, Richwhite & Company had offices in Auckland and Wellington, New Zealand; Sydney, Melbourne, Perth, and Adelaide, Australia; and London and Hong Kong. A Tokyo office was about to be born. Much of the funding for *New Zealand* came from Fay, Richwhite & Company.

Fay is essentially a "spectator." Wrote Bruce Ainsley in the *New Zealand Listener*, "Who is Fay like then, in the long history of the America's Cup? He is closer to the Australian raiders, the Hardys and the Bonds. But the talk in Fay, Richwhite offices is more of the ancients, the Liptons, Sopwiths, and Vanderbilts. But despite plots on shore, they all competed on the water. Fay's real race is outmaneuvering the Americans before they get to the starting line. . . ."[3]

If a spectator, he appears athletic in an owlish way. He is a lean, boyish, and bespectacled man who bubbles with energy. Like Lipton, he seems even to enjoy the press. Through them, he turned moral indignation into an art form—always taking the high ground.

Fay watched with interest when, in 1983, Alan Bond's *Australia II* captured the greatest prize in yachting. "When Bond won the Cup we were all at the office watching the celebration on television. It was impressive. What a mighty and successful endeavor it was for Bond," he said.

Fay might have gone too far this time, Ainsley suggested before the match was sailed: "We love winners, of course, and if he cleans up in San Diego, all will be forgiven. In the meantime, he tries to hold the public relations line, puts the blame on the Americans, while all the time he is having a ton of fun. The America's Cup is a bloody great mud-fight! And he loves bloody great mud-fights! There's no fun if there's no wild ball. He's on a roll, it feels good."

When you get down in the mud with the pigs, you lose, as a saying, more or less, goes. The America's Cup of September 1988 was a lose-lose situation for me—the sort of thing I hate. If I won in the catamaran, as I did, everyone would say, and some actually did, "There goes Dennis in a cheater boat." If I lost, they'd say, "There goes Dennis, losing the America's Cup again."

---

3. This quote is revealing about Fay, if flawed. Jim Hardy, who skippered *Gretel II* in 1970, *Southern Cross* in 1974, and *Australia* in 1980, was hardly an "Australian raider," and Thomas Lipton never "competed on the water."

I wasn't enthusiastic about sailing a catamaran, at least initially. Like many monohull sailors, I considered multihulls "biker boats"— fast but vaguely unsavory. More roller coaster than sailboat; more "muscle car" than sports car. That is a commonly held prejudice in the sailing community. Such prejudice was, I believe, one reason why our response to Fay's renegade challenge—and that's what it was— proved so abhorrent to so many.

The battle lines between monohull and multihull sailors were formed in 1876, when America was exactly 100 years old. That year Nathanael Herreshoff, who would become *the* legendary American yacht designer and boatbuilder, crashed the supposedly "open" Centennial Regatta of the NYYC with a spidery 30-foot catamaran, *Amaryllis*. Herreshoff would later design and build five winning America's Cup monohulls, including *Reliance*, but at this point there was no Herreshoff Manufacturing Co. in Bristol, Rhode Island, where he would work his magic.

As Herreshoff wrote, "In 1875 . . . I conceived the idea of making a double-hulled sailing boat, by which great stability could be obtained with little weight and easy lines. To make the thing practical in a seaway, I devised a system of jointed connections between the hulls and intermediate structure that carried the rig, so the hulls could pitch and dive independently with but little restraint. These catamarans would sail very fast, and would make 20 m.p.h. on a close reach, also 8 m.p.h. dead to windward. For actual sailing, I enjoyed these craft more than any other I ever owned."

Amaryllis was the first of seven catamarans Herreshoff built. He even patented the design. His affection wasn't shared by others. Despite two victories in the NYYC regatta over the 90-boat fleet, she was disqualified on a technicality: a lack of "accommodations." As the saying has it, "East is east and west is west . . . ," and there has been a dearth of accommodations since.

The next year, 1877, another catamaran, *Nereid*, tried to join the NYYC's fleet. The commodore of the club termed her "an abomination," but the owner argued that the club's purpose, according to its charter, was to encourage "yacht building and naval architecture and the cultivation of naval science." She was granted a certificate to race; however, she was no world-beater. There's even a model of *Nereid* on the wall of the NYYC.

Several friends advised me to avoid the America's Cup of 1988 altogether. Let someone else drive the boat—even organize the defense—they said. Randy Smythe, for example, a leading multihull sailor, was on our team. He'd won an Olympic Silver Medal in the Tempest Class and was a Formula-40 champion—both multihulls. Smythe would have done an admirable job, I'm sure. As would Cam Lewis, a two-time winner of the Finn Gold Cup (world championship) and noted multihull sailor, who was also on our team.

Finally, Malin Burnham, my lifelong friend, and other members of the SDYC came to me and asked me to participate in the defense. After all the yacht club had meant to me throughout my life, it wouldn't have been appropriate to quit just because the prospects were unpalatable.

WHEN WE WON the Cup in Perth, Western Australia, in February 1987, Malin and I didn't immediately name the site of the next defense. A year before the competition in Western Australia started, the SDYC, under whose banner we sailed, was worried about the costs of keeping the America's Cup and staging the next event, should our group be successful. To indemnify them, we had signed a management agreement back in September 1985. The agreement protected the club from financial liabilities of being the trustee of the Cup. In return, we got marketing rights to the event to pay the bills.

Under the agreement, our syndicate nominated an America's Cup Committee to decide, among other things, the venue and dates of the next competition. The SDYC could accept or reject the members we nominated but could not name its own committee. Or so the eight-page document read. Malin and I named an America's Cup Committee made up of local sailors and others from around the country. We hoped the committee would make the best decision for the event. SDYC rejected this committee and tried to name one of its own.

Malin and I hoped that the SDYC, where both of us have sailed all our lives and both served as commodore, and the city of San Diego, our home, would make an emotional and financial commitment to help keep the trophy. The Australian government, for example, gave $50 million for waterfront and civic renovations before the America's Cup in Western Australia. It seemed to have been a worthwhile investment, as Western Australia businesses reportedly grossed $700 million from the 1986–87 America's Cup. Plus, it showed the world the area's abundant charms—a lasting legacy.

When I challenged for the America's Cup through the auspices of the SDYC in 1986–87, less than $300,000 came from the SDYC membership. Thus, I had to turn elsewhere. While we were raising money in other parts of the country, we were often asked if we would consider holding the event in some other place. We'd consider it, we said, but made no promises.

Hawaii, where we trained in preparation for Perth, had been very good to us. America's fiftieth state was also most eager to stage the event. By any measure, it is a wonderful place to sail, like Western Australia, only better. As I said, in Western Australia, the "Fremantle Doctor" only makes housecalls during the antipodean summer months; in Hawaii those raucous winds blow year-round.

In truth, it was never our intention to steal the America's Cup from San Diego. We feared, however, that if we gave it to the SDYC and to San Diego, we'd never get their support after they had our commitment. Who's going to pay for something you've already been given? It wasn't handled well, however: The yacht club was angry at me because they thought I had some conspiracy to take the Cup out of San Diego. I was angry at the club and the community for what I perceived as a lack of support.

As we quarreled amongst ourselves—a "lover's quarrel" might be the best way to characterize it—Michael Fay pounced. The weapon he used was the Deed of Gift. This document is under the jurisdiction of the New York State court system.

The Deed was first drafted in 1857. The original Deed was about 240 words, and it and later versions that became ever more legalistic and impenetrable proved ill-suited to withstand the assault mounted by Fay and his attorney. Before this America's Cup, I doubt if anyone had seriously studied it in decades. I know I never did. After Fay began to beat on us with it, it found a new audience. If tough sledding, the Deed, for that matter Fay's entire challenge, was a history lesson in the America's Cup. That, at least, proved positive.

The original Deed promised: "Any organized yacht club of any foreign country shall always be entitled through any one or more of its members, to claim the right of sailing a match for this Cup . . .

"The parties desiring to sail for the Cup may make any match with the yacht club in possession of the same that may be determined upon mutual consent . . .

". . . The challenging party being bound to give six months' notice in writing, fixing the day they wish to start. This notice to embrace the length, Custom House measurement, rig and name of the vessel."

It shall be a "friendly competition between foreign nations." The conditions specified that the challenger must travel to the competition "on its own bottom."

The Deed was rewritten in 1881—specifically to keep Alexander Cuthbert, a Canadian boatbuilder and yacht designer, from challenging again. Cuthbert's *Countess of Dufferin*, the challenger in 1876, and *Atalanta*, the challenger in 1881, had been unfortunate, lopsided affairs. For example, *Atalanta* lost to *Mischief*, the defender, by 33 minutes on average.

When Cuthbert announced *Atalanta* would remain in New York for another go next year, the NYYC had seen enough. Such one-sided affairs were killing the America's Cup, it believed. Perhaps to members of the NYYC, Canada didn't have the same *cachet* as England, from whence the first two challengers came. The NYYC must have considered Canada—or at least Cuthbert—an engaging, if slightly disreputable, neighbor. For example, to get through the locks, before entering the Erie Canal on his way to race the New Yorkers, Cuthbert's *Atalanta*, more than a foot too wide, was reballasted so it heeled over, and was pulled by mules. Even though reballasted, *Atalanta* barely fit in the locks, and the boat's side and bottom were scraped raw by the passage. By any measure, it was bad form. Likely, the New Yorkers also worried that the America's Cup was in danger of becoming a parochial affair.

So it turned to George Schuyler to amend the deed. Schuyler was a member of the NYYC and part of the original *America* syndicate.

The new Deed was twice as long as the original. It now read

that no losing vessel can return unless "some other [challenging] vessel has intervened, or until after the expiration of two years." More specifically, it banned Great Lakes clubs. A challenging yacht club, it said, must hold races on an "arm of the sea."[4]

The next major rewrite of the Deed came in 1887. It was more than five times the length of the original and read, according to one writer, like a "mortgage."

Wrote Thompson in *Lawson*: "In the old deed the clause providing for mutual agreement on all terms was the initial basis of a match; in the new deed it could not be." Before getting to "mutual agreement," the club had a whole series of new demands. Previously, the NYYC demanded six months' notice of a challenge; now it wanted ten. The club demanded to know the name of the challenging vessel, its load waterline length, beam at the load waterline, beam on deck, and draft—these dimensions, then, could not be exceeded—as well as the type of rig. Also, a custom house registry of the vessel must be sent to the NYYC as soon as possible. It was, some said, tantamount to sending the lines of the challenger to the NYYC for study before producing a yacht.

The result was a brouhaha both abroad and at home. Wrote *Forest and Stream*, an American publication, "The whole future of international racing was, and still is, in our opinion, centered on the question whether the America's Cup . . . is . . . to be raced for on fair terms, or whether it is in effect the private property of the New York Yacht Club, the privilege of competing for it being accorded foreign clubs as a favor and not as a right." It described the new Deed as, "an act to prevent yacht racing."

In a defense of the dimensions' clause in the 1887 Deed, Schuyler, by then an old man, who had been consulted on the new Deed, wrote, "The main reason we ask for the [dimensions] is to know what kind of a vessel we have to meet. I believe the challenged party has a right to know what the challenging yacht is like, so that it can meet her with a yacht of her own type if it be desired." Those last four

---

4. This would prove troublesome to Buddy Melges in the 1986–87 Cup when his *Heart of America* syndicate challenged under the auspices of the Chicago Yacht Club. Melges had to prove to a New York court, which he did, that the Great Lakes are "an arm of the sea."

words—"if it be desired"—would have considerable import over 100 years later.

Schuyler is the Thomas Jefferson or Alexander Hamilton of the America's Cup. He was, in fact, married to two granddaughters of Alexander Hamilton—a Founding Father of America and the first Secretary of the Treasury. When Schuyler's first wife died he married her sister. For those who care about such things, Hamilton's grand-daughters were also George Schuyler's cousins, or cousins once-removed. Hamilton had married a daughter of General Philip Schuyler, of Revolutionary War fame. General Schuyler was George Schuyler's grandfather.[5]

George Schuyler is described in *The Lawson History of the America's Cup* in this way: "Although interested in the business of steam navigation in Long Island Sound, and in the vicinity of New York, Mr. Schuyler devoted much time to the pleasure of outdoor life . . . His interest in yachting was unflagging . . ." Schuyler died on July 31, 1890, aboard *Electra*, a yacht belonging to NYYC Commodore Elbridge T. Gerry. Dead or alive, his name would echo through any number of New York courts a century later. So would phrases like "friendly competition between foreign nations," "a match," and "mutual agreement."

Another historic exchange would have import and ultimately affect the stewardship of the America's Cup in 1988. This occurred after the 1903 match, where Sir Thomas Lipton's *Shamrock III* lost 3-0 to the abundant *Reliance*. Lipton challenged for 1907, but on the condition smaller boats be used. He proposed that the Cup be sailed in yachts of about 110 feet overall and 75 feet on the water.

The yacht club rejected this, as such boats were of "insignificant power and size." It wrote that the trustee (NYYC) could not accept any challenge that purported to add any design limitations beyond those expressly stated in the Deed. In fact, the New York membership unanimously adopted a resolution, which, in part, states, "That no agreement should be made with any challenger which imposes any

---

5. Fort Schuyler, the home of the Maritime College, part of the State University of New York (SUNY) system, was named for General Schuyler. The Maritime College sponsored America's Cup syndicates in 1977, '80, and '83. The latter two times were for *Freedom* and *Liberty*—boats I skippered.

other limitations or restrictions upon the designer than such as is necessarily implied in the limits of water-line length expressed in the deed."

As the NYYC wouldn't budge, you will recall, there was no match in 1907. In 1913 Lipton challenged for 1914. He again asked that the competition be held in smaller boats. The club said that challengers don't write rules, the defender does. Finally, Lipton backed down and challenged without conditions. The yacht club accepted his original terms—the match would be sailed in 75-footers. Because of World War I, this challenge was finally sailed in 1920, when *Resolute*, the defender, barely beat *Shamrock IV* 3-2. In fact, Lipton's boat won the first two races.

Resolute and *Shamrock IV* were forerunners of J-Class boats but they weren't exactly J-Class boats. From 1930 to 1937, J-Class boats that conformed to all class rules were used. World War II ended the reign of the J-Class boats. Even these "diminutive" boats—and that's what they were when compared to the Great Sloops—proved too expensive. In 1956, after a 20-year hiatus, NYYC Commodore Henry Sears traveled to England to discuss with Sir Ralph Gore, Commodore of the Royal Yacht Squadron, whether there was interest in continuing America's Cup racing in boats much smaller than J-Class yachts. This resulted in the 12-Meter era that had its debut in 1958.

Two rule changes were significant. The Deed of Gift was amended in 1956 to read, "The competing yachts or vessels, if of one mast, shall be not less than forty-four feet nor more than ninety." This allowed 12-Meters because 44 feet is about the minimum waterline length for a 12-Meter. ("Ninety feet," on the other hand, would have significance to Fay's challenge.) Also waived was the condition that required challengers to sail to the competition on their own bottom.

The NYYC issued a memorandum on December 7, 1962, saying that in the event it successfully defended the Cup in 1964, and, within thirty days, received more than one challenge for the next match, it would regard the challenges as "received simultaneously"; and "after due consideration [would] determine which to accept." Also, that it expected to defend the Cup in 12-Meter yachts (and would give two years' notice of a change in class); and that it believed that "it would be in the best interest of the sport and of the competition for the America's Cup if such matches were not held more frequently than once every three years."

This removed an important prerogative from the challenger. Before 1962, a challenger challenged and the NYYC responded. A challenger could be working on its design for years, and New York had only 10 months, or less, to meet it. Now New York was establishing the timing—"once every three years"—as well as controlling the yacht, "12-Meters." Also, prior to this memorandum, the club could have been forced to race yearly—something that could sorely strain resources and, even more important, the will to win.

Within three days of the conclusion of the 1967 match, in which *Intrepid* beat *Dame Pattie*, from Australia, New York received bids from several challengers, all of whom agreed to an elimination series of races, with the winner earning the right to challenge New York for the Cup. Thus began the multiple-challenger era. The club made a formal arrangement with a "challenger of record"—one of the challengers—who agreed to abide by the Deed of Gift. This Challenger of Record, in turn, dealt with the other challengers. Similar procedures were followed for each America's Cup match until 1983, when the New Yorkers lost the America's Cup.

To prevent unruly challengers and other embarrassments that had characterized this contest since 1870, the New Yorkers did another very significant thing that only became known to outsiders after Fay's challenge. Before challengers were formally accepted, it had a challenge in hand. Called a "vest-pocket challenge," this challenger agreed in writing to follow the procedures in the Deed of Gift and other interpretations. This way the NYYC didn't have to deal directly with unruly challengers. Being both the competition and the apparent enforcer of the rules has always placed the trustee of the Cup in a difficult position. New York continued to exercise some control with the challenger it favored and considered first among equals but did so more in the background.

Having had 100 years of experience in both defending and running the Cup competition, the New Yorkers were remarkably adept. Had we known about the existence of "vest-pocket" challenges, the litigation that characterized the 1988 match, and the poison it spread, might well have been avoided. (It is interesting that New Zealand used a vest-pocket challenge in 1995, when it finally won the America's Cup. Whom did it turn to? The NYYC—bringing it back to the fore. The club had been sitting on the sidelines for nearly a decade.)

FOLLOWING HIS STINGING defeat on the water, Michael Fay had "not yet begun to fight," to quote John Paul Jones, the American naval hero. Fay returned to Judge Ciparick's court. New Zealand argued that a catamaran versus a monohull was an unfair "match," as described in the Deed of Gift. Further, that the defender is bound to compete on equal terms in a "like or similar boat." San Diego argued the only design limitation in the Deed of Gift was that the competing vessel must be "propelled by sails only . . . and if one mast, shall not be less than forty-four nor more than ninety feet on the load water-line." Its boat fitted comfortably within those two dimensions.

Judge Ciparick saw it otherwise. ". . . The conclusion is inescapable that the donor contemplated the defending vessel to relate in some way to the specifications of the challenger."

Persuasive to the judge was the fact that there are no references to multihulls in the Deed, despite the fact that multihulls were in existence when the Deed was rewritten in 1887. Recall Herreshoff's catamaran *Amaryllis*, which sailed 11 years before, and *Nereid*, which sailed in NYYC regattas in 1878 and 79. Then the judge seemed to lose her way, at least in my opinion. (This opinion was apparently shared by the Appellate Division and then the State of New York Court of Appeals.)

Important to her were these lines in the Deed: "Centreboard or sliding keel vessels shall always be allowed to compete . . . and no restriction whatsoever shall be placed upon the use of such centreboard or sliding keel . . ." She wrote, "The use of the terms 'centreboard or sliding keel' in the singular would tend to indicate that the donor did not contemplate multihulled vessels competing for the Cup." The reasoning here appears to be that a catamaran has two hulls and, thus, typically two centerboards (to use the modern American spelling). Certainly *Stars & Stripes '88* did. If the donor anticipated catamarans competing in the America's Cup, the judge believed the word centerboard would be plural.

One wonders what would the court have ruled if the San Diego catamaran were like a Hobie 16, a catamaran with no centerboards? Or what if it was a trimaran—a three-hulled boat—that typically has only one centerboard in the center hull? And since the organizers knew about multihulls and their speed, why didn't they specifically ban them? More intriguing, John Cox Stevens, head of the *America* syndicate and the first commodore of the NYYC, not only knew about catamarans, he *owned* one, *Double Trouble*, in 1819. In view of these catamarans, George Schuyler had to know about them, too. It seems to me that if he wanted to ban them, he would have. All he had to say was "no catamarans."

Also persuasive to the judge were the lines in the Deed, "This Cup is donated upon the condition that it shall be preserved as a perpetual Challenge cup for friendly competition between foreign countries." The judge determined that "the emphasis of the America's Cup is on competition and sportsmanship. The intention of the donors were to foster racing between yachts or vessels on somewhat competitive terms ... While this may not rise to the level of a 'like or similar' standard, the import is clear from the provision of the Deed ... the vessels should be somewhat evenly matched."

So on March 28, 1989, Judge Ciparick awarded the America's Cup to the Mercury Bay Boat Club in New Zealand. Thus, Fay became the first challenger to win the America's Cup without winning a race. As the headquarters of the Mercury Bay Boat Club are in a small sedan, an English Ford—its horn starts the races—100 miles east of Auckland, one wonders how Fay planned to display the Cup and protect it. Lock it in the trunk?

However, on September 19, 1989, a divided Appellate Division reversed Judge Ciparick's decision. It declared that *Stars & Stripes* was an eligible vessel and the winner of the two races. Referring to Judge Ciparick's decision, the Appellate Court wrote, "In finding that the vessel must be 'somewhat evenly matched,' the court promulgated a rule that is neither expressed in, nor inferable from, the language of the Deed ..."

The court emphasized Schuyler's explanation of the dimensions' clause, following the release of the 1887 Deed. Recall he wrote: "The main reason we asked for the [dimensions] is to know what kind of a vessel we have to meet. I believe the challenged party has a right to know what the challenging yacht is like, so that it can meet her with a yacht of her own type *if it be desired* [authors' emphasis]." Wrote the court, "There can be no clearer expression of the intention of the donor that the defender was not required to meet the challenger with a similar vessel."

Also important was the letter the club wrote to Lipton in 1907. It said, "That no agreement should be made with any challenger which imposes any other limitations or restrictions upon the designer than such as is necessarily implied in the limits of waterline length expressed in the deed."

Fay appealed this, and the State of New York Court of Appeals concluded on April 26, 1990, that there is a difference between whether a contest is "sporting" or "fair" and whether it is "legal." "Sporting" and "fair" are not subjects for judicial review. It decided to view the match in the legal sense only. The issue was, it said, "Whether the donors of the America's Cup . . . intended to exclude catamarans or otherwise restrict the defender's choice of the vessel by the vessel selected by the challenger?"

The court ruled that nowhere in the Deed of Gift have the donors expressed an intention to prohibit the use of multihull vessels or to require the defender of the Cup to race a vessel of the same type as the vessel to be used by the challenger. "In fact," wrote the court, "the unambiguous language of the deed is to the contrary."

The court also rejected Mercury Bay's contention that the phrase, "friendly competition between countries" connotes a requirement that the defender race a vessel that is the same type or even substantially similar to the challenging vessel. It said that neither the words nor their position "warrant that construction."

Rather the court saw the phrase "friendly competition between countries" as a spirit of cooperation. "It was in this spirit of cooperation," wrote the court, "that the competitors had, since 1958, agreed to race in 44 foot yachts [i.e., 12-Meters]."

Then it spanked Fay. "Indeed, it was Mercury Bay, not San Diego, that departed the agreed-upon conditions of the previous thirty years. San Diego responded to Mercury Bay's competitive strategy by availing itself of the competitive opportunity afforded by the broad specifications in the deed." The court returned the Cup to San Diego.

For Fay, not all of 1990 was a loss. That year Queen Elizabeth II knighted him, "For service to banking and yachting."

"THOSE WHO CANNOT remember the past are condemned to repeat it," wrote George Santayana, the philosopher. So what can be learned from 1988 to prevent its repetition? Sir Michael Fay found a loophole in the rules large enough to drive a monohull 90 feet on the water (133 feet overall) through. Fay's miscalculation was in thinking he'd found the only loophole. We found one large enough to drive a 60-foot catamaran through. It's that simple.

Frankly, Fay underestimated us. I was defending the America's Cup—a trophy I hold dear. It is, to me, a line drawn in the sand. "Anyone studying why nations go to war would do well to examine the America's Cup," wrote Bill Center in the San Diego *Union*. I don't find that comparison odious, even though I'm probably supposed to.

As I said at the end of the match to a writer, "We didn't ask for this match. We didn't concoct it—Fay did. Then he said, 'Hey wait! I didn't want you to defend yourselves.' It was an alley fight. He jumped us, and I turned around and decided to fight to the death. I got a little bloody, but we kept the Cup. I had a job to do. I could have walked away and let America lose. It was a thankless job, but someone had to do it. I'll let history decide, and I think I'll come out all right."

Sir Michael, however, would be condemned to repeat the past: This "backdoor man," who came to Perth with a plastic 12-Meter in 1986–87, and to San Diego with a superyacht in 1988, returned to San Diego in 1992, as we will see, with an oddly designed boat that flew and jibed its spinnaker in an unorthodox fashion.

Once the Kiwis came through the "front door," in 1995, they left with the America's Cup. Although by that time Sir Michael Fay— the Mouth That Roared—was gone.

CHAPTER 11

1992

WHEN MONEY TALKED

—⟡—

ONE SALUTARY AND lasting by-product of 1988 was a new boat: the International America's Cup Class (IACC) yacht, that made its official debut in 1991. It was as brand-spanking new and as high-tech as the 12-Meter, the IACC yacht's predecessor, was dated. By any measure, except by perception, the 12-Meter was an ancient warrior.

Despite its technical pretensions America's Cup yacht design—even with its winged keel—has been hidebound since the 1930s, when class boats were used for the first time. It could be described as modern ideas rubbing up against old-fashioned constructs. These were the International Rule, to which the 12-Meter was designed, and the Universal Rule, to which its predecessor, the J-Class boat, was designed.

While the J-Class yacht had a brief flowering in the America's Cup, from 1930 to 1937, the 12-Meter ruled from 1958, the first postwar match, through 1987, the first match not in America. These two classes of boats were used in thirteen defenses, or from the fourteenth defense in 1930 to the twenty-sixth defense in 1987.

If it didn't surface in the America's Cup until 1958, the 12-Meter actually dates back to 1907, when *Heatherbell* was designed and built in England. Even then it was not an up-to-date design. It was a reaction to extreme boats such as Nathanael Herreshoff's *Reliance*, which defended the Cup in 1903. The 12-Meter represented a swinging back of the pendulum.

As noted, the sail area on *Reliance*, the largest single-masted boat ever built, was 16,600 square feet of sail—the equivalent of 8 12-Meter yachts. She was 143 feet, 9 inches overall but a mere 89 feet, 9 inches on the water. Her forward overhang, which provided unmeasured waterline when the boat heeled, was 28 feet. From the end of her boom to her bowsprit, she was 201 feet overall. She was disparaged as a "skimming dish"—more a theme taken to its extreme than a yacht. Indeed, it was Herreshoff who penned the Universal Rule, perhaps to make amends. The rule took overhangs and hull shape into account.

The IACC yacht began with a blank sheet of paper. She would be built of high-tech carbon fiber; the 12-Meter was built of wood until 1974, and then aluminum.[1] (The only exceptions to this were the two fiberglass 12-Meters that Michael Fay's New Zealand syndicate built for 1986–87, and *France II*, which was built in wood by Baron Rich, for 1977.)

With the new IACC rule and this carbon-fiber material, you can build these boats as light as you want, or as light as you dare—witness the sinking of *oneAustralia* in the next (1995) America's Cup. By way of contrast, the construction of the 12-Meter was strictly controlled by Lloyd's—the worldwide insurance concern. That is one reason why so many 12-Meter yachts are still alive and sailing.

The IACC yacht is 20 percent longer on the water than her predecessor, the 12-Meter, carries 66 percent more total sail area, shows 40 percent more draft, and weighs 34 percent less. While not so extreme as *Reliance* and her Herreshoff-designed predecessors, *Vigilant, Defender*, and *Columbia*, every number that produces speed in the art and science of yacht design is pushed toward the limit.

Extremes, however, are held at bay by the rating-rule formula that looks like this:

---

1. If an aluminum 12-Meter didn't appear until 1974, the first aluminum America's Cup defender was *Defender*, designed and built by Nathanael Herreshoff for the 1895 match. Herreshoff's *Reliance* had a bronze hull over steel frames with an aluminum deck. She was called a "damn bronze scow."

$$\frac{\text{Waterline Length} + 1.25 \times \sqrt{\text{Sail Area}} - 9.8 \times \sqrt[3]{\text{Displacement}}}{0.388} \leq 42 \text{ Meters}$$

While there are numerous layers to that fairly simple-appearing formula, enough to fill many pages and enrich many yacht designers, builders, and technicians, the significance of it to the layman is expressed in the plus and minus signs. They show that it is a rule, as are most modern rules, for "horse traders." A designer can trade the amount of sail area and waterline length, which increase speed, and thus get a plus sign, against displacement, or the weight of the boat, which decreases it. In other words, if you're going to go long on the water, with a lot of sail area, you must pay the piper with a heavy boat.

Having praised it, honesty compels me to say that I wasn't in favor of the new boat. In the America's Cup, the only ones who seem to get rich, in sickness or in health, are the yacht designers. Giving a yacht designer a new America's Cup design is like turning over the asylum keys to the inmates. Thus, it should be no surprise that yacht designers, like Iain Murray and Britton Chance, spearheaded the switch in boats.

Even men of great means had sizable reservations. Consider Bill Koch (pronounced Coke), a man with more money than God. Koch, who headed the *America³* syndicate, said, after sailing the first race in the 1991 IACC Worlds, where the boat made its debut in what happened to be tempestuous conditions, "I think the guys that made up the rule that designed these boats are idiots." A year later he amended it slightly: "These are great boats to sail—*if* you are not paying the bills."

THE TRIALS OF the 1992 America's Cup could be characterized as the haves versus the have-nots. There was no dearth of have-nots, on the defense and challenger sides—including yours truly. The finals could be characterized as the fabulously rich versus the fabulously rich. And not only were they powerful and rich—men who could afford to leave "no stone unturned"—but they were practically instant yachtsmen. Just add water, money, and stir.

The American giant, or defender, was Koch, whose personal wealth was estimated by *Fortune* magazine to be $650 million at the time. He runs Oxbow Corporation, which includes energy-producing operations all over the United States. His budget for 1992 was $70 million. Of that, $50 million came from the tax-exempt *America³* Foundation. Sponsors, such as Chevrolet, provided "in kind" products, etc. The balance came from Koch. His effort included four new boats, two full-blown crews, and 150–200 people on his payroll. Every time we drew a bead on him, managed to catch up, Koch reinvented himself with a new and better design: *Jayhawk, Defiant, America³*, and *Kanza*, in chronological order. His third boat, *America³*, proved to be the world-beater.

Fred Koch, Bill's father, ran Koch Industries, a privately held oil business, which is the "second largest closely held company in America," so says *The Wall Street Journal*. The senior Koch built oil refineries for Stalin in the Soviet Union, among other places. In Fred Koch's case, to know them apparently wasn't to love them, as he was a co-founder of the ultraconservative John Birch Society. Today Koch Industries is a $23-billion-a-year company with 13,000 employees worldwide.

Raised in Wichita, Kansas, Bill and his fraternal twin brother, David, were the youngest of four children in, according to Bill, a rather cold family. As he said, "There wasn't much love there, and what there was, we all had to compete for it." From the varsity basketball team at Massachusetts Institute of Technology to the offices of Koch Industries, Bill, who received a Ph.D. from that substantial school in chemical engineering, often found himself overshadowed by David and older brother Charles.

In 1980 Bill and his other brother Frederick battled David and Charles for control of the family business—a "coup" it was called. Siding with David and Charles was J. Howard Marshall II, who held 16 percent of the stock and had been a friend of the senior Koch. Fourteen years later, Marshall, an 89-year-old millionaire who was wheelchair-bound, became better known when he married the 26-

year-old *Playboy* Playmate of the Year, Anna Nicole Smith. He died the following year, 1995.

While Bill and Frederick didn't prevail, the brothers paid the former a reported $470 million and the latter $320 million to turn in their stock and go away. (They went away, but would return in 1995, during the next America's Cup, for another run at the family fortune.) There have been a total of nine different lawsuits that have been heard by 25 state and federal judges, said *The New York Times*. "It is no secret that the courts have become the stage for the unraveling of a family," commented Sam Crow, a U.S. District Court judge.

The challenging giant was Raul Gardini, of Venice, Italy, who built an astounding five boats, called *Il Moro di Venezia*. Gardini was born and raised in Ravenna, an agricultural and industrial center in the Emilia-Romagna region of northern Italy. He was known in Italy as "*Il Contadino*"—the peasant, wrote Jane Kramer in *The New Yorker* magazine.

Gardini owned a palace, Ca' Dario, in Venice that supposedly came with a curse. When he first entered the America's Cup he was head of the Ferruzzi empire, started by his father-in-law, Serafino Ferruzzi. An important part of Ferruzzi, garnered by Gardini in 1988, was Montedison S.p.A., the largest chemical concern in Italy. It was also the second largest privately held company there—after Fiat.

This was no happy family either. In the midst of the 1992 America's Cup, Gardini was fired from Ferruzzi by his wife Idina's family and replaced by his brother-in-law Arturo Ferruzzi, a pig farmer. A "divorce" it was called in Italy. It must have been a "Divorce Italian Style," as it didn't seem to trouble the Italians in the least. More than 20 million of them watched on television Gardini's yacht, *Il Moro di Venezia*, lose to Koch's *America³*, 4-1. Twenty million is one-third of Italy's population, and this was the largest television audience there since 1990.

Sadly, the America's Cup of 1992 proved to be Gardini's last hurrah. A year later, he put a bullet through his head when a warrant for his arrest was issued. The parallels to Shakespeare's tragedy *Othello, the Moor of Venice*, for whom his boats have always been named, were astounding.

Gardini was the tenth suicide in what the Italians called *Mani Pulite*, or clean hands, a political and social upheaval in Italy that focused on big business. He was to be arrested for political payoffs of an astonishing size. It was described in Italy as *La madre di tutte le tangenti*—the mother of all bribes. The bribe was reportedly $140 million.

A question worth considering: Had Gardini been successful in the 1992 America's Cup, would he have been too important to indict? Also, would he still be alive?

Other intrigue entered the 1992 competition. On December 12, 1991, we had television cameras and the media in the compound. As *Stars & Stripes* was being lowered into the water, she wore her "modesty skirt," which covered her keel from prying eyes. Greg Prussia, a crew-member, noticed a scuba diver swimming under the skirt. First, he tried to harpoon the diver with the boat's kelpstick—a long stick used to remove kelp from the keel. When that failed, he dove in after him. Meanwhile, all of this was being filmed by the media.

San Diego is headquarters for the 11th U.S. Naval District. Perhaps it is the plethora of navy installations that makes it illegal to dive in San Diego Bay. So whoever was down there was breaking the law. The diver went swimming off toward Campbell Ship Yard, next door, and Prussia, without scuba tanks, was unable to follow him. Later, under the boat, we found a hollowed-out flashlight that contained what appeared to be a depth-measuring device.

Several of our "ribs" (rigid-inflatable boats), were dispatched to try to find the diver or divers. There were no telltale bubbles, as emitted by a diver using scuba tanks, to follow. That was strange.

While unable to find the diver, one of our team members in a rib saw a man in a pickup truck with wet hair. He jotted down the license-plate number. Our assumption then was that this was just someone who was freelancing, hoping to get some pictures to sell to the highest bidder. That night, the video of the diver and Prussia's dive into the murky waters of San Diego Bay appeared nationally on CNN and on local television. The hometown media speculated that I, considered the "Machiavelli of the America's Cup," staged the event. My motivation was, they said, to prove that other syndicates were spying on us.

One of our team members had connections in the navy. He did

a little checking and discovered that the license plate of the wet-head in the pickup belonged to a Navy Seal, or Sea-Air-Land team of the Naval Special Warfare. The Seals, who do underwater demolition work and the like, are trained and stationed in San Diego. They don't get much tougher than these guys; the San Diego *Weekly Reader* magazine, for example, described them as "America's roughest, toughest, meanest mothers." When Prussia learned whom he'd been tangling with, he got a little weak-kneed.

Was this the Seals practicing their craft on America's Cup sailors or was it Seals, or former Seals, working for a syndicate or freelancing? We wondered. And if they were working for a syndicate, which one? While we had our theories, we had no proof.

ON THE SURFACE, at least, Koch's genius in 1992 was the triumph of pure science—something that he holds so dear. This man, whose doctoral thesis was titled "The Flow of Helium Through Porous Glass," put an exponent after the name of his syndicate and the name of his prized yacht: *America*^{3}. He further highlighted that exponent by informally calling his syndicate "the Cubens"—a name that caught on, first with a smirk but later with admiration.

Eight years before Koch successfully defended the America's Cup, he started racing sailboats in the Southern Ocean Racing Conference (SORC). There he saw Maxi boats racing. Koch purchased a used 80-foot Maxi, *Huaso*, which he renamed *Matador*, after his father's Texas ranch.

For his second Maxi, Koch organized a unique design competition, by asking 20 designers of varying reputations and accomplishments to submit lines for a new boat. These designs were tested in wind tunnels and in a computer-driven, velocity-prediction program (VPP). He also had yacht designer German Frers submit the lines of six of his best-known Maxis. Twenty-two-foot models were made from these designs, and they were rigged and ballasted as small boats. These models were tested on the water extensively against candidate designs. For a man with three technical degrees from MIT, it must have been the ultimate high-tech game.

Eventually Koch built *Matador*^{2}—another exponent. The boat was considerably faster than any boat out there, and Koch spent so much money making it and keeping it so, that *Matador²* ostensibly killed off Maxi racing. She won the Maxi Worlds in 1990 and 1991. Even these guys couldn't keep up with Koch.

The technology Koch used in the designing and building of *Matador²* was groundbreaking and relevant to the new IACC design, as the boats are similar in size and construction. He was, he claimed, approached by every American defense syndicate; there were nine of them at one point. I know I approached him. Rather than being an accessory to me or to someone like me, Koch decided to go it on his own. He hired yacht designers John Reichel, Jim Pugh, Doug Peterson, Phil Kaiko, and Jim Taylor, and technicians such as Dr. Jerome Milgram, a professor at MIT, and Dr. Heiner Meldner, a physicist at the Lawrence Livermore National Laboratory, to begin work on a series of IACC designs.

A lack of interest in "stars," or name-brand sailors, would characterize his America's Cup team and his *Matador²* team before that. It wasn't that way in the beginning, however. Early in his Cup campaign Koch hired Gary Jobson, then and now a television commentator on ESPN. Jobson, who had been tactician for Ted Turner, eventually departed, to "return to his other love, television." Cam Lewis, a Finn world champion and multihull sailor—he sailed with me on the catamaran in 1988—came and went, too. Other helmsmen who passed through the revolving door included Larry Klein—since deceased—and John Kostecki. Alumni of the program had an expression: "Touch the wheel and lose your deal."

Steering his own boat was, unambiguously, what Koch wished to do, even though he'd only sailed for eight years. He took considerable heat from the press and public for this. One profile of Koch in the San Diego *Union* newspaper began with the definition of the word *dilettante*.

Koch, in truth, had stars, but they weren't stars with overfed egos. Most obviously a star was David Dellenbaugh, his tactician. Dellenbaugh made his America's Cup debut with *Heart of America* in Perth in 1986. Of measured words, he is a talented man. When Koch tapped him, he was marketing director of North Sails, the largest sailmaker in the world.

Keeping his ego in check must have been more of a character stretch for Harry "Buddy" Melges, Koch's chief helmsman. Age 62, he had won the Mallory Cup, the U.S. Men's Sailing Championship, in 1959 and 1960, a Bronze Medal in the Flying Dutchman Class in the 1964 Olympics, a Gold Medal in the Soling Class in the 1972 Olympics, and two World Championships in the Star Class. Melges won his first Star Worlds when he was 48. In 1986, he skippered *Heart of America* in the America's Cup when he was 56.

Melges is neither a shrinking violet, nor is he a kid. How he did not run afoul of Bill Koch is a mystery to me. Perhaps he viewed it as a last hurrah to a brilliant career. The America's Cup was one of the few competitions in the sport on which he'd never had much of an impact.

Dellenbaugh characterized Koch's strategy for the trials: "It was always our plan to eliminate *Stars & Stripes* as quickly as possible, to guarantee ourselves two boats in the Defender Finals and a berth in the Cup match."

In Round I of the defense trials *Defiant*, skippered by Melges, beat my *Stars & Stripes* in all three matches, and *Defiant* beat *Jayhawk*, skippered by the rookie Bill Koch, in their three intramurals. Of course, Koch might have been a rookie, but he owned the "bat and ball." *Stars & Stripes*, which finished second, beat *Jayhawk* in our three meetings.

In Round II, we went with our trick tandem, or forked keel, something the Kiwis were trying on their side of the fence in the Louis Vuitton challenger trials. It showed no rudder but two trim tabs, used to steer the boat, on the back of both keels.

In the first race, *America³*, which debuted in this round, won by a monumental 6:23 over my floundering *Stars & Stripes*. With the new keel, the hull seemed at war with the watery world, although it was pretty quick going sideways. Race 2 was a breezy 18 knots, and Koch, driving *Defiant*, beat *Stars & Stripes* by 4:16. This was Koch's first victory over me. In race 3, *Defiant* lost for the first time, to stablemate *America³* by 49 seconds. In Race 4, *America³* beat *Stars & Stripes* by 6:00. In three races, my losing margin averaged 5:33.

It must have been as ugly from ahead as it was from behind because a meeting was held at Koch's compound to decide whether to allow me to make what was termed a "mid-series mode change." This was contrary to the rules. Keel changes and the like were only permitted between rounds unless both syndicates and the defense committee agreed otherwise. Internally, Koch's syndicate voted 14-1 against it. The dissenting vote was cast by Koch, which, of course, carried the day. Koch retained the right to make a mid-series mode change when and if he wished.

While I'm hesitant to highlight it, letting me off the mat is not a good idea—indeed, 1995 would prove that. With my boat back in its original configuration, I subsequently won two races in that round, which I certainly wouldn't have won. These two victories, seemingly of little import back then, allowed me to carry one bonus point into the semifinals. Without that point, there wouldn't have been a sail-off between *Kanza*, Koch's fourth and final word on the subject, and *Stars & Stripes*, my first and only word on the subject. We won it to get into the finals.

Dellenbaugh put this moment into perspective. "You have to look back at it now and say [letting Dennis make the change] was the right thing to do. It was always our plan to eliminate *Stars & Stripes* as quickly as possible, to guarantee ourselves two boats in the Defender Finals, and a berth in the Cup match. As it turned out, we just missed doing that. I think, emotionally, it was disappointing for everyone. On the other hand, everyone knew in their heads it was going to be better for us to race Dennis in the finals than to sail against ourselves."

America³ proved to be a super boat. She was the narrowest boat in San Diego, and this narrowness made the boat very effective in light winds and turbulent seas—the typical San Diego condition. Beyond this, the boat performed exactly how Koch's design team said she would, which gave the syndicate huge and deserved faith in its designers. In later rounds, the syndicate would trust its designers sufficiently to make changes—even radical changes in the midst of playing a winning hand—with little or no on-the-water testing. Yacht design strolling down such a logical path was contrary to my experience. Koch's design team, most of whom were not that well known in our little fraternity, appeared to have a crystal ball.

In a best-of-thirteen final, Koch, with *America³*, won the first three races and four of the first five. By this time, there was a re-volving door in the back of the boat with Dellenbaugh starting her, Melges steering upwind and down, and Koch steering her through the three reaching legs.[2] Then I won the next three races, tying the score at four. Said Dellenbaugh, "We kept asking ourselves: What do we have to do to knock this guy down and to keep him there?"

The ninth race, with the score tied at four, proved critical in the defense trials, with the lead changing hands four times. On the first leg, I was in front. Then *America³* passed us to round the weather mark 14 seconds ahead. On the run, *Stars & Stripes* seemed to have a little better speed downwind, and we got ahead again to round the leeward mark in front by 9 seconds.

On the next weather leg, *America³*, on port, tacked inside and ahead of us very near to the mark. At this point, it seemed as if we'd slightly overstood it. Exhaust from *America³* began to hurt us. *Stars & Stripes* began to sag off the layline and slow precipitously. I went to the low-side wheel at this point and watched in both frustration and admiration as *America³* began her inevitable march into the America's Cup match and *Stars & Stripes* into oblivion. The time difference at the finish was 25 seconds for *America³*. This Cup season proved to be my earliest exit ever. It hurt like a kick to the gut.

THE LOUIS VUITTON Cup, held to choose an America's Cup chal-lenger, began with eight entries: *Il Moro di Venezia, New Zealand, Nippon* (Japan), *Ville de Paris* (France), *Challenge Australia, España* (Spain), *Tre Kronor* (Sweden), *and Spirit of Australia*. Eighty-five races later, the field was reduced by half: the last four boats were excused from the competition.

This must have been a bitter blow for Iain Murray, skipper and designer of *Spirit of Australia*, who seemed about to get what he had always wanted. In 1992 Murray was to be the beneficiary of Alan Bond's largess. Bond, you will recall, had rejected Murray's offer to sail for him in 1986–87, so Murray sailed for Kevin Parry. Their

---

2. The course in the 1992 America's Cup was windward-leeward-windward. Then there were three reaching legs, then windward-leeward. I can't recall a single boat being passed on the reaching legs. They were dropped for 1995.

Kookaburra III easily eclipsed Bond's *Australia IV* to become the defender, before falling to us. Ben Lexcen had died in May 1988, so Bond turned to Murray, who was instrumental in formulating the new IACC rule.

Then Bond got into financial troubles and pulled the plug on Murray and 1992. Forced to go it alone, Murray mounted a low-budget "people's challenge," which translates to no big sponsors. It showed prodigious effort but precious little success. It was a one-boat program, as was mine, which didn't measure up in 1992.[3]

"Of course I was disappointed," said Murray of his riches-to-rags tumble. "So was Alan Bond, I'm sure. We'd started to build momentum. Bond had made a pretty significant investment in development, and all of a sudden the cloth got pulled from under him."

And how. If his America's Cup ship sank in 1987, Bond's business interests and lifestyle sailed on seemingly in untroubled waters. Later, that year, in November, a rare painting went on sale at Sotheby's in Manhattan. The auctioneer announced "Lot Number 25" and then named the painting: "*Irises* by Van Gogh." He opened the bidding at $15 million. It may have seemed pricey but earlier that year Van Gogh's *Sunflowers* had sold for $40 million—a record.

The world had changed, however, since then. This auction was less than three weeks after the stock market crashed on October 19, 1987—"Black Monday"—losing 508 points. There was talk of another Depression.

There was silence when the auctioneer asked for $15 million, but it only lasted for a few seconds. Soon the bidding went upward at million-dollar clips. Finally, *Irises* was sold over the telephone to an anonymous bidder for $53.9 million—a record. That included a 15-percent commission to Sotheby's.

The world waited a year before learning that the winning bid was cast by Alan Bond, the former sign-painter from Ealing who had developed an appreciation for fine art. It was the first Van Gogh

---

3. Of the match participants, Koch built four boats; the Italians, five. The New Zealanders, the other finalist in the Louis Vuitton Cup, built four boats. Of the semifinalists, the Japanese built three boats, and the French, the same number. No one-boat effort on that side made the cut. It was a Cup when money talked.

to go to Australia. Said Bond then, "This isn't just a great painting! It's the greatest painting in the world."

In time, it was revealed that Sotheby's, the auction house that conducted the sale, loaned Bond more than half the money, or $27 million, to buy the painting. Further, the painting would serve as collateral for the loan. The loan was made, speculated *Time* magazine, so Sotheby's could claim that art holds its value in troubled times.

A year later, Bond and his various companies, including the Bond Corp. Holding (BCH), his chief public company, were more than $9 billion in debt. He couldn't pay the $27 million he owed to Sotheby's, so the company rolled it over for another year. Sotheby's, like most of Bond's creditors, was extremely accommodating.

The way Bond purchased *Irises* was apparently typical of how he conducted his business. He used other people's money and paid top dollar for assets. Those who owned such treasures were extremely anxious to help him make the deals. Further, Bond paid top dollar for the dollars he borrowed; that appealed to the greedy side of his bankers until they realized they weren't getting paid. It was, apparently, a house of cards that grew so huge that no one was willing to knock it down. You don't knock a building down while you're waiting in line in the lobby to be paid.

For example, Bond bought Channel Nine television stations in Australia for more than $700 million, turning its former owner Kerry Packer into a billionaire overnight. Packer, son of the late Sir Frank Packer, is quoted as saying, "You only get one Alan Bond in your life." Two weeks before the stock market crashed, Bond bought G. Heileman, a U.S. Brewery, for $1 billion, but by 1989 it was worth half that. He bought the St. Moritz Hotel in Manhattan from Donald Trump at a $110 million profit, according to the former owner. This was supposedly a half hour after Bond first walked through the door.

Describing his foray into the art world, *Time* magazine's Robert Hughes described Bond as a "Billionaris ignorans, a species now almost extinct in the US, but preserved (along with other ancient life-forms) in the Antipodes."

Earlier, the question was posed about Gardini: Could America's

Cup success have saved him? It couldn't save Alan Bond, although it likely delayed his downfall. Eventually, Bond was indicted, and later convicted, of acting dishonestly in a 1987 bailout of Rothwell Ltd., an investment bank in Perth. He had served 90 days in jail before the conviction was overturned on appeal. He was later acquitted in a separate trial.

His legal problems aren't over, however. Alan Bond is presently serving a prison term for siphoning $1.2 billion from Bell Resources, a Bond Corp. affiliate. The sentence was increased from four to seven years upon appeal. He will be eligible for parole in April 2001, when he is sixty-three years old.

Bond was formally declared bankrupt in April 1992. (This was during the Louis Vuitton Finals, where he and Murray had hoped to make such a splash.) He personally owed creditors $598 million.

In 1995 Bond settled with creditors for $3.25 million—or half a cent on the dollar. Long gone was the Van Gogh, sold to the J. Paul Getty Museum. Long gone, too, were the yachts.

It is, as I've said, a story we apparently never grow tired of.

TWO MORE BOATS fell after the Louis Vuitton semifinals: *Nippon*, which had started the semifinal round in first place—a surprising debut for the Japanese—and *Ville de Paris*, sailed by Marc Pajot, the hero of French yachting.

Left were the heavyweights: *New Zealand*, skippered by Rod Davis, an American living in New Zealand, and *Il Moro*, skippered by another American, Paul Cayard. With so many Americans skippering foreign boats, no wonder they call it the America's Cup.

Paul Pierre Cayard was born in San Francisco in 1959. His father, who lost his parents during the war, lived in France until he immigrated to Canada when he was 22. From there he went to San Francisco, where he built sets for the San Francisco Opera. He married a San Francisco girl in 1958, and Paul Cayard followed the next year.

Cayard started sailing when he was eight. At age 12 he reached the semifinals of the Sears Cup, the U.S. National Junior Sailing Championship. That success brought him notice from the St. Francis

Yacht Club, the prestigious San Francisco club in the shadow of the Golden Gate Bridge. The St. Francis Junior Program is like a farm team for future champions.

In 1978 there was a match-racing event between St. Francis and the Balboa Yacht Club. Cayard was invited to participate. "I conned Tom Blackaller, who I'd met once, into teaching me how to match-race," he said. "That was really nice of him. Blackaller was a big deal at the St. Francis Yacht Club; he'd just opened the North Sails loft in San Francisco. I was basically an unknown, just another junior kid hanging around."

Despite almost a generation of difference in their ages, a significant friendship developed between Blackaller and Cayard. After Cayard graduated from college, Blackaller landed him a job at North Sails San Diego, selling one-design sails. Cayard's parents were skeptical about a career in sailing, but Blackaller counseled that professional sailboat racing was about to become a viable career. Later Cayard sailed with Blackaller on *Defender* in the 1983 America's Cup, and on *USA* in 1986–87.

Cayard got a call to sail in Italy on a boat called *Nitissima*, a 50-footer. His decision to go to Italy proved pivotal: He placed second in the Sardinia Cup, and this success, in turn, brought him to the attention of Gardini, who invited Cayard to skipper his *Il Moro di Venezia II*. This 67-footer won two of five races.

When Gardini decided in 1988 to make a run at the America's Cup, he turned to Cayard to be his helmsman. While perfectly legal under the rules at the time, an American skippering an Italian boat proved particularly offensive to Koch, who labeled Cayard a "soldier of fortune" and a "mercenary." I called him, simply, "Cayardini"— but it was mostly for psychological effect.

Suffice it to say there was little love lost between Cayard and Koch, while Cayard would sail with me as my co-helmsman in 1995. I have great respect for his talents. He's an interesting amalgamation of Blackaller, who would die in 1989 of a heart attack while racing automobiles, and me. As Cayard said, "Tom, I think, was more of a natural sailor, and, I think, that's one of my strengths . . . I have a much higher tolerance for practice and testing, which is an attribute of Dennis."

If a soldier of fortune, Cayard learned to speak Italian; he often translated Gardini's words to the press. Cayard, who also speaks French, like his father, seems true to his European roots. He is more a citizen of the world than are most Americans. Being no lucky seed—or not to the manor born—he has to earn a living. Opportunities in sailing are limited and only occasionally lucrative.

In the Louis Vuitton Finals, the Kiwis, who built four boats to the Italian's five, started strongly, going up 4-1—the same quick start as *America*³. Needing but one more victory, they seemed to have their arms not merely around the Louis Vuitton Cup but, if you believed the pundits, the America's Cup.

However, at this point Cayard, taking a page from my book, fanned into flames a technical issue that had been smoldering for 92 days: how the Kiwis used their bowsprit. The issue was first: Does the bowsprit, which helps keep the asymmetrical spinnaker extended, provide an unfair advantage when jibing? Then later: Does it provide an unfair advantage when straight-line sailing? It seems silly now, and about as much fun as a legal brief, but America's Cup fortunes often revolve on minutiae such as this. The war, led by General Cayardini, soon spilled into the protest room and, more important, into the press center.

The Louis Vuitton Series and the bowsprit issue actually began on January 26 in a race between the New Zealanders and the Italians. When the Kiwis jibed their spinnaker for the first time, the Italians protested. Said Cayard, "We're not protesting the bowsprit. We're protesting how the Kiwis are using it for an advantage when maneuvering."

Two rules would figure prominently in this dispute. International Yacht Racing Rule (IYRR) 64.4 reads, in part, "... No sail shall be sheeted over or through an outrigger.... An outrigger is any fitting ... so placed that it could exert outward pressure on a sail ..." Also important was Challenger of Record Committee (CORC) Condition 8.9 that reads: "A bowsprit which exerts downward pressure on a spinnaker pole does not infringe racing rule 64.4."

Careful reading shows the second rule seeks to explain the first one by making a distinction between "outward" and "downward." Also, the second rule was a CORC condition that likely would have no bearing on the match conducted under the IYRR. Indeed, on March 5, the Match Jury, asked jointly by CORC and the America's Cup Organizing Committee (ACOC) to rule on this matter, said the way the New Zealanders used their bowsprit violated Rule 64.4. Further, that rule would be enforced in the match. Nevertheless, the Louis Vuitton Cup (LVC) Jury that night dismissed Cayard's protest.

CORC obviously had a problem. Its LVC Jury and the Match Jury—higher on the food chain—were at odds. CORC could have stopped the Kiwis from jibing this way or even taken points away in protested races. They did neither, however. CORC wrote with a very fine pencil in its Condition 8.9: "... When a spinnaker boom is not in use ... a line which is attached to the spinnaker and is *controlling* [authors' emphasis] the setting of the spinnaker and is led over or through a bowsprit, infringes Rule 64.4."

This was a subtle wording change. In essence, the LVC Jury made it double-conditional. To violate Rule 64.4, a line had to be run through an outrigger *and* be controlling the sail.

Hindsight, of course, beats foresight. Had the Kiwis changed their jibing technique between rounds two and three, when after the March 5 ruling it became obvious that they wouldn't be allowed to maneuver that way in the America's Cup match, they might well have won the Louis Vuitton Cup and the America's Cup. Their boat was significantly faster than the Italians'.

It was another "backdoor maneuver" by the Kiwis, led by Sir Michael Fay. It seemed to be their tragic flaw. Rather than conforming, or coming through the "front door" like everyone else, the Kiwis made a video of how they used the bowsprit when jibing and presented it privately to the LVC Jury, which approved its use. This was highly irregular.

On Saturday, April 25, the Italians led the Kiwis by 4:20 at the final windward mark in very light breezes and a foul current. On the last leg, the Kiwis gained an astounding 6 minutes and 58 seconds to win the race by 2:38. As described, the Kiwis needed but one more victory to win the Louis Vuitton Cup. However, *Il Moro* sported a red protest flag.

The hearing lasted through the night. Eventually, the jury annulled the results of this April 25 race under Rule 8.9. Cayard was not mollified; at the very least he wanted a victory, not a resail, and he wanted the jury to address 64.4, too.

On Sunday, April 26, he turned to the press. At a packed 8:00 A.M. press conference, Cayard, who looked like he'd slept in his face, said, "First, this jury, in my thinking, is consistently in New Zealand's camp on this issue...." Cayard mentioned the video and the fact that a member of the LVC Jury, which made the decision, was the father of a crew-member on *New Zealand*. This man, Don Brooke, subsequently became a rules consultant to the Kiwis, said Cayard. "The point of this whole thing is that the gennaker on *New Zealand* is being flown by a rope that goes directly from the bowsprit to the tack of the sail. The rope which controls the tack of the sail is not led through the spinnaker pole."

At the same press conference, Raul Gardini, head of the *Il Moro* syndicate, told the assembled crowd through a translator that "*New Zealand* has been racing in the Louis Vuitton Cup regatta [in] an unsportsmanlike manner and with the same unsportsmanlike attitude using this bowsprit in this way."

The America's Cup is won "if by land; two if by sea," to paraphrase poorly that immortal line of Henry Wadsworth Longfellow. Cayard knew that. It had been a full night for Cayard in the protest room, and a difficult press conference the next morning; nevertheless, he converted his advantage by winning race six later that day by 43 seconds. It was done on pure adrenaline—something he seemed to be mainlining.

He wasn't done yet, as he protested this race, too. The protest was based on how New Zealand was carrying its spinnaker when "straight-line sailing." That night, with both skippers again in attendance, the LVC Jury dismissed the protest.

There was a hue and cry. The next day Dr. Stan Reid, head of CORC, and the LVC Jury faced the press to explain. Dr. Reid, an Australian physician, said that Condition 8.9 had been deleted. The amendment now follows the exact wording from the interpretation of the America's Cup jury. "*New Zealand* has told me that they will be complying with this amendment in today's race."

America's Cup jury members are like Supreme Court justices— their decisions are rarely subjected to direct questions. That changed this day when Graeme Owens, chairman of the LVC jury, said pedantically, "We do not believe there is a change in the meaning. There has been a change in wording to keep a number of people happy." At which point Barbara Lloyd, of *The New York Times*, asked, "I am confused. If the change in the wording does not change the meaning, then why are the New Zealanders changing the way that they are sailing today?"

What followed was an odd colloquy. "Who said they are changing today?" Owens asked.

"Stan Reid," said Lloyd, pointing out what had been said but minutes before.

"Well," replied Owens, "obviously Stan knows something that we don't."

The New Zealanders did change the way they flew their gennaker that day, April 29. The issue was apparently becoming a huge distraction. More important, and most inexplicably, they changed skippers that day, from Rod Davis to Russell Coutts. The move appeared to be engineered by Peter Blake, operations manager.

It might have made sense for Coutts to start the boat and for Davis to steer it after that, as the "whirling dervishes" were doing on *America³*—but that didn't happen.

Steering *New Zealand*, with its two trim tabs and no rudder, wasn't intuitive. I know that from trying to steer the similarly configured *Stars & Stripes* in the second round. Coutts, while a talented and aggressive match racer who would positively shine in 1995 when aligned with Peter Blake, had only steered *New Zealand* three times in actual races. It was no surprise that he couldn't do a good job of it when called upon in the final races. Coutts and New Zealand lost the next two races and, on April 30, the Louis Vuitton Cup. The sinking was as unexpected as that of the *Titanic*.

Turnabout is fair play, and in the final act, the Kiwis protested the Italians under Rule 75, the Fair Sailing Rule. The flash point was, apparently, Gardini's charge that the Kiwis had been cheating. On the way in after winning the final race, Gardini went aboard the Kiwi tender and offered his apologies to Sir Michael Fay. Sir Michael accepted it, but demanded it be done publicly. He told Bruno Troublé, media director of Louis Vuitton, that he was willing to go back to New Zealand as a loser, but not as a "cheat."

At the press conference that evening, Gardini offered a formal apology. Sir Michael nodded to Stan Reid, signaling that he was dropping the protest. After four months, and 119 races, Reid presented the Louis Vuitton Cup to *Il Moro di Venezia*, which would meet Bill Koch's *America³*. There was little love lost between these two groups.

AND WHAT DID the pundits think of the America's Cup match? Peter "Crash" Gilmour, helmsman on *Spirit of Australia*, wasn't impressed by the defenders. After his ride failed to reach the challenger semifinals, Gilmour stayed in San Diego and studied the defenders from a rubber boat. His conclusion: "The challengers are, today, well ahead of the defenders. In fact, I would go so far as to say, if *America³* and *Stars & Stripes* had been racing in the Challenger Selection Series, they would not have qualified for the Louis Vuitton semifinals. In current configuration, *Il Moro di Venezia* would be five to six minutes faster around the course than *America³* in nine knots of wind, and between three and four minutes faster in 13 to 14 knots of wind."

History would prove the death of the defender was a bit premature. The defense committee, in fact, cleverly changed the length of the legs, as well as the overall length of the race, to invalidate such comparisons.

America³ had a makeover between the trials and the America's Cup match—a period of eight short days. She certainly wasn't broke, but Koch decided to fix her. Who else but Koch and his designers, with their all-knowing crystal ball, would do that? I wouldn't.

Of the 28 IACC boats built for the 1992 Cup, likely 27 of them had carbon-fiber keels. Carbon fiber is stronger and stiffer than steel. However, the material gets its stiffness through a honeycomb core—a sandwich construction that acts like an I-beam. While a carbon-fiber keel doesn't weigh much, it is thick, and thickness, a yacht designer knows, translates to increased drag. This is between the hull and keel and water.

During the hiatus, Koch's designers replaced the carbon-fiber keel on *America³* with a steel one. The steel keel wasn't as stiff—it flagged, or flexed, more under the weight of the lead bulb than a carbon-fiber keel would have—but it presented less wetted surface. Minimal wetted surface was the absolute theme of *America³*.

There wasn't much time to test the new keel on the water. Also, there would be no turning back. The tank, the wind tunnel, the computer codes, and the design team liked it—so they went with it. Only Bill Koch, a man who believes utterly in the religion of science, would have taken such a risk.

As I wrote earlier, I'm all in favor of pooling resources *after* you're eliminated from the competition but not before. In the limited time available, *Stars & Stripes* did help *America³* tune up. It is interesting to note that Bill Trenkle thought the changes to *America³* actually slowed her.

No conclusions could be drawn from race one of the 1992 America's Cup, on May 9. At 30 seconds to the gun, Cayard on starboard tack headed for the pin end of the line. He had a head of steam and should have had a great start. To avoid being early, he had at least a couple of boat lengths before the starting mark to fall off and to kill time. At the gun, however, he was 16 feet over the starting line—a major misstep—and had to recross. By the time he extricated himself, *Il Moro* was at least 30 seconds behind at the start. That was the time difference at the finish.

For the second race, the next day, the wind was again light at 8 to 10 knots. This was one of the best races in the modern era of the America's Cup match—not to be confused with the trials—and, thus, it is worth expanding upon.

America³, at the pin end, was across the line first by 1 second, but *Il Moro*, starting at the committee-boat end, seemed to have the better start on the right-hand side of the course that turned out to be favored. The first crossing went to *Il Moro*, if just barely. Had *America³* been bolder—brave enough to risk a port-starboard crossing—she might have been ahead.

America³ ducked *Il Moro*, and with the duck, *Il Moro* tacked on top of the American defender, executing the perfect slam-dunk. *Il Moro* controlled the defender to the layline, rounding the first mark with a 33-second advantage.

The American boat, able because of her design to sail with a bigger spinnaker, gained on the first downwind leg by sailing a lower and faster course. This is a punishing combination on a run. *America³* jibed first onto starboard for the mark. This put her upwind of *Il Moro*. *Il Moro* jibed back to port first. The defender's first jibe had been unworthy, but her next three were worse—her spinnaker fell limp on each of them.

One more time they came together, *Il Moro* on starboard, *America³* on port. *America³* jibed to starboard, just upwind of the Italian boat, and for the fourth time her spinnaker collapsed. Cayard, to leeward, then sharply luffed *America³*, and a protest flag erupted from *Il Moro* with the claim that the spinnaker of the defender had touched its boat. The protest was nullified, or "green-flagged," by the on-the-water umpires; however, as a result of the luff, *America³* continued almost into the wind and stopped, with her spinnaker flagging, ineffectually. *Il Moro* bore away with speed. It took a full minute for *America³* to refill her spinnaker. *Il Moro* rounded the second mark with a 32-second lead.

That luff could have been a death knell for the defender, but *America³* clawed away at the challenger's lead, gaining 12 seconds on the next weather leg. The time difference, or "delta," at the second weather mark was 20 seconds in *Il Moro*'s favor. On the three reaching legs, Koch's moment in the sun, *America³* brought that down further to 13 seconds.

In a spectacular 30-tack duel in light air on the seventh leg, *America³* eroded the challenger's lead to one boat length. Then, near the mark, *America³* tacked in a vacuous hole, and the Italians regained about three boat lengths. The delta at the seventh mark was 31 seconds. The Italian boat had recovered 18 seconds on that weather leg—but could she hold on through the final leg downwind where *America³* had appeared so potent?

On that last leg *America³* gained slowly but surely. Nearing the finish, with both boats on starboard tack, *America³* was to windward, with mast-abeam, and was hurting *Il Moro* with her wind-shadow. Twice within a minute, *America³* protested *Il Moro* for sailing above her proper course without luffing rights. Both protests were properly green-flagged by the umpires.

Finally, Cayard jibed onto port to keep *Il Moro*'s wind clear. The defender held on for 40 seconds before jibing. After *America³*'s jibe, both boats sailed on port tack. So light was the wind, however, they more paralleled the line than sailed for it. *Il Moro* jibed to starboard to cross *America³* with rights. *America³*, still on port, had to come up substantially to keep clear. Both boats jibed at the same moment, putting *America³* on starboard, with rights; *Il Moro* was now on port. However, with the jibe, the spinnaker on *America³* collapsed completely; this was her fifth unworthy jibe. The crew had to drop the halyard more than 20 feet to clear the sail, which was fouled on the top jumper strut.

America³ tried to cross *Il Moro*, but her spinnaker was still not full. Rather than crossing, however, Cayard jibed to windward of the American boat and bore away for the finish line. As they approached the line, neither boat carried much speed. Cayard, however, was to windward, blocking the American boat's wind. *Il Moro* crossed the finish line 3 seconds ahead. The score was tied at one. This was—and remains—the closest race in the history of the America's Cup. The previous record was a 26-second difference, in 1962, when *Weatherly*, the defender, beat *Gretel*, from Australia.

After that, it was relatively easy, as *America³* won the next three races and the 1992 America's Cup. When it was over, Cayard came close to *America³* to congratulate the crew. He pointedly avoided shaking Koch's hand—even though Koch reached for his. Photographed by many, it proved to be the summarizing moment of the 1992 event.

It was a triumph of science and, yes, money. I, for one, was awestruck by what Koch accomplished in his first attempt. He moved from a blank sheet of paper to the best design in San Diego. "This is a triumph for American technology and American teamwork," Koch crowed after winning the Cup on May 16, 1992.

CHAPTER 12

1995

THROUGH THE FRONT DOOR

———

ON WEDNESDAY, APRIL 26, 1995, *Mighty Mary* rounded the fifth mark in the Citizen Cup Finals 4 minutes and 8 seconds ahead of us. If not in a different time zone, this boat, sailed almost entirely by women, certainly warranted a different area code. At one point, her lead was 45 boat lengths—nearly 3,400 feet. This was a do-or-die race for us, and only 3 miles separated her from an easy victory, and us from oblivion. Our 1995 America's Cup effort appeared doomed.

ESPN, the all-sports television network, apparently concluded that the race was over as it cut to different programming, just as "once upon a time"—in 1968, actually—NBC switched from an important NFL game between bitter rivals, the New York Jets and the Oakland Raiders, to the children's movie *Heidi* when the ending seemed all but written.[1]

Dave Dellenbaugh, the tactician and lone male on *Mighty Mary*, took them left on port jibe for the 4 minutes and 8 seconds it took us to reach the weather mark. Sure this jibe was favored, but why

---

1. With 65 seconds left, the Jets led 32 to 29. Then, while out of sight and out of mind, the Raiders came back to win it 43-32. This became known as the "Heidi Game." To be fair, ESPN transferred its coverage from ESPN to ESPN2—its sister station. However, the latter station was new, and thus seen on far fewer cable outlets.

he didn't split the difference—go 2 minutes on port and the same on starboard, to put *Mighty Mary* back in the middle of the track at about the time we rounded the mark—I don't know. Dellenbaugh commented later that the battens on *Mighty Mary*'s mainsail often didn't flip in a light-air jibe. This meant the mainsail would be flying inside out and act as a brake rather than an accelerator.

As we reached the mark, I told the crew, "Stranger things have happened . . ." We did a bear-away set and soon after jibed to starboard where there was more, if certainly not much, wind. As we made that turn, *Mighty Mary* turned with us in an awful last tango where only one partner would be left standing. It was a dance to the death.

When we turned again for the first cross, we'd cut her lead. We'd found more breeze. This allowed us to sail lower and faster. What followed then were two crossings that saw us close the gap ever farther. This was helped inordinately by the crew of *Mighty Mary*, who, perhaps because of the mounting pressure, did a series of leaden jibes.

Halfway down the leg we started to roll over them to weather. To prevent this, *Mighty Mary* luffed us. A mast-abeam call curtailed that defensive move, and we passed her—the first time we were ahead in this race. Then her gennaker collapsed. However, our into-the-wind response to her luff turned a small hole in our gennaker into a complete luff-to-leech blowout. Like wind rushing from a ripped balloon, our lead and, perhaps, our America's Cup run appeared lost again. The crew of *Stars & Stripes* responded with another gennaker in 40 seconds, however. The glad rags were hacked away along with the halyard. We hardly missed a beat. Thereafter, we covered their boat jibe for jibe.

We crossed the finish line 52 seconds ahead of *Mighty Mary*, which had waged a Herculean battle. We were almost giddy. "God must like *Stars & Stripes*," I said then.

"Is that the race of a lifetime or what?" asked Paul Cayard, my co-helmsman.

ESPN's Jim Kelly described me as a "Houdini with a keel." Adrian Karsten, also of ESPN, described this race as "the greatest comeback in America's Cup history." Unfortunately, no one cried,

"Cut! Print it! That's a wrap!" because New Zealand's *Black Magic* and the America's Cup match lurked ominously over the horizon.

FOR ME THE twenty-ninth defense of the America's Cup in 1995 was a roller-coaster ride: towering highs and bruising lows; for a group of women sailing for Bill Koch under the banner of *America³*, it was a historic ride; for others—the French, Spanish, and one of two groups from Australia—it was practically a nonstop voyage to oblivion; for the John Bertrand–led *oneAustralia*, it was a shockingly quick voyage to the bottom of the deep, blue sea; but for an inspired and focused group of Kiwis, representing the Royal New Zealand Yacht Squadron (RNZYS), it was practically dead-solid perfect.

In 1995 seven syndicates from five nations descended upon San Diego with the hopes of wresting the "auld mug" from the San Diego Yacht Club (SDYC), its ambivalent keeper. The challengers collectively built 11 new boats. Three syndicates vied to be the defender— the San Diego Yacht Club's standard-bearer. They built three new boats, and one, *Mighty Mary*, didn't race until the fourth round. For the challengers, there was certainly strength in those numbers. Sadly, we defenders sailed in our little world, only vaguely aware of what was percolating elsewhere. It was reminiscent of 1986–87, when the Australian defender, *Kookaburra III*, was so overwhelmed by the challenger, my *Stars & Stripes*. The reason the Australians failed in 1987, and the SDYC failed in 1995, were the same, too: internecine battles that sapped the defense.

As opposed to helping the defenders, the yacht club seemed more interested in being a proper host and then sending the guests on their merry way. So what if they stole the silver! Lacking firm leadership, we beat each other up unmercifully. It was as inappropriate as a brawl at a wedding.

In keeping with an ugly end, it was an inauspicious beginning for the defenders. A week before the trials were scheduled to begin, a wicked wind whipped through the compound of PACT or *Young America*, as they also called themselves, strewing destruction in its path. One of its sails, which weighed 90 pounds, was found a mile away in the Sea World parking lot. Another sail, a new and unused carbon-fiber North 3DL mainsail, valued at about $50,000, was wrapped incongruously around a tree, like a fabric sculpture by wrap-artist Christo. The boat, but a few days from its christening, was blown off her cradle. This caused consequential damage to the hull.

PACT was an acronym for Partnership for America's Cup Technology, a group spawned by John Marshall, my design chief in two earlier America's Cups, and my mainsail trimmer in 1980 and 1983. In 1992 the two defense efforts supported PACT, financially if not enthusiastically. Certainly Bill Koch, skipper of the victorious *America³* in 1992, was not enthusiastic about supporting PACT. This time PACT was a full-blown syndicate—sprung not a little from Bill's and my support in 1992. It was like having a child that seems intent on destroying its parents.

Their boat was decorated by that incongruous (at least in my opinion), if eye-catching, Roy Lichtenstein mermaid. What that mermaid had to do with high technology or the America's Cup I could never fathom. Their tender was painted a patriotic red, white, and blue, and was called *Old Glory*. They were "old"; they were "young"; they were a blue and yellow mermaid; they were "red, white and blue." I mean: Who were these guys? That question could ultimately be asked of their uneven performance, too.

These were innocent days in the timeline of the America's Cup, and in the interest of good sportsmanship, *America³* and my Team Dennis Conner agreed to reschedule our races to give PACT, again led by Marshall, more time for repairs. Said *Young America* skipper Kevin Mahaney, "I think the other defenders understood the severity of our circumstances and exhibited great sportsmanship in agreeing to reschedule the races." Mark those words.

Young America's tornado was one act—not the first, and certainly not the last—of the demolition derby that characterized the 1995 America's Cup. This edition had chills and spills galore. Two months before the racing started, the first boat of the Nippon challenge, from Japan, was dismasted. Marc Pajot's *France 2* was next to fall from grace when this boat, France's first of two, fell from the crane and landed on the concrete, doing $1.5 million worth of damage.

The inauspicious beginning continued for defenders when *Stars & Stripes* and *America³*, the boat that preceded *Mighty Mary*, were blown off the race course on January 12, the first day of racing, because of high seas. Then on January 13—Friday the thirteenth—we were beaten by *America³*, "the women"—a rubric that followed them through much of the competition.

Bill Koch's plan to field an all-women's crew in the America's Cup was audacious, to be sure. I don't pretend to know Bill's innermost thoughts, but it would keep him before the cameras, something he seems to enjoy. The Sunday, November 20, 1994, *The New York Times* reminded us that Koch was again involved in a lawsuit with his family back in Kansas, this time for $1 billion. Koch admitted that such a politically correct gesture like the all-women's defense might enhance his image with the jury. In 1992 Koch was named "Kansan of the year" for winning the America's Cup as well as for charitable contributions that included the Wichita Boathouse.

Whatever his motives, it made wonderful sense from a marketing standpoint. He sold it well and brought a number of new and unlikely sponsors, like *Glamour* magazine, Yoplait yogurt, Gillette Dry Idea (deodorant), and L'Oreal (bottled hair color), to the ball. He then recruited a number of well-respected women sailors, like Dawn Riley, J. J. Isler, Leslie Egnot, Annie Gardner-Nelson, Courtenay Becker-Dey, and Susie Nairn.

For the strength positions, like the grinders, he recruited Olympic rowers and even, for good measure, if for an abbreviated stay, a bodybuilder, whose *nom de guerre* was "Siren." She made her living on the *American Gladiators* television show.

Their motto, "We Can Do It!" appeared on ubiquitous T-shirts accompanied by a "Rosie the Riveter" graphic. For you who missed World War II, Rosie appeared on posters aimed at recruiting women to work in factories to build war goods while their men were off fighting the war. I don't think Koch really cared, at least in the beginning, whether his team won the 1995 event or not. Bill has never been enthusiastic about the San Diego Yacht Club's stewardship of the Cup. He believes he was ill-treated by the club, and I was its favorite son. That was Bill's complaint about his own family, as well. Perhaps he figured, why win it for them? That will only prolong the agony. If the Cup was lost, he could go win it back and situate it in a place more to his liking.

In words that came to haunt him, he solemnly avowed to ESPN's Jim Kelly that he would never put a man aboard the boat. Said Koch, "This team is dedicated to a principle, and we're going to see it through."

"You told them that?" asked Kelly, sounding like a prosecutor.

"Absolutely!"

"And they're buying it?"

"You can play this tape the first of May, and the answer is the same: You will not see a man on this boat."

Video tape doesn't lie—you can't claim to be misquoted—and once the all-women's sanctuary was violated by a man, the red-bearded David Dellenbaugh, Bill's words were aired time and again.

Only three women had ever sailed in the America's Cup match: Hope Goddard Iselin sailed aboard such successful defenders as *Defender* in 1895, *Columbia* in 1899, and *Reliance* in 1903. The wife of syndicate head, C. Oliver Iselin, she sailed aboard these behemoths as timekeeper. During the J-Class era, Phyllis Brodie Gordon Sopwith sailed in that same position aboard *Endeavour* in 1934 and *Endeavour II* in 1937, alongside her husband, T. O. M. Sopwith, the famous British aircraft manufacturer. Also, Gertie Vanderbilt sailed with her husband, Harold S. "Mike" Vanderbilt, in 1934, on *Rainbow*, which nearly lost the America's Cup that year, and aboard the speedy *Ranger* in 1937. Mrs. Sopwith and Mrs. Vanderbilt faced each other in these two Cups, 1934 and '37, making these the only two America's Cup matches where a woman sailed against another woman.

In the 1992 trials, Dawn Riley worked the pit (raising and lowering sails) for Bill Koch's *America³*; she didn't sail in the match, however, which, perhaps, shows Bill's conversion to the women's movement was a recent one. Then, Christy Steinman, who sailed as backup navigator on *Freedom* in 1980 and *Liberty* in 1983, and Dory Street Vogel, who sailed in that same position on *Stars & Stripes* in 1986–87, sailed in the trials but not the match like Riley. I skippered the latter three boats.

That Friday the thirteenth, victory over us proved to be *America³*'s only victory in the first round. On January 29, *America³* won the first race of the second round, this time against *Young America*. That proved to be her only win in the second round. Then *America³* beat us in the first race of the third round. Again, *America³* didn't win another race in that round.

It was then we began to hear rumblings that *America³*, "the women," weren't "one for all and all for one." A male coach for *America³* actually told us the problems had to do with leadership and the decision-making process. At least some of the women weren't comfortable, he said, taking orders from other women. As if it were an anthropological curiosity, he advanced the theory that when men are put in a group, inevitably a leader will come forward; a pecking order will emerge. All the men will work together toward whatever the goal is. Women, on the other hand, he claimed, don't want strong leaders. They all want to have their individual space, don't want anyone telling them what to do, and they break up into all these little cliques. This coach claimed that a number of the women on *America³* seemed to gravitate more to the grinders and others in the strength positions than to the leadership at the back of the boat.

J.J. Isler, the tactician on the boat, an Olympic silver medalist, and the wife of Peter Isler, ESPN's sailing commentator, was the focus of at least some of this attention. Before her, Annie Gardner-Nelson, an Olympic medalist, a strong leader, and the wife of Bruce Nelson, rival PACT's chief designer, had received similar attention before being knocked down to B-boat status.

Then, on March 18, David Dellenbaugh joined *Mighty Mary* as tactician and starting helmsman. Dellenbaugh, who did these same jobs for Koch in 1992, replaced J. J. Isler. It was done, Koch explained, "to strengthen the experience at the back of the boat . . ."

After Koch announced this change at a team meeting to a surprised group, he tactlessly passed out designer scarves. It was an awkward gesture by an awkward man.

Replacing J.J. with a man was for some the shot heard 'round the world. Bill claimed the women came to him and proposed the change. Many of them later denied that.

Said Koch, "After the last round several of the women came to the management and asked us to do something to improve their lack of experience in the America's Cup. We looked at our objectives. Are we here to win or [to] further the cause of women's sailing? We decided we were here to win, and we made our choice.

"The afterguard chemistry, experience, and mix is absolutely critical to getting the best out of the boat.

"We talked to a number of our sponsors this morning, including one that has a contract with us precluding us from putting a man on the boat, and they were all supportive.

"I sought advice from a number of prominent women, including the governor of Kansas [Joan Finney]. They all said, do what you have to do to win and ignore the torpedoes and don't read the press for two weeks."

Then, in an unfortunate metaphor, Koch told John Phillips, of Reuters, about a caribou hunting trip in Alaska. He saw "the cows, the females, were all moving together . . . and they were all supporting and nurturing each other and looking after each other's calves.

"Whereas the bull would be . . . spending all day butting one bachelor away from his herd." That shows "men are extremely competitive with one another. One man has to be top dog . . . Whereas the women want to nurture."

Later, Riley, captain of the women's team, and the skipper of *Heineken*, an all-women's effort in the 1993–94 Whitbread Round the World Race, sounded a similar, if better reasoned, refrain. Or maybe it was just coming from a more credible source. She told Reuters's Phillips that women aren't emotionally suited to skipper an America's Cup yacht. They don't take readily to a chain of command, like men do. They are more comfortable running things by committee. Also, women don't leave negative things that happen on the boat, like men tend to do. Rather, they take it home and stew about it.

My guess is that Bill brought a man in because he started enjoying what he had wrought and saw clearly that maybe they could "Do It!" All it involved was a little tinkering with the concept. His new boat, *Mighty Mary*, was about to be launched and optimism must have been spilling over there. The new boat was named for Bill's mother, whom he and brother Frederick sued in 1988 for $10 million when she was dying of cancer. She, in turn, disinherited them. Explaining this unlikely choice, Koch said, "I did not have the best relationship with my mother. This is my way of paying tribute to motherhood as well as to her. She did the best she could."

With Dave—the "bearded lady"—in the crew, the new boat went from being *Mighty Mary* to *Mostly Mary*—a joke ESPN's Jim Kelly couldn't tell often enough.

I think Bill also wanted to prove to himself or to the world that his latest yacht was a worthy successor to his previous one, *America³*—that "triumph for American technology and American teamwork." Finally, I don't think he could tolerate losing, going quietly into obscurity.

In casting an infringer—and infidel—Koch could have done far worse than Dellenbaugh. He is a man who likes, respects, and lives surrounded by women: his wife, Susan, and their two young daughters. After graduating from Cornell University, he drove a school bus in South Boston in the 1970s, when the courts ordered the schools to be desegregated there. He did it because he believed in the cause. Dellenbaugh has to be the world's most politically correct sailor.

WHAT DROVE PACT skipper Kevin Mahaney was equally perplexing. Jerry La Dow, my syndicate head, had a conversation with Mahaney that struck him as odd. At a party Mahaney came up to him and said that as far as he was concerned, it didn't matter if *Young America* won another race, as he'd accomplished all his goals. Jerry stopped him and said, "What are you talking about? Aren't you here to win?" Mahaney said no, that his goal was to form a syndicate. He then related how he had approached John Marshall about being his syndicate's head, but Marshall had turned him down. But his persistence had persuaded Marshall to reconsider. In view of such humble goals, it is not surprising that PACT, or *Young America*, practically invincible up to the finals, proved deficient in the end. Indeed, all the defenders did.

The challengers had their moments and issues, too. The French, under Marc Pajot, an Olympic medalist and world champion in ocean-girding multihulls, have enjoyed relatively successful runs at the America's Cup. In 1986–87 Pajot made the final four with his 12-Meter *French Kiss*. He got equally far in 1992 with the IACC yacht *Ville de Paris*. Pajot had the largest budget in 1995: 200 million francs, or $40 million—much of it public money. Nevertheless, for Pajot and for France it proved to be another Waterloo.

After rebuilding *France II*, the boat they dropped in December, they further modified it extensively between Round I and Round II. The boat emerged from the shed, before the second round started on January 29, with flaps on the keel's trailing edge to minimize drag. However, the measurer rejected them. "We did seek clarification of the ruling during the design period," said a spokesman. "Perhaps we were not clear enough . . . We did not want to let anyone know exactly what we were doing."

This boat would later capsize when its keel fell off during training on February 20. By this time, however, it had been replaced by *France 3*. Then, *France 3* was dismasted on March 5—"Black Sunday," as it came to be called.

With so much of it public money, and so little to show for it, the budget of the French syndicate was under scrutiny by the French press and sponsors, like Jean Michel Tissier, head of Stardust Marine, which owned Pajot's two boats. Tissier wondered where the money had gone. The French built 120 sails when only 45 could be used. Also, the sails were handmade, paneled sails, while the most successful syndicates used North's 3DL molded sails. The articles further alleged that sponsors paid 80 million francs to build and equip two boats that actually only cost half that much.

When the French didn't make it into the Final Four, or semifinals, in 1995, Pajot's house in La Baule, France, was defaced with the graffiti: "Pajot, you're no good," and "Pajot, you're the shame of French yachting." Perhaps it loses something in the translation.

On that same day, March 5—Black Sunday—we raced *America³*, "the women." Before the start, Ralf Steitz, a foredeck-man on our boat, was aloft repairing the mainsail. With the mast carving large ovals in the sky, Steitz lost his footing and swung back into the backstay, where he hung upside down for an agonizing time. Greg Prussia went aloft and righted Steitz, and both returned safely to the deck. Nevertheless, we dropped out of this race at the end of the second leg. Like the French dismasting, this was but a footnote on this weighty day.

Certainly the most dramatic failure of the day, and undoubtedly ever, in the America's Cup, struck *oneAustralia*, skippered by John Bertrand, who had bested me in 1983. The wind was in the 20-knot range, and the seas were about 7 feet. After winning the IACC Worlds in 1994 with his first boat, the Bertrand-led Australians seemed off the pace. Their second boat started fast, however, winning three races and almost beating the invincible *Black Magic*—the race wasn't decided until the final leg.

Before the start, Bertrand shared his opinion with the race committee that conditions weren't appropriate for racing. A corresponding sentiment was proffered by the crews of *Black Magic* and *France 3*. However, Race Committee Chairman Pat Healy, whose committee boat was a mile away, saw things differently: "Before the racing, we were looking at 14 to 16 knots, within the criterion we have agreed to sail in [20 knots].

"A number of boats called and asked us to consider not to sail. In that situation you have to make a discretionary call, but as long as winds are within the agreed criteria, we should go ahead and start racing."

Bertrand said that *oneAustralia* came off a wave, and they heard a cracking sound. "It was a sickening sound as the boat broke in two, and it was obvious a major disaster was taking place."

Bertrand continued at the press conference that followed this race, "Half the crew went forward as the boat was folding through the center, and the remaining team went to the stern. The boat was unzipping in front of our eyes—the sound of an unzipping. We abandoned the yacht." Chase boats from *oneAustralia* and *Black Magic* began picking up the sailors. "About half of the team was still in the water when the tip of the mast disappeared. I remember watching the wind gear and the carbon-fiber sensor at the top of the mast just disappear under the ocean. It was just unbelievable."

Bertrand promised to return another day. "It's all about adversity. Australia is renowned for adversity. This is a tough blow to the program, but we come from very strong stock. We have to focus all our energy into our first boat; we have to go on with that equipment and win the America's Cup."

So the Australian second boat—or was it their third?—went to the bottom of the deep, blue sea in under three minutes.

The previous Cup, in 1992, had been the year when money talked. With a reported budget of $70 million, Koch built four boats in his winning effort. The Italians built five boats but lost the Cup. The New Zealanders built four boats but lost to the Italians. To keep costs in check, a limit of two new boats that would be *eligible* for the America's Cup was imposed.

There were at least two problems with this rule, however. First, when boats could be modified so extensively, were they still the same boat? *Nippon 94*, for example, underwent major—not just cosmetic—surgery following the 1994 World Championship in San Diego. She emerged from the shed with a new bow, stern, and underbody and was wholly unrecognizable from the previous design. On the eve of the second round, and with *Nippon 95* on its way to San Diego, the Japanese were protested by Team New Zealand, led by Peter Blake, who picked up the pieces from Sir Michael Fay. (Blake worked for Fay in 1992.) New Zealand maintained that the reworked *Nippon 94* was this group's second boat, and thus, the new boat was ineligible. The International Jury dismissed the protest on a technicality, however. They said the Kiwis didn't file it in a timely fashion. Said Sean Reeves, rules adviser for Team New Zealand, "It is unacceptable that the jury uses technicalities to avoid dealing with issues that are crucial to this regatta." It was gutless, in my opinion.

The second problem was equally as complex: What would happen if two challenging syndicates came from one country, and the same principals designed and built all the boats? Where does one syndicate end and the other begin? And is one syndicate but a puppet, or front, for the first?

Enter a compatriot of Bertrand's, the 68-year-old Syd Fischer, who has been involved in the America's Cup wars since 1983. His efforts, which included *Advance* that year, *Steak 'n Kidney* in 1986–87, and *Challenge Australia* in 1992, were primarily self-funded—more a gentleman's efforts—and not particularly successful. After 1992, it seemed as if he'd had a bellyful. Fischer commented, "I don't think I could do another one. I'm too old. It knocks you around too much."

However, it's certainly a gentleman's prerogative to change his mind, and Fischer was back in 1995 with *Sydney 95*, a boat designed by Fluid Thinking and built by John McConaghy. The two *one-*

Australia boats belonging to John Bertrand were designed and built by the same entities. In Australia, they'd trained together, and in San Diego, their compounds in Mission Bay were next to one another. More than a few of us, both challengers and defenders, wondered if *Sydney 95* wasn't Bertrand's first boat. If it was, then Bertrand had circumvented the rule and built three boats.

An October 1994 protest unleashed the Trustees Committee—those august, wise men, representing the New York Yacht Club, Royal Perth Yacht Club, and the San Diego Yacht Club. Being august, they bounced it back to the International Jury, led by Britain's John Doerr, who found no evidence of collusion.[2] After *oneAustralia* ducked under the waves, more than a few of us wondered if perhaps a higher authority saw things differently.

Beyond a Two-Boat Rule, there was, as mentioned, a 45-Sail Rule to keep costs in check. Since 11 of its first-line racing sails had gone to the bottom with its boat, the Australians asked for permission to build extra sails. To do this, they would need unanimous support from all the challengers and defenders. Chris Dickson's *Tag Heuer* challenge from New Zealand, and all three defenders, wouldn't agree. Said Dickson, "We are in favor of looking at a change of ruling in the case of an incident occurring outside of a team's control . . . When the opposition tries to make gains in design and construction those gains are not without risk. We believe that if *oneAustralia* had more sails it would be an unfair advantage in this situation."

However, in the America's Cup, as in life, what goes around often comes around. A similar occurrence would nearly sink my campaign—literally and figuratively—a few weeks later.

Around this time, an issue that had been smoldering on the table from the word *go* flared. This was the contention of the SDYC, the trustee of the Cup, and America's Cup '95, SDYC's organizing body,

---

2. The Two–Boat Rule recognized that there was no way to prevent a syndicate from building any number of IACC-*type* yachts as trial horses. What the rule endeavored to do was to limit the number of America's Cup–*eligible* yachts. Before a boat was built, the syndicate was to supply the measurer, in this case Ken McAlpine, with the lines drawing. This boat would be given a sail number, as would a second boat, with accompanying lines plans, if desired. Any other boats would *never* be eligible to sail in the America's Cup. In hindsight, it might have been more advantageous to protest Syd Fischer, who seemingly got a sail number for one of these boats, than Bertrand, and to let Fischer and Bertrand fight it out. That would have been interesting.

that it could name "Either Citizen Cup Finalist as its AC XXIX Defender." I wasn't the one who pushed this, at least not initially.

The Notice of Race and Conditions Governing the Races for America's Cup XXIX contained the language: "AC '95 agrees to name the yachts in the finals of the Citizen Cup Defender Selection Series and provide a copy of the front page of each yacht's valid IACC measurement certificate to SDYC prior to 1200 on April 8, 1995 and agrees to have these nominated yachts to participate in an unveiling ceremony on April 9, 1995. One of the yachts so named shall be selected by SDYC to represent it in the America's Cup match... Prior to 1800 on May 1, 1995, the CORC [Challenger of Record Committee] shall be informed in writing of the yacht so selected to defend the America's Cup."

From May 1993 on, every subsequent draft of the document contained those words, and CORC never objected to it. On the other hand, the document continued, "CORC shall have the right to name the challenging club and its challenging yacht at any time provided that: (a) its yacht won the Challenger Selection Series."

Then, in March 1995, the challengers must have finally understood the import of these words, because their combative leader, Ernie Taylor, an Australian, and Chief Executive Officer of the Challenger of Record Committee, objected strenuously. He was quoted as saying: "We made an agreement to level the field. Now the San Diego Yacht Club [Defense Committee] are saying either of the boats in the defender trials can go forward into the match. We're in disagreement and have taken it to the Trustees Committee."

Warming to the subject, Taylor told the press that the San Diego Yacht Club was killing the America's Cup. The Cup's very survival depended upon the SDYC losing it, he warned. Like in bra-burnings of yore, he then tore up his SDYC guest card and threw it on the table. It was all too theatrical and not helped by the fact that it was a *guest* card that he ripped up. It was about as meaningful as burning a borrowed bra.

The Royal New Zealand Yacht Squadron, for whom *Black Magic* sailed, was embarrassed by these remarks. In a letter written by Peter Blake and Alan Sefton, public relations manager, it said, "Mr. Taylor did state that the views expressed were his own, but we are concerned that the challenging syndicates may be judged by association. It is Team New Zealand's objective to remove the America's Cup from San Diego, but in the spirit of friendly competition intended by the Deed of Gift.

"Team New Zealand has received nothing but friendly hospitality since we have been here and our relationship with AC '95 and Chuck Nichols [President] is excellent. Of course, we don't agree on everything, but we do find solutions. May that situation prevail."

The Trustees Committeee eventually reaffirmed the defenders' right to name its defender from any of the finalists. The New Zealanders changed their tune considerably once we won the Defender Trials and announced our intention to use PACT's *Young America*. They took the issue yet again to the Trustees Committee, which, only four days before the first race of the actual Cup, reaffirmed its earlier decision. Perhaps this, together with its handling of the Bertrand two/three boat controversy (pick one) is why New Zealand so summarily erased the Trustees Committee (see chapter 1) immediately after it garnered the America's Cup.

Then on Sunday, March 26, our keel nearly fell off when we were but 13 seconds behind *Young America*, toward the end of the semifinals. We were at this moment one thin point ahead of *Mighty Mary* for the second and final berth in the finals. *Young America* would clinch the first spot if she beat us this day.

Jim Brady, our navigator, noticed water leaking copiously where the keel joins the hull. We immediately waved our rubber boat over, effectively dropping out of the race. On it were Tom Ehman, our rules adviser, and Dave Pedrick, our chief designer. Afraid we were going to sink like *oneAustralia* had before us, and *Young America* nearly did three weeks before when she dropped off a 12-foot wave, we began unloading expensive sails and other gear onto our chase boat. At the same time, air bags were put aboard the boat and a marker float was raised to the top of the mast. Unfortunately, pumps put aboard *Stars & Stripes* from our tender, *Betsy*, didn't work at first. Most of the crew, including Pedrick and Ehman—"white-collar" types—formed a bucket brigade to keep the yacht afloat.

The Coast Guard brought pumps over that finally kept up with the influx of water. Then, Tom Whidden, my tactician, Paul Cayard, tactical strategist, and I caucused with Ehman and Cy Gillette about repairing the boat from the standpoint of the rules. Specifically, there was a "no-change" rule that forbad boat changes in a round. This could be interpreted to mean even in the face of damage. Obviously, if we couldn't repair the boat we were through. That was the tack Koch's *America³* syndicate and its *Mighty Mary* would soon take in a flurry of protests. Like the Australians, we had taken risks in construction, Koch's syndicate maintained, and would now have to pay the piper. "What goes around comes around," as I've said.

A crew-member half–seriously suggested we claim we hit a whale—meaning this was an act of God, not man—but no one, least of all me, wished to lie.

Mick Harvey, in charge of building and repairing my boats, recognized there was no way to fix this keel in time. Before we were even back in San Diego Harbor, we had decided our only option was to replace the damaged keel with our old one (a keel discarded as hopelessly slow at the end of the first round). That would require a tremendous Herculean effort by Mick and his team if we were to get the old keel back on in time. If we missed more than two races, we were finished.

On shore, the Measurement Committee deferred the decision to the Defense Committee. The Defense Committee agreed we had the right under the rules to fix or replace our broken appendage. The measurer's only caution was not to exceed the maximum draft measurement. Thus, much of our team, including most of the crew, spent the next 48 hours replacing our new keel with the old one, fairing, and repainting it. In view of the measurer's words, we shimmed it in such a way that it was 7 mm, or one-quarter inch, shallower than the keel it replaced. Then we had to have the boat remeasured.

Somehow we made it to the starting line on Tuesday, March 28, and miraculously beat *Mighty Mary*. Our success this day was, in part, responsible for the conspiracy theory that we deliberately damaged our keel to replace it with a faster one. Nothing could be further from the truth. This was an unimproved keel that hadn't distinguished itself in the first round, where we won three races and lost four. The only change was we put wings from the damaged keel onto the old one.

Our argument, crafted by Tom Ehman, was that the "no-change" rule was there to keep you from *improving* your boat in the midst of a round, not to prevent you from *repairing* it.[3] Also, there's a rule that says a damaged appendage may be replaced by one that is "like and similar." We threw that one in the hopper, too; however, Chief Measurer Ken McAlpine didn't agree that this keel was "like or similar" to the one it replaced. It was, in essence, a quarter-inch shallower than the first, and by any measure or measurer, shallower means slower on the important upwind legs.

Mighty Mary protested us because our keel was not "like and similar." That was one rule—we had several others, we believed, on our side.

We had an agreement with Vincent Moeyersoms, *America³*'s Chief Executive Officer, and Tom Stark, PACT's Chief Financial Officer, not to use the press as a judge and jury. However, Cayard and Ehman felt sure that *America³* would go public with its charges and wanted me or Ehman to call a press conference and present our side to preempt them. Cayard used that tactic most effectively in 1992. By the time he was finished, the Kiwis were so tied up in knots they never won another race. However, Jerry La Dow, my syndicate's Executive Officer, and I did not want to influence the situation. Thus, the press conference was never held.

Sure enough, the night our keel nearly parted company with the boat, Roy Bell, a lawyer working for *America³*, launched a blistering criticism of us through Bill Center, of the San Diego *Union Tribune*. Basically, Bell accused me of duplicity.

Meanwhile, after PACT clinched its berth in the finals on the day our keel nearly fell off, it secretly petitioned the Defense Committee for the right to make a mid-series mode change, which had been specifically prohibited. It wished to add wings to the rudder— what became known as "Nelsons," in honor of *Young America's* designer, Bruce Nelson. The Defense Committee apparently countenanced this mid-series mode change because a new certificate was issued. This was discovered by Barbara Lloyd of *The New York*

---

3. IYRU Rule 70.4 and 20.1 say if a yacht's measurement certificate becomes invalid during a race due to damage or wear and tear, the yacht shall repair it, put it back to right, before racing again.

Times, who had requested to see the first page of all certificates, as was the media's right, indeed, anyone's right. The date on the new certificate was March 26, in the midst of the current round.

There were a total of five protests, filed primarily by *America³*, but also by PACT that, in particular, strikes me as being remarkably gratuitous. Here we're fighting for our lives to make a mid-series mode change—to salvage our boat and remain in the competition— while PACT has been secretly given that right to make a mid-series mode change to improve its boat. They were just jumping on top of the pile, in my estimation. Long forgotten was the extra time we gave them to repair their boat on the eve of the first round.

One protest was against the Race Committee, one against America's Cup '95, and three against us. That included a Rule C "Fair Sailing" protest filed by Koch that basically accused me of cheating.[4] *America³* wanted the hearing to be before the International Jury, which it saw as less partial; however, the Defense Committee rejected that saying it was a defense matter. When Koch threatened a lawsuit—his weapon of choice—the Defense Committee caved in like a house of cards, and the International Jury was convened to discuss the matter. The aforementioned Roy Bell, a local attorney and noted litigator, represented *America³* at the protest hearings.

The International Jury had a history in 1995 of "splitting the baby," if you'll forgive another cliché. And after 20 hours of deliberation over three days, it didn't throw us out of the competition, but it did nullify our Tuesday win over *Mighty Mary*. It said the no-change rule doesn't prohibit a change to a boat as long as the numbers in the certificate aren't changed. The only number in the certificate that had changed was the draft, which was now one-quarter inch shallower. Said John Doerr, head of the jury, "If they had put a self-tapping screw into the bulb at the point of measurement that would have sufficed."

"Doerr is so literal," a friend of his commented, "that if he saw a sign saying, 'Wipe Your Feet Before Entering,' he'd take off his shoes and socks to do that." Not surprisingly, the jury required us to lengthen the keel that quarter inch.

---

4. Koch later apologized to me for this.

From our perspective it was a huge penalty, as victories were precious at this point, and we'd just lost three races in a row. Also, we're talking about a quarter inch here on a 13-foot keel. To put it boldly and in accurate if inappropriate language: We got screwed.

On Saturday, April 1—April Fool's Day—we lost to an apparently speeded up *Young America* by 52 seconds. This day, a crewmember on *Stars & Stripes* commented dejectedly, "What really sucks about this whole thing, America, is that we didn't give this bitch a proper burial when the keel fell off." For better or worse, that comment was overheard by the television audience.

The Defense Committee's secret deal with PACT, or *Young America*, allowing the mode change, was unconscionable, I believe. In the beginning, the Defense Committee reported to the SDYC board. America's Cup '95 (AC '95), a separate entity, was the event-management organization, hired by SDYC to run the event. At the insistence of Frank Hope, Chairman of AC '95, control of the Defense Committee was eventually turned over to his AC '95. The president and general manager of AC '95 was Chuck Nichols, who worked for SAIC—a sponsor of PACT. It was Nichols, in fact, who got Marshall's program up and running in 1992.

It seemed to us that the committee (or committees) had already made its decision about who the defender would be: *Young America*. History would prove they got that much right.

The deal would have been draconian enough if *Young America* beat us in our two remaining races, and beat *Mighty Mary* in their two remaining races. Indeed, the boat was unbeaten at this point in this round and gave every indication of remaining so. However, on March 27, the spinnaker pole on the freshly reminted *Young America* broke when she was leading *Mighty Mary*. The women and one man, sailing superbly, passed *Young America*, not once but twice, to tie us in the overall standings.

That brings us to Sunday, April 2, where we had a do-or-die race with *Mighty Mary*. This was to make up for the annulled race. A win by us would tie the score and force a sail-off; a loss would force our departure—my earliest ever. Meanwhile, the challenger finalists, *Black Magic* and *oneAustralia*, had been off the water for days, improving their boats and crews. We defenders burned while the challengers fiddled—methodically improving their machines and men. Further, once New Zealand beat the Australians in the Louis Vuitton Finals, they would have 16 days to prepare for the match; we'd have but half that time.

Looking back, there are moments or decisions that you realize caused you to win or lose the America's Cup. They could be presented as snapshots. Looking at these particular snapshots, I know the America's Cup was lost in this bickering.

The race was something of an anticlimax. Dellenbaugh, who'd joined *Mighty Mary* two weeks before, crossed the starting line two seconds early. The Associated Press described this start somewhat uncharitably as, "The worst by any crew, challenger or defender, in nearly 150 races so far in the trials." We led at the first mark by 1:18. Then on the fourth leg, a gennaker on *Mighty Mary* burst. It took nearly two minutes to hoist and fill its replacement. Syndicate Head Bill Koch, who was along for the ride as the nonsailing "seventeenth man," pounded his leg in frustration. We won by 4 minutes and 49 seconds. The sail-off was set for Tuesday, April 4.

While these scenes were playing out publicly, behind the scenes the San Diego *Union-Tribune*'s Bill Center was at the center—or at least was a sounding board—for much of this controversy. He sent a private memo to America's Cup '95, saying since PACT had already clinched, the racing between *Mighty Mary* and *Stars & Stripes* should be decided on the water, not in the protest room. Center was seemingly troubled by the harsh penalty we'd received for making a mid-series mode change to stay in the racing, and the murky deal between the Defense Committee and PACT, allowing it to make a mid-series mode change to improve its boat. He proposed a best-of-three match, or something like that, rather than a sail-off. This memo got circulated among the defenders. While we didn't do what Center suggested, everyone began searching for a compromise.

Jerry La Dow, Vincent Moeyersoms, and Tom Stark began looking for some way to salvage the trials. It was then the suggestion arose that all three boats should matriculate to the finals as equals. PACT, who had won the semifinals outright and which had a record at that point of 21-7, wouldn't go for that. The next suggestion was that *Young America* get two points, equal to two wins in the finals, and *Mighty Mary* and *Stars & Stripes* get zero points. Neither of us went for that. So as late as 10:00 P.M. on Monday, April 3, the day before the Tuesday sail-off, the deal seemed dead.

The weather forecast for Tuesday was for light winds and lumpy seas. If we had a strong suit, this was it. Perhaps it was because these were our conditions that Bill Koch continued to push so hard for a deal. Koch had a roomful of lawyers and rules experts working through the night to try to put something down on paper that we all could sign. Like flood insurance, I wanted this deal for the crew, for myself, and for our sponsors.

America's Cup '95 was in charge of making the television deal. They'd promised us television time, and we'd promised it to our sponsors, but up to this point most of the racing had been on ESPN2. Further, this three-boat final would give us time to fix our boat; the design team had some radical ideas how to slice the boat open, down the middle, and make it narrower and, thus, less troubled by the seas; comparatively, *Stars & Stripes* was a wide-body boat, like an aircraft carrier, while the others were pencil-shaped, like a destroyer.

The negotiations began anew at 4:30 A.M. Tuesday. Finally, the deal was cut by 9:00 A.M. PACT would get two points; the winner of today's race would get one; and the loser, none. The finals were changed from a best-of-11 series between two yachts to a 12-race sail-off between three yachts. If there was a three-way tie at the end, the boat that had entered the finals with no points would be excused. This latter rule would prove significant.

After receiving word of the deal by cell phone from Jerry La Dow and Tom Ehman, I told my crew. There was considerable disappointment. Koch, for his own reasons, didn't tell his crew. His team sailed a great race and beat us by nearly six minutes. At the finish, they were so high, they appeared to be floating two feet above the deck. When told of the deal by ESPN's Gary Jobson, they seemed positively deflated—lead balloons. As Koch later explained, "The team was fired up; they were ready; they wanted blood; and they wanted to go out on the race course; they were extremely focused. We did not want to distract them."

That night, John Marshall, Bill Koch, and I faced the world's press, which collectively was not in a congenial mood. Explaining the deal, Marshall, a graduate of Harvard with graduate work at Rockefeller Institute, said, "I spent some time with the help of mathematicians at Science Applications last night analyzing the statistical probabilities of various scenarios that had been put forward in negotiation and concluded that a two-point bonus coming out of our very successful semifinal series was sufficient to make this a very good deal from our point of view."

Koch, who has a Ph.D. from MIT, commented similarly. "We wanted to maximize our chances of getting into the America's Cup and winning it. We did a careful analysis."

With a couple of years at San Diego State, I said simply, "It was our conclusion that you can't fight if you're dead."

BETWEEN THE SEMIFINALS and the finals, we cut a lengthwise slice out of *Stars & Stripes* to reduce its beam. It was fairly agricultural or rough and ready, in implementation, as the America's Cup World would see on unveiling day, on April 9, but it seemed to make us relatively faster.

That was a historic day; for the first time since 1983 and *Australia II*'s secret keel, all boats in the finals "lifted their skirts" publicly, and the gates of the compounds were thrown open to any curious observers. On the eve of unveiling day, Peter Blake described it best: "When this idea was first presented a couple of years ago it seemed good. Now we're all a little nervous. A bit like a bride on her wedding night."

We won the first two races in the finals. At this point, the three boats were tied at 2-2-2. So much for Marshall's "statistical probabilities"; they must have been fairly twisted up over there after having allowed us to get up off the mat. *Young America* beat *Mighty Mary* on April 14 to take the lead, but we beat *Young America* the next day—by one thin second. In both of these races, *Young America* again wore those wings on her rudder—a first in the America's Cup as far as I know. All the defenders agreed that each boat could make one mode change this round; it could change back if it wasn't satisfied with the change.

The next day of racing, April 17, *Mighty Mary* beat us, and now the score was tied at 3-3-3. Around this time, *Mighty Mary's* crew and coaches held a meeting, at the former's behest. The crew asked that J. J. Isler be brought back aboard. As one of them said, "Dave has not proved the shining knight everyone made him out to be. He has made a lot of bad calls, which we don't believe JJ would have made." It didn't happen, however.

On April 21, we were alone in first place, having beaten *Mighty Mary* this day and *Young America* the day before. Just before the finals began Kevin Mahaney was served with divorce papers by his wife. Perhaps this affected how he sailed, or perhaps, as he told Jerry La Dow, he'd accomplished all his goals. They'd lost a surprising five of seven races in the finals. Whatever their problems, there could be no doubt about it: Lazarus—yours truly—had risen from the dead.

The only hope for *Young America* and *Mighty Mary* was for us to lose two straight races, which would give each boat five victories. With this tie I'd be eliminated in keeping with the amended rules. Then, *Young America* and *Mighty Mary* would have a sail-off.

Young America, sailing without her "Nelsons," beat us on April 24. No "Nelsons" perhaps, but *Young America* had ladies' panties on its running backstay. They were a gift of the *Mighty Mary* crew. Said Kevin Mahaney, *Young America's* skipper: "The girls said the other day when they beat us they had on their lucky panties, so they lent them to us. So we have our lucky charm up there, it worked today, and we'll probably have to send them back tomorrow." A message was emblazoned on the panties. It read: "Good luck, Kevin. Don't get bunched up." Turnabout is fair play, and Mahaney promised to send *Mighty Mary* a pair of PACT 95 boxer shorts for its race against us on Tuesday. The latter proved to be less potent.

Boys will be boys and, I guess, girls will be girls, but more sinister, we believed, was the teaming up of *Young America* and *Mighty Mary* to oust us from the competition. It was now two against one. The race we lost to *Young America* was actually a makeup for an April 23 race that had been canceled.

That morning, *Mighty Mary* tuned up *Young America*, and the two pooled weather information. This included the use of *America³'s* helicopters that could help predict windshifts.

Before the start, we noticed Vincent Moeyersoms, Chief Operating officer of Koch's syndicate, on *Young America*'s tender. He was dressed incognito in a *Young America* jacket. That very tender got in our way after the starting sequence had begun. Moeyersoms was laughing and applauding. To signal our displeasure unambiguously Paul Cayard took aim at an *America³* tender that carried syndicate head Bill Koch. Wrote Tony Chamberlain in the Boston *Globe*, ". . . [This] gave the crowd the ohh-ahh thrill of the day by slicing dangerously close."

"It's an eye-opener how much of a help it is to have a second boat out there, even for an hour," said PACT's John Marshall.

Monday was not a good day. Besides losing to *Young America*, we received threatening phone calls at the base camp and at the *Stars & Stripes* store. We'd received one like it the previous week. Then my wife, Daintry, called to tell me that the house we'd rented in Point Loma was on fire. Spooky, but it turned out to be an electrical fire. Damage was minimal.

The Flag Officers of the San Diego Yacht Club ended this unholy alliance between *Mighty Mary* and *Young America*. It sent a letter to G. Wytie Cable, Chairman of the Defense Committee, saying "We ask that you advise the individual Defense Syndicates and demand that they cease and desist or face risk of disqualification as spelled out in Article 3.4 of the Defense Plan." *America³* decided to respond publicly. In an open response, it wrote, "This letter is another example of Dennis Conner's long-time friends at the San Diego Yacht Club attempting to tarnish and discredit the Women's Team . . ."

As described at the beginning of this chapter, we won the next race of the 1995 America's Cup trials against *Mighty Mary* to move on to the America's Cup match. Said Cayard at the end, "We got lucky and we won, but before we got lucky and won, we got tough."

We received more than a thousand faxes at our compound in San Diego after this win. Many of them were from old friends, like Fritz and Lucy Jewett, Mike Dingman, and Ed and Eleanor du Moulin. There were messages from our sponsors: Citizen Watch, Sears, Cadillac, American Airlines, Toshiba, Ocean Spray, and Sperry Top-Sider. Many more of them were from new friends. A number of them invoked the story of the tortoise and the hare or of the singing fat lady.

Bruce Farr, the New Zealand yacht designer, wrote, "Your performance will go down in history as a demonstration of your team's talent and determination . . ." Farr and I have had our differences, most notably after the debacle in 1988, where he designed Michael Fay's abundant boat, but he later designed *Winston*, my Whitbread boat in 1994 and *Toshiba*, my Whitbread boat in 1997. His words, for one, were appreciated. John Bertrand, who beat me in 1983, but who had just lost to the Kiwis in the Louis Vuitton Cup, wrote, "Well, you and the team hung in there with an incredible result. Congratulations!"

One of my favorite quotes came from John Marshall, head of PACT, who said to the press, "The next time I have a snake at my feet I'll know to cut its head off."

The door was left open by the Trustees Committee to choose another boat to defend the Cup. While we won the trials, *Young America* had sailed to a 21-7 record, while our record was 13-15. As I announced at a press conference, "I don't think anybody that's in touch with reality looks forward to defending the Cup with this boat." So when Marshall offered to lend me *Young America*, I jumped at the chance. Of course, John's idea of a loan and mine were different things. Indeed, I almost needed a loan to finance the "loan."

As I said at a press conference following this arrangement, "Talk about sacrifices for the good of the Cup. . . . There are some substantial financial obligations that I incurred here that I had to decide what to do, and it was a tough decision. But I told John on the phone the other day that what really made me decide to do this is that I'm not sure what the America's Cup brings to Dennis Conner down the road. I don't know where I'm going. And if this turned out to be my last America's Cup, and we sailed on the blue boat [Stars & Stripes] and lost, I think there would have been big emotional baggage for me to always wonder the rest of my life, what would happen if I had sucked it up and made a deal to sail a faster boat . . ."

The boat switch proved to be an unpopular choice, but I can stand the heat in the kitchen. In my estimation, the America's Cup has never been a popularity contest. The switch also had its risks. Members of my syndicate, including rules adviser Tom Ehman, whom I came to respect, feared the Kiwis were merely biding their time—that they would protest us just before the match. As mentioned, this they did, but it seemed more perfunctory than real. After 1992 with Cayard, the Kiwis weren't about to lose their focus over a technicality. Too bad for the home team.

THAT BRINGS US to the 1995 America's Cup match. I will be brief. In the first race we won the start on *USA 36*, my "borrowed" boat. We were ahead and to leeward of *Black Magic*. However, before we could "gas" her, the New Zealand boat sailed higher *and* faster than we could and, more distressingly, in windy and rough conditions. It was like *Australia II* in 1983 sailing lower and faster on the downwind legs. In hindsight, it was "checkmate" at that moment.

While I'd rather bury Caesar than praise him, it was as dominating a performance as I've ever seen in the America's Cup and, perhaps, will ever see. As the world well knows, *Black Magic* not only shut us out 5-0 in the America's Cup match, but they won a total of 41 races in 43 attempts since the trials began in January. In the America's Cup match, the New Zealanders led at all 30 marks and made up time on 25 of 30 legs. That, in my opinion, outshines *Ranger*, the last of the J-Class yachts, considered by the cognoscenti to be the greatest racing yacht in history.

Black Magic was only beaten once on the water, on April 15, during the Louis Vuitton Finals—losing to *oneAustralia* by 15 seconds.[5] Explaining the loss, Kiwi skipper Russell Coutts said, "The short version is, I stuffed up the start. The long version is, I really stuffed up the start."

Peter Blake, the syndicate head, wasn't aboard for this loss. "It wasn't him we missed," said Coutts, "but his lucky red socks." Instantly, red socks became the clothing symbol of the Kiwis' 1995 America's Cup campaign. Spurred on by TV New Zealand, 100,000 pairs were sold between the one-and-only on-the-water defeat of New

---

5. The boat lost an earlier race to that same group on a technical protest in the second round. John Bertrand, skipper of *oneAustralia*, successfully protested the Kiwis for having crew-member Murray Jones up the mast during the prestart maneuvering and the downwind legs. The Australians claimed Jones was outside the sheer line of the boat when it heeled.

Zealand and the culmination of the America's Cup match. This added $500,000 to the syndicate's coffers that it used to buy new sails.

In the fifth and final race, the crew of *Mighty Mary*, reduced to spectators, wore red socks, too, while their fellow Americans were being slaughtered in the winds off Point Loma. It was, wrote *Outside* magazine's Randy Wayne White, a "brattish stunt [which] if pulled by Conner would have made national headlines."

It wasn't easy, but it was easier losing the America's Cup the second time than it was the first. The America's Cup got off to a rocky start here, in San Diego, in 1987—with the renegade challenge of the Michael Fay–led Kiwis and our equally unpalatable response to it—and it never recovered. A poll of San Diego Yacht Club members in 1995 showed that 70 percent wished it would go elsewhere. They got their wish.

With age comes some wisdom, and I have come to realize that if properly nourished, the America's Cup grows stronger and more illustrious when planted on new—especially foreign—soil.

After the match, I congratulated the Kiwis with these words: "They had a fabulous campaign. If the Cup had to leave San Diego, there could be no better home for it than Auckland. This team really earned it, and, I know, they will enjoy it and take good care of it. New Zealand can be proud of its heroes."

BIBLIOGRAPHY

—◦◦◦—

Auchincloss, Louis, *The Vanderbilt Era*, Charles Scribner's Sons, New York, 1989.

Barry, Paul, *The Rise and Fall of Alan Bond*, Bantam Books, Sydney, Australia, 1990.

Bertrand, John and Smith, Patrick, *Born to Win: A Lifelong Struggle to Capture the America's Cup*, Hearst Marine Books, New York, 1985.

Bray, Maynard and Pinheiro, Carlton, *Herreshoff of Bristol*, Woodenboat Publications, Brooklin, Maine, 1989.

Conner, Dennis, *Comeback: My Race for the America's Cup*, St. Martin's Press, New York, 1987.

Conner, Dennis and Rousmaniere, John, *No Excuse to Lose*, W. W. Norton, New York, 1978.

Dear, Ian, *The America's Cup—An Informal History*, Dodd, Mead & Company, New York, 1980.

Dear, Ian, Enterprise *to* Endeavour: *The J-Class Yachts*, Dodd, Mead, New York, 1977.

Harrington, Melissa H., *The New York Yacht Club 1844–1994*, Greenwich Publishing Group, Inc., Lyme, Connecticut, 1994.

Heckstall-Smith, Anthony, *Sacred Cowes*, Allan Wingante Ltd., London, 1955.

Herreshoff, L. Francis, *The Wizard of Bristol*, Sheridan House, Dobbs Ferry, New York, 1953.

Hoyt, Sherman, *Sherman Hoyt's Memoirs*, D. Van Nostrand Company, New York, 1950.

Illingworth, John H., *Twenty Challenges for the America's Cup*, St. Martin's Press, New York, 1969.

Jones, Theodore A., *Challenge '77: Newport and the America's Cup*, W. W. Norton & Company, Inc., New York, 1978.

Jones, Theodore A., *Racing for the America's Cup, 1974: A View from the Candy Store*, Quadrangle/*The New York Times* Books Co., New York, 1975.

Lawson, Thomas W. and Thompson, Winfield M., *The Lawson History of the America's Cup, a Record of Fifty Years*, Southampton Ashford Press Publishing 1986 (a reprint of the original version published privately in 1902), Hampshire, England.

Levitt, Michael, *America's Cup 1851 to 1992: The Official Record of the America's Cup*, Publish 92, San Diego, 1992.

Levitt, Michael and Lloyd, Barbara, *Upset: Australia Wins the America's Cup*, Workman, New York, 1983.

Meyer, Elizabeth, "Powerful in Every Way," article published in *Nautical Quarterly*, Autumn 1985, New York.

Mitchell, Carleton, *The Summer of the Twelves*, Charles Scribner's Sons, New York, 1959.

Morris, Everett B., *Sailing for the America's Cup*, Harper & Row, New York, 1964.

Riggs, Doug, *Keelhauled: Unsportsmanlike Conduct and the America's Cup*, Seven Seas Press, Newport, Rhode Island, 1986.

Rousmaniere, John, *America's Cup Book, 1851–1983*, Overseas, s.r.l. Milan, Italy, 1983.

Rousmaniere, John, *The Golden Pastime: A New History of Yachting*, Nautical Quarterly Books, Essex, Connecticut, 1986.

Salisbury, Bill, "Koch Overboard," San Diego *Weekly*, San Diego, May 4 and May 7, 1995.

Stone, Herbert Lawrence, *The America's Cup Races*, Van Nostrand, New York, 1958.

Vanderbilt, Arthur T., II, *Fortune's Children*, William Morrow and Company, New York, 1989.

Vaughan, Roger, *America's Cup XXVII*, Dennis Conner Sports, San Diego, 1988.

Vaughan, Roger, *The Grand Gesture*, Sports Illustrated Books, New York, 1975.

Vaughan, Roger, *Ted Turner: The Man Behind the Mouth*, W. W. Norton & Co. New York, 1978.

Waugh, Alec, *The Lipton Story*, Doubleday & Company, Inc., Garden City, New York, 1956.

Whall, Hugh, *The* Southern Cross, *Australia's 1974 Challenge for America's Cup*, Admiralty Publishing House, LTD., Annapolis, Maryland, 1974.

INDEX

—◦◦◦—

Page numbers in **bold face** indicate photographs